A COMPREHENSIVE GUIDE TO LAND NAVIGATION WITH GPS

(THIRD EDITION)

BY

NOEL J . HOTCHKISS

PUBLISHED BY:

ALEXIS U.S.A.
1037 Sterling Road • Suite 201
Herndon, Virginia 20170

First Edition 1994
Second Edition 1995
Second Edition 1997 Revised
Third Edition 1999

Published by:
Alexis Publishing
A Division of Alexis USA, Inc.
1037 Sterling Road • Suite 201
Herndon, Virginia 20170

Library of Congress Catalog
Card Number 98-074914

ISBN Number 1-892688-00-X
Printed and Bound in Hong Kong

GRAND CANYON, W. H. HOLMES CIRCA 1882

ABOUT THIS GUIDE

This practical hands-on guide was written to meet the needs of those who wish to apply the advantages of the new Global Positioning System (GPS) technology to their navigational requirements on land. Unlike many publications on the subject, this one does not dwell upon how the system works. Instead, it is focused on what GPS can do and how it can best be used by you in a variety of everyday circumstances. The book is intended to be read, enjoyed, and easily understood.

The content organization and presentation of the material are based upon sound principles of instructional design. The navigational concepts and strategies presented here were discovered, refined, or developed and tested through professional research.

In fact, the book draws heavily upon the extensive land navigation research conducted by the U.S. Army Research Institute in the years just prior to the Gulf War and the introduction of GPS technology to military operations in Saudi Arabia during the training of Royal Saudi military personnel by Alexis International, Inc. immediately thereafter. The author of this book is an accomplished trainer and he was a key participant in both of these projects.

The first edition of this book in 1994 blazed the trail by responding to the needs of those who realized early the value of this new technology. The second edition kept pace by incorporating the new receiver functions, features, and characteristics then being developed by the manufacturers. Now, this third edition not only keeps pace with the progress of GPS, it continues to lead the way with some important additions. There is now a chapter focused upon vehicle navigation; Alexis Publishing introduces its revolutionary new GPS-compatible road maps with the handy Universal GPS Grid™; there is an expanded discussion of the coordinate systems and map datums used by GPS units to report positions, and, finally, this new edition presents some highly innovative techniques for identifying and confirming individual terrain features both in the real world and on topographic maps. These new topics are not only useful but they add to the fun of using GPS.

Although this publication is written to address the needs of general and recreational consumers, as well as highway motorists, it will also be of great interest to those who wish to explore the applicability of GPS to their professional land navigation (LN) requirements. This includes public safety, forestry and even military personnel.

This technology is new, so its utility is not yet fully understood by many who could take advantage of it. This is especially true for potential land-based users because they have had less experience with some of the techniques associated with using maps and charts, coordinate systems, and the more formalized navigational practices commonly employed in both flight and nautical situations. Nevertheless, this lack of familiarity should not deter anyone. This guide contains all the information needed to make navigating with GPS easy for everyone, even for the novice.

In addition to the general lack of awareness people may have regarding GPS's great utility to the land-based navigator, there are some serious misconceptions that must be dispelled. First, there is the belief that GPS user equipment is too expensive to purchase and employ for general use by average consumers, state and local public safety agencies, or volunteer emergency organizations. The fact is that the prices of GPS receiver units have fallen dramatically since they were first introduced a few years ago.

Another widely held misconception is that consumers must purchase, install, and carry with them expensive and bulky electronic equipment for accessing and displaying digital or interactive videodisk maps in order to effectively employ their GPS units. While there are now available some complex and expensive integrated systems using various digital map data sources, such as the Geographic Information System (GIS), there is still a very attractive alternative available: paper maps.

For centuries people have been using good paper maps to help them find their way. There is no reason they cannot continue to serve us well as we enter this new era of navigation with the GPS.

In summary, adding the advantages of using GPS to your current repertoire of navigational skills and capabilities is the most convenient and cost-effective way to ensure that you will arrive at your destination quickly and without difficulty.

Finally, this Guide is organized in a way that makes it easy to use and understand.

Chapters 1 through 4 focus upon how to fully exploit and integrate GPS capabilities into a variety of navigational situations while using a map and compass. This is done without delving into the specific instructions for using the various functions and features of GPS equipment. That discussion is reserved for Chapter 5. Learning how to employ the GPS receiver comes more logically after you know about its advantages and how it can and should be employed. The equipment, itself, is not difficult to operate.

Chapter 6 explains what is needed to navigate over mapped trails, streets, roads and highways. Furthermore, it introduces Alexis Publishing's revolutionary highway map series of the United States utilizing its easy-to-use *Universal GPS (UGPS) Grid*™. These maps can be used with virtually every hand-held GPS receiver unit manufactured to date. Chapter 6 is a completely new addition to the third edition.

Chapter 7 provides a few suggestions for both developing and participating in a short practice navigation field exercise designed to apply the skills learned about LN while using the equipment. This chapter will focus on how best to use your hand-held unit and a map - both in setting up the course and running through it as a participant.

The final chapter (Chapter 8), provides a short glimpse into the future by forecasting the impact GPS will have upon how we do things. This chapter has also been completely revised for the third edition.

In conclusion, the Global Positioning System was planned, designed, and developed by the United States Department of Defense as a navigational aid for military operations. But, without question, it is of equal or, perhaps, even greater utility to civilian consumers.

This Guide will introduce you to the unparalleled advantages and unexpected operational simplicity that is built into this revolutionary new GPS land navigation equipment.

After you have read the manual, we invite you to send your questions, reactions, and suggestions along to us at:

**Alexis Publishing
1037 Sterling Road
Suite 201
Herndon, Virginia 20170**

alexispub@aol.com

We will attempt to answer your questions and will consider your reactions and suggestions as we develop future publications and products.

For up-to-date information about new products and/or to place an order, visit our web site at http://www.alexispublishing.com

TABLE OF CONTENTS

GPS OVERVIEW

All the great navigators - including Marco Polo, Magellan, Lewis & Clark, and you - have shared a common problem over the ages. Until recently, there was no surefire way to quickly and easily determine a position. Now, with GPS, this problem has been solved.

BACKGROUND

Always knowing your location is the fundamental key to finding your way along a selected route to your destination. It is the most fundamental requirement for any type of navigation.

Over the years, several aids and techniques were developed and used to help guide our movements. They included the drawing of crude portolan charts of the Mediterranean during the Middle Ages and use of the astrolabe, sextant, and printed almanacs that predict the "movements" of celestial bodies across our skies. More recently, we have employed modern radio-based systems, such as the Navy's low-orbit Transit SatNav (satellite navigation) and surface broadcasting concepts like Omega and Loran-C.

All of these aids had limitations associated with their use that are not encountered when using Global Positioning System (GPS) equipment. These limitations included poor visibility related to weather, the necessity to refer to endless tables, and the requirement to follow mathematically complex and time-consuming procedures. In the case of electronic navigation, the limitations were restrictive times and areas of coverage, increasingly questionable accuracies at greater ranges, and atmospheric and ground interferences that often resulted in poor signal reception. Low altitude and ground-based radio systems are particularly impractical on land.

NAVSTAR GPS, an acronym standing for **Nav**igation **S**ystem with **T**ime **A**nd **R**anging **G**lobal **P**ositioning **S**ystem, is a revolutionary development that is designed to provide highly accurate, reliable, continuous 24-hour, worldwide coverage for position reporting. It was created by the United States Department of Defense and is operated by the Air Force. The satellites that make up the space segment of the system broadcast the information required for the small lightweight user unit (receiver/computer) to determine its precise location. While the design of the system and the hand-held GPS receiver are highly complex, use of the equipment is simple. You can have your position reported on the display screen in seconds with the push of a button.

During the development and testing of the **NAVSTAR** program, the United States Government made decisions to extend its use to both domestic and international communities. Its applications range from navigation over the land, in the air, and on the seas to precision surveys, tracking the whereabouts of trains and trucks, knowing where and how much to fertilize agricultural fields, which club to use on the next golf shot and even tracking oil spills. Our imaginations seem to be the only limits to the applications that may be developed for GPS. Of course, our discussion here will be limited to those closely related to its use as an aid to our movements over the land.

Some describe GPS as a new man-made form of celestial navigation because a constellation of 24 artificial satellite "stars" (including three spares) has been placed in high orbit circling the globe about every 12 hours at an altitude of approximately 12,500 statute miles (about 20,200 kilometers). Each satellite vehicle (SV) tells an unlimited number of GPS receivers anywhere in the world the current date, time, and locations of all other NAVSTAR SVs both now and into the immediate future. It also sends out a precise timing code. This timing code makes it possible for each navigational unit to calculate its distance from either three or four SVs presently "in view" and then determine its position.

Information from three SVs is needed to calculate a navigational unit's horizontal location on the earth's surface (2-dimensional reporting); but information from four SVs enables it to determine its altitude in addition to its horizontal location (3-dimensional reporting). Three-dimensional reporting is more crucial on land because, unlike the surface of a large body of water, ground surfaces are not constant and the elevation of the receiver antenna is considered when the unit calculates its horizontal position on the ground. Ninety-five percent of all position fixes (position calculations) are accurate to within from 25 to 100 meters. This is close enough for nearly all land navigation applications. Without question, it will keep you from being lost.

This system could be even more precise if the U.S. Department of Defense were to drop its **Selective Availability (SA) Program** that makes GPS less accurate for security reasons. On the other hand, it is possible to overcome the SA and various natural inaccuracies through use of a special, yet somewhat expensive, application called **differential GPS**. This will be discussed later.

If you wish to further explore a layperson's discussion of the technical aspects of this new space-age technology, please refer to Appendix A in the back of the Guide.

GPS APPLICATIONS FOR LAND NAVIGATION (LN)

Many of you first learned about the GPS on TV or in newspaper stories reporting the progress of our allied forces during OPERATION DESERT STORM. Some of the popular hobbyist- and scientifically-oriented magazines then followed-up with short articles reflecting the enthusiasm expressed by our troops for this new navigational aid. As the result of the Gulf War, many soldiers discovered its advantages when they were issued (and some even purchased) this new equipment. More recently, we saw news stories telling us about soldiers being trained in the use of GPS just prior to their deployment as part of OPERATION RESTORE HOPE in Somalia and during our military deployments in Haiti and Bosnia. And now, GPS is entering the main stream of American Life with references to it in a wide range of publications and on television. Now you can find it being referred to in everything from comic strips and soap operas to newscasts and films such as James Bond. Chances are also good that you personally know someone who has purchased and uses a GPS receiver.

What is important is that you understand **GPS is for everyone**, not just for soldiers, jet pilots, or ships' captains. GPS has and certainly will continue to be integrated into a growing variety of advanced "heads-up" displays, digital computer and CD-ROM map call-ups, as well as sophisticated nationwide vehicle location and tracking systems. But, without question, its largest user group will consist of individuals using relatively inexpensive nonintegrated GPS equipment while carrying paper

maps of the areas in which they must find their way.

Next, we will briefly introduce some of the navigational advantages offered by GPS receivers. Later chapters will help you to better understand and utilize their many useful characteristics, features and functions.

FOR GENERAL NAVIGATIONAL USE

THE EAGLE EXPEDITION II ™

NAVSTAR GPS (the system) has only one fundamental purpose. It sends out radio signals carrying the information needed by your receiver unit to compute its position. It provides continuous, worldwide coverage under any atmospheric condition.

On the other hand, receiver units are designed to perform a multitude of functions. They are extremely versatile navigational tools.

For example, the GPS receiver not only determines and reports where you are located, it also remembers where you have been. Thus, it can tell you how to get back (direction and distance) to any location you have asked it to recall or that you may wish to punch in with a few strokes on the keypad.

Since it can tell you where you are and remembers where you were, it can also determine the **direction** you have gone, calculate the **distance** you have moved during a given period, and report your **average speed** over the ground. Finally, after you have established and programmed the route you wish to follow (intermediate checkpoints and final destination) and begin to navigate over it, the unit will provide you with a wealth of navigational information to assist you with your movement. It will display, both in numbers or words and graphically, the name and relationship of your next checkpoint (landmark/waypoint) to your present position and to north or south, its direction and distance, your actual direction of movement, and the estimated time of arrival from your present position at any point along the route. In addition, it will report your velocity over the ground and the rate at which you are making progress toward your destination. Finally, it will show you which direction and how far you may have drifted off your intended route and allow you to either get back on course or proceed directly to your next checkpoint.

How can the GPS receiver accomplish so much more for the land navigator than basic location reporting? Because, in addition to collecting, processing, and reporting positioning information from the NAVSTAR SVs, it can store and integrate this information with other data in various ways for later use. For example, the unit can draw upon and utilize a vast pool of pre-programmed formulas and reference tables held permanently in its memory, and it will accept a number and variety of information inputs and preferred reporting format selections made by you.

The pre-programmed reference information held within the unit's permanent memory is what makes it a comprehensive navigational aid. This information in-

THE MAGELLAN GPS 4000 XL ™

cludes: (1) tables containing magnetic variations (declinations) for all parts of the world, (2) formulas for calculating and reporting coordinate locations on maps using any one of several geodetic datums (theorized earth surface shapes) upon which various map drawings are based, and (3) the tables and equations needed to report positions in either True Geographic Coordinates (Latitude and Longitude) or Universal Transverse Mercator Grid - based coordinate systems (false easting and false northing): as well as a number of other map coordinate systems from around the world.

Chapter 3 will take an in-depth look at three of these standard coordinate systems. **Latitude and longitude** is universally used for reporting positions around the world and found on most maps. Next, the **Universal Transverse Mercator Grid** (UTM) is included on all maps published by the U.S. Geological Survey (USGS) and many other governments' mapping agencies. It forms a perpendicular grid with constant distances among its lines that makes it superior to latitude and longitude for use on land. And, finally, the **Military Grid Reference System** (MGRS) - not really a separate coordinate system at all - is a variation of the UTM grid system that makes it much easier to use. Whenever possible, use of the MGRS format of the UTM grid is the

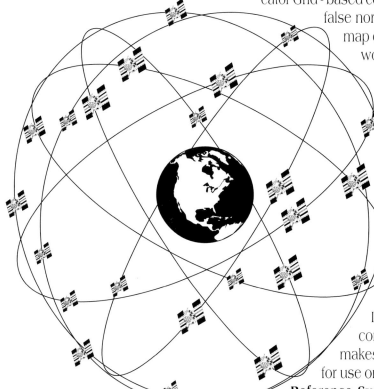

VECTOR ILLUSTRATION OF 24 SATELLITE GPS CONSTELLATION BY FRANCK E. BOYNTON

best bet for any type of land navigation. Presently, not all GPS units report UTM positions in MGRS format, but many do.

The information inputs and reporting format options that you can program into most units allow you the flexibility to configure and re-configure it to meet your changing needs. For example, you may (1) **enter your initial position** to reduce the time it takes to obtain your first position-fix; (2) **save current and/or enter up to hundreds of positions to be used as landmarks** (waypoints) for use in route planning; and (3) **program a multi-segment reversible route** with up to several legs that the unit will track in the navigation mode.

In addition, you can tailor the reports rendered by your receiver by making selections from among several available formats. They include: (1) **time and date information** (local or universal 12 or 24 hour time), (2) **azimuth directions** (true, or magnetic values), (3) **distance, elevation, and speed readings** (metric or British units), and (4) **position-reporting modes** (3-D, 2-D, or automatic).

There are also several other functions and new features that make the equipment more accurate as well as easier and quicker to use. However, they will be reviewed in more detail in Chapter 5, where you will read how to specifically employ the many features available on the majority of GPS receiver units.

THE EAGLE EXPLORER ™

IN SUMMARY

If you are an experienced navigator, your thoughts may already be racing toward new applications for GPS. And, if you are not that experienced, this comprehensive Guide will help you to more fully explore and exploit the many navigational advantages it makes available to you.

THE LORANCE GLOBALNAV 212 ™

THE GARMIN GPS III ™

It should be of little concern that you may not already understand such concepts as magnetic variation, map projections, coordinate systems, or datums because these and many other aspects of using maps in conjunction with GPS will be fully explained in Chapter 3. In fact, this Guide will teach you all that is necessary about reading maps, observing the terrain, and using a magnetic compass to move over the land with skill and confidence while employing this revolutionary new equipment.

Whether you are an outdoorsman, highway traveler, part of a civilian public safety organization, forester, soldier, or anyone else wishing to improve your ability to navigate over the land, you will find both GPS and this Guide quite helpful. Sometimes, improved capabilities in LN may be only a matter of convenience; but it is frequently essential for getting the job done and done safely.

THE MAGELLAN 6000 ™

Photo: U.S. Geological Survey

2

THE UTILITY OF GPS ON LAND

Navigation is basically a problem-solving activity. It consists of a series of requirements or problems (many unforeseen) that are unique to every situation, each demanding the development of a strategy to meet or solve it. The purpose of this chapter is to show you how GPS technology and equipment can help you handle these challenges.

BACKGROUND

The fundamental concepts behind successful LN are not difficult to understand. In fact, there are only **four steps, one rule, and three movement techniques** to be employed as you find your way.

The FOUR STEPS are:

Step 1 -   **Know where you are,**

Step 2 -   **Plan the route,**

Step 3 -   **Stay on the route, and**

Step 4 -   **Recognize the destination.**

The **steadfast LN rule** is that you should **always navigate with a correctly oriented map**. In fact, the amount of error should not exceed 30°. This practice of always keeping your map oriented to the ground as you make changes in direction is sometimes referred to as "steering" or "driving the map."

The three **movement techniques** that land navigators employ are **(1) terrain association, (2) dead reckoning, and (3) highway or trail following**. **Terrain association** consists of the navigator's use of the many features encountered in the real world and portrayed on maps to help determine position and guide movements. **Dead reckoning** (altered over the centuries through common language usage from deduced reckoning) is simply the application of an old nautical navigation technique to movements on land. The navigator uses a compass to follow a specific directional bearing and some means for measuring the distance traveled (e.g., an odometer, pacing, or lapsed time) to keep track of position and guide movement along each segment of the route. Finally, **highway or trail following** generally refers to a navigator's use of well established and mapped highway, street, and trail networks to track his position and guide him along to the destination. Obviously, these techniques can be employed separately or in concert.

GENERAL APPLICATION

Now it's time to take a closer look at the requirements and techniques associated with LN and how the Global Positioning System (GPS) can be applied in helping you to accomplish them. Let's first examine the four steps and three movement techniques.

FOUR-STEP LN PROCEDURE

STEP 1 (KNOW WHERE YOU ARE)

Yes, you must continually know where you are located, both on the map and on the ground, in order to navigate effectively. This includes when you start your journey, while moving along the route, and as you reach your destination.

Before the advent of GPS, land navigators were required to almost constantly relate the features they saw in the real world around them with the map's portrayal in order to keep track of their locations. For even the most experienced navigators, there was always an element of uncertainty for a number of reasons. First, no map presents a perfect portrait of the terrain. Due to scale limitations, maps are severely restricted as to how much detail they can include in a limited space without becoming an illegible mass of clutter. Next, there are always many changes made in the real world after any map is produced. This is particularly true with regard to man-made features and vegetation. And finally, mistakes are occasionally made by those who compile the maps we use.

Map interpretation, at best an imprecise science, can also present a difficult challenge for navigators. Each individual brings to the task different experiences and skill levels, and some terrain is more difficult to read than others. For example, the relatively featureless areas found along the borders of Saudi Arabia, Kuwait, and Iraq were nearly impossible for the allied Coalition Forces to use in determining their locations during Operations DESERT SHIELD and DESERT STORM.

All of these factors serve to erode any navigator's confidence during movements in those areas which are unfamiliar. Using maps, compasses, and protractors, military navigators and others who moved cross-country often completed time-consuming triangulations from two or more known features in the distance as a means to restore a degree of certainty and confidence in their position estimates.

Now, using GPS equipment, you can quickly learn your precise location anywhere at anytime. After dark or at midday, in rain or shine; or whether the surrounding countryside presents a featureless plain or numerous easily identified landmarks; the push of a button quickly calls-up a position reading that you can use with confidence. That, in itself, is reason enough to employ this new equipment, but there is much more.

**STEP 2
(PLAN THE ROUTE)**

Land navigation's second step reminds you to plan the route. Let's imagine for a moment that you have decided to go hunting with your camera in search of wild game or some beautiful scenery. You pull the car over and stop along the edge of the logging trail you have been driving, jump out, and then push the button on your GPS unit fixing your current position. After obtaining that information, you store it as a landmark or waypoint you name as "CAR.". Now, you move on quickly through the woods with your camera in hand. Several rolls of film and a few hours later, you decide it's time to return to the automobile. But which way must you go? You really haven't been paying attention to where you walked and did not bother to write the coordinates for the location of your parked car.

There is no problem. You can simply ask your GPS receiver to tell you where you are located and in what direction and how far you must go in returning to your car's location at the stored waypoint you named "CAR." In fact, the unit can tell you the distances and either the map or compass directions between any two or up to hundreds of locations that you may have saved or wish to program into the unit at any time. It can even tell you whether travel between them would be generally up or downhill by checking the elevations reported for each position's description. Incidentally, you can determine compass directions on the ground (by trial and estimate) using only your GPS receiver, but it is certainly quicker and easier to carry and use a magnetic compass for this purpose (Chapter 4).

Unlike movements at sea or in the air, the quickest way to proceed between two points on land most often will not be a straight line. Mike Hagedorn, a New York State Forest Ranger working in the vast six million-acre Adirondack Preserve in upstate New York (one of the world's largest protected wilderness areas), warns that when selecting a route over land, you must consider its "functional distance." He determines the **functional distance** of any potential route segment through a careful assessment of the **time**, amount of **effort**, and **the level of difficulty** required to move over it. For example, there may be a cliff, swamp, or a steep hill located directly between you and the destination. This means the selection of a less direct route will be longer and not necessarily faster or even less difficult to negotiate but it is a route you have chosen for a specific purpose (leisure or rigorous training). In this case, you would not want to plan straight line movements over the mountainous terrain shown in the next photograph.

In regard to highway travel, we know that few roads follow straight lines. Also, some roads are easier and quicker to drive than others, so you are always

MAGNETIC LENSATIC COMPASS
STOCKER AND YALE, INC.
SALEM, NH U.S.A.

confronted with choices and decisions when planning any route.

Obviously, Step 2 (plan the route) is made easier by using a GPS receiver because it can quickly tell you the relationship between your location (your **starting point**) and anywhere you wish to end up (your **destination**) in terms of direction and distance. However, it is just as obvious that you must also know how to use a map in order to effectively apply this information to the selection of a good, **practical** route over the ground.

PHOTO: U.S. GEOLOGICAL SURVEY

You will find Chapter 3 (Navigating With GPS And A Map) quite helpful in this regard.

STEP 3
(STAY ON THE ROUTE)

Without question, the essence of navigation is staying on the route. You will recall that there are three **movement techniques** generally used for accomplishing this task: (1) terrain association, (2) dead reckoning, and (3) highway or trail following. Remember, they may, be used separately or in concert.

As long as visibility conditions are good (usually related to light and weather conditions or the density of vegetation) and adequate concentrations of identifiable terrain and other landmark features are available in the immediate area, experienced navigators prefer to move by **terrain association**. When employing GPS, this will still be the case, but with GPS all the uncertainty is gone. You can get a reliable position-fix at any time. The terrain will still provide the guidance needed to wend your way over the selected route to the destination, but you can now move more quickly, with greater confidence, and with far less mental concentration on the navigation task itself. You are free to concentrate on other factors such as enjoying the beautiful scenery or getting a job done.

On the other hand, when movement by terrain association is not possible, navigators proceed by **dead reckoning**. Prior to the advent of GPS, they moved by sighting with their compasses on a series of steering marks encountered along the designated azimuth (compass bearing) while measuring or pacing-off the prescribed distances over each segment of the route. These steering marks were uniquely-shaped bushes, trees, rocks - anything they could use to guide them along the way. When steering marks could not be seen due to visibility conditions or in barren landscapes, a man was often sent out ahead to create a steering mark along the prescribed azimuth. (NOTE: An **azimuth** is defined as a 0° to 360° angular directional value measured - by a compass out on the ground or by a protractor on a map - clockwise from a north reference line (e.g., north = 0° or 360°, east = 90°, south = 180°, and west = 270°)).

Generally, when using GPS, the compass should be used to set your general direction of progress without regard to specific steering marks because the GPS unit will keep track of your actual progress. However, **when great precision is required** in moving along a narrow corridor, it may be still easier to sight on steering marks with your compass and utilize the GPS receiver as a backup to insure that you do not wander out beyond your safety limits.

If you are following a dead-reckoned course cross-country with your GPS receiver, it will tell you anywhere along the way what directional azimuth to "steer" and how far it is to the next checkpoint (waypoint or landmark).

The navigational information a GPS unit will report when a route has been set in its memory includes: (1) the name of the leg destination waypoint, (2) a graphic schematic showing north or south, movement direction, and the relative location of the leg destination waypoint , (3) an azimuth (bearing) and distance from the present position (PP) to the leg destination waypoint, (4) TTG (time to go), (5) ETA (estimated time of arrival), (6) VMG (velocity made good - velocity running a line parallel to the course line), (7) SOG (speed over ground - speed of movement in relation to the earth's surface, and (8) the amount and direction of your deviation from the planned course.

Before GPS was available, the navigator **traveling on paths, streets, and highways** was required to recall, identify, and negotiate key turns by spotting, in time, the various landmarks and signs previously keyed in his mind to each of these decision points. Given the many other details and events demanding his attention and the lack of information included on most published road maps, this was often a difficult task to accomplish.

With GPS, staying on all the correct pathways or roads is a simple matter of periodically checking your position using the receiver unit and mentally placing yourself on the map. You'll know well in advance when you are approaching a key turn, route change, or the destination. If you do happen to miss a turn or drive by a desired stop, you can quickly determine where you are located, check the map, select a return route, and get back to the plan with little difficulty.

STEP 4 (RECOGNIZE THE DESTINATION)

The final step is to recognize the destination. Before the development of GPS, unless you were familiar with your destination, it was frequently no easier to identify than any of the other checkpoints, critical turns, or intermediate objectives you were required to find along the way. Fortunately, now with GPS, recognizing these crucial locations is no longer a challenge.

As part of its route-following function, the GPS receiver **informs you when you have arrived** at your intermediate and final objectives. More specifically, the unit tells you when you have crossed a line drawn perpendicular to your direction of travel through the waypoint located at the end of each route segment. After reporting your arrival it automatically begins to navigate the next leg of the route and render its reports regarding your progress as soon as the previous one has been negotiated.

THE STEADFAST LN RULE

Always navigate with a correctly oriented map. There is no reason to perform the difficult mental gymnastics necessary to get properly oriented on a map that does not display its features in the same pattern as those it represents in the real world. You may have already attempted this frustrating exercise while examining an improperly oriented graphic floor plan shown on the directory of a large airport terminal or shopping mall.

Even when employing GPS, it is important to keep your map properly oriented. Although you can get a position-fix at any time and may do so frequently, you will find that you should still make good use of terrain and other features, your map, and magnetic compass readings to guide your movements between these position checks. It is not practical to continuously operate and read the GPS equipment when other matters may require your attention. Use of GPS will give you more freedom from concentration on the navigational task - not less.

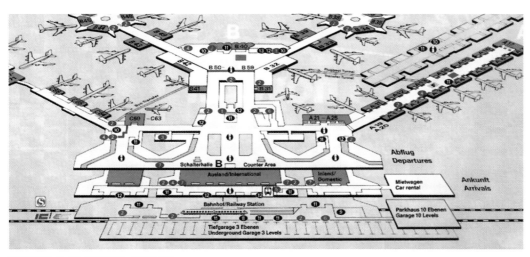

TERMINAL B, FRANKFURT, GERMANY
LUFTHANSA BORDBUCH

You will learn specifically how to orient your map in Chapter 4 when we discuss the use of the compass.

ADDITIONAL FEATURES, CHARACTERISTICS AND OPTIONAL ACCESSORIES OF GPS UNITS

GPS receivers have many valuable features and characteristics that enhance their utility as tools for the land-based navigator. First, they can provide position updates every second and their average position accuracies are within about 25 meters (disregarding the effects of the U.S. Government's Selective Availability (SA) security policy). Next, they report on the strength of the signals received and the quality of the geometry used (based upon the positions of the satellites) to calculate this data. Most units will warn you when a fix should not be used or when signal strength is so weak that contact with a particular satellite may soon be lost. It should be noted, however, that signal strength has little impact upon the accuracy of a unit's calculation of a position.

Furthermore, some units have the capacity to simultaneously track up to 12 satellites, allow you to either automatically or manually store an inventory of hundreds of landmarks/waypoints, and enable you to backtrack through the dozen or more positions held in a "lastfix buffer." In addition, these units permit you to establish and navigate multi-leg routes using waypoints you have held in memory. Their special navigational features include on-screen graphic steering aids, course correction information related to direction and distance, a "go to" feature that acts as an instant single leg route from your present position (PP) to any stored waypoint, and various time/speed/distance reports.

Finally, today's portable GPS units fit easily into the palm of your hand as well as being lightweight, rugged, and waterproof (non-submersible). Most models have easy-to-learn keypads and backlit LCD graphic display screens with contrast and light intensity controls. They also come with lanyard straps and carrying cases and offer a variety of accessories such as external power supplies, antennas, data ports, cigarette lighter plug-ins, and rechargeable batteries

Most GPS receivers are incredibly easy to use and will revolutionize the way you approach your outdoor adventures. Now you can get where you want to go—anywhere in the world, at any time, and under any conditions—simply, quickly, and with confidence. Whether you are deep in the wilderness or moving along a trail or highway, it will give you a quick, accurate fix on your position and other vital information to help you proceed along the way. To avoid lawsuits, most GPS receiver manufactures include a disclaimer warning the user not to rely solely upon the GPS unit. Regardless of its purpose, this is sound advice. Use of your GPS in conjunction with a map and compass provides the best possible approach to meeting the challenges presented in land navigation.

IN SUMMARY

If you are an experienced navigator, GPS receivers will be easy to use and integrate into your well-established repertoire of knowledge and skills. It will also eliminate the guesswork, uncertainty, and demand for focused concentration with which you have always had to contend in continually tracking your position and staying on the route. Your navigational quickness, safety, and assurance for success in arriving on time at your destination with a minimum of difficulty will greatly increase. The number of mistakes you make, amount of time wasted while enroute, and stress level related to directing any movement will significantly decrease.

If you are a new or somewhat inexperienced navigator, GPS will make it possible for you to achieve the navigational prowess previously attained by only the most gifted practitioners. This is the case because the GPS unit derives all the vital information formerly available only to individual navigators using every meager clue they could glean from years of study and practice in using the terrain, map, and compass. Simply applying this vital information now provided by the GPS receiver unit - the **easy** part of LN - is all that is left to be accomplished by you.

ILLUSTRATION BY: MATTHEW DWYER

FIGURE 3-1   WORLD MAP FROM THE FIRST COMPLETE PRINTED ATLAS, THE 1482 ULM EDITION OF COSMOGRAPHIA

NAVIGATING WITH GPS AND A MAP

This chapter will help you to read and interpret maps so you can effectively navigate on land while using GPS. Its objectives are to teach you to (1) locate and report your position using map coordinates, (2) understand the language and techniques used by map makers to portray real world features and convey other related information, and (3) apply a carefully researched strategy for identifying specific terrain features - both when encountered on topographic maps and on the ground - as guides to your movements. Finally, this third chapter also includes a thorough discussion of map datums so you will better understand why it is important to set the correct datum on your GPS receiver before attempting to navigate with a map.

BACKGROUND

Psychologists remind us that we must always deal with two forms of reality - the one we think exists and the one that is actually out there. When our mind's reality deviates too much from the genuine one, we cease to function effectively at whatever we are doing. That is especially true for navigation. The conceptualizations we form in our minds about the physical shape and content of the real world area in which we are operating are the only basis we have for our navigational decisions and actions.

In order to navigate effectively in any area, it is a great advantage to know it as well as your own neighborhood. Other than living somewhere for an extended period of time, the only way you can seize this "home court" advantage is through an ability to use maps.

Further, without the information maps convey, GPS position reports are nothing more than a meaningless series of letters and numbers. Also, GPS cannot tell us where we may wish to go or which route is the most functional to take us there. We must decide these things for ourselves after consulting a map. Although the GPS receiver reports our location, it is the map that tells us if we are located where we wish to be. And, if we are not, it allows us to determine how best to proceed in making our corrections.

Unquestionably, land navigators using GPS need maps just as medical doctors utilizing advanced CAT SCAN technology still require a comprehensive understanding of the human body. Without them, the vital information being provided by the sophisticated tool has little meaning.

FINDING & REPORTING POSITION

All maps use colors, symbols, labels, and marginal notes to portray the real world around us. But **good maps** also include a coordinate system that facilitates our ability to locate and report any position within the areas covered. In fact, when employing GPS, this becomes the map's most fundamental use. The coordinate systems used for this purpose must be understood by you, any other persons to whom you may wish to communicate your location, and the GPS receiver you employ.

The idea is that the coordinate system used on the map allows you to apply the locational information developed by your GPS equipment to the matrix of lines placed there to define it. In turn, the map's portrayal of the real world's features, as drawn and labeled within that network of lines, allows you to further relate that position to the many characteristics found on the ground in the area through which you are navigating. These characteristics may include both natural and cultural features such as hills, valleys, ridges, bodies of water, forests, trails, highways, towns and cities, man-made structures, and so forth.

There have been several coordinate systems developed over time to define the position of any point on the globe or map. For example, it is quicker and easier to tell someone that you will meet them at the intersection of 2nd Avenue and 8th Street, rather than saying they will find you in front of the 12th white house north of the museum (**Figure 3-2**). Urban street patterns form a simple, yet usable, grid coordinate system. Their limitations are that they are irregular in street spacing and can not be used with a worldwide electronic navigational system or even a small scale map that does not show all the streets and their names. Nevertheless, the concept behind the use of this street grid is very similar to that of reading the standard coordinate systems used by cartographers (map makers) and by GPS units.

A large percentage of the world's base information maps (including most large and intermediate-scale topographic maps) display both geographic coordinates (latitude and longitude) and the Universal Transverse Mercator Grid (UTM) or some similar regional coordinate system (e.g., the British and Irish grids). For example, the U.S. Geological Survey (USGS), as do many other nations' mapping programs, includes the UTM Grid on all published maps at a scale of 1:1,000,000 and larger (**Figure 3-3**).

These maps are frequently used by those engaged in hiking and other forms of outdoor recreation, park and forest management, and search and rescue

FIGURE 3-2
SEGMENT OF LE MARS, IOWA
1:24,000 SCALE MAP SHEET
USGS.

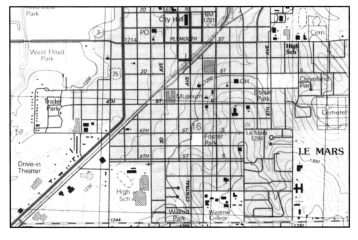

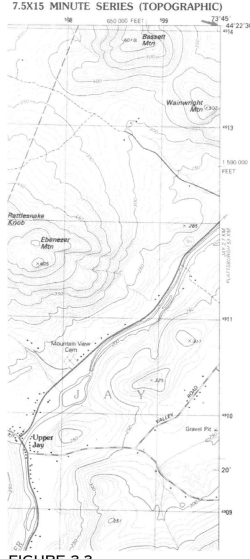

FIGURE 3-3
SEGMENT OF LAKE PLACID, NY
1:25,000 SCALE MAP SHEET
USGS

operations. Just as importantly, they are also used by commercial map producers in their development of standard highway, street, and other types of travel maps. Thus, both geographic and UTM grid coordinate information is easy to obtain and add to your maps when it is not already found there. No doubt, most commercial producers will soon add this type of information to their maps as the increased employment of GPS creates a demand for its inclusion.

The UTM grid coordinate system was specifically designed by the French military during World War I to overcome its frustration with the use of True Geographic Coordinates (Latitude and Longitude) by ground forces. It has proven to be far better suited for land-based navigation than the previously used lines of latitude and longitude. Soon thereafter, the U.S. military refined and simplified this coordinate system by developing the Military Grid Reference System (MGRS) which actually utilizes UTM grid lines and parts of its labels. The MGRS was ultimately adopted by the military forces of all NATO countries, as well as many other nations not affiliated with the former Soviet Block. Canada, for example, uses the MGRS on all its large- and intermediate-scale topographic maps; both military and civilian. This will all be more fully explained later in the chapter.

Virtually all makes and models of hand-held GPS receivers report positions in both LAT/LON and UTM Grid coordinate values. Eagle, Magellan, Garmin and Trimble also market units that include the MGRS coordinate format option (**Figure 3-4**), which is unquestionably more advantageous during highway travel (see

FIGURE 3-4
EAGLE EXPEDITION II™
MGRS COORDINATES

Chapter 6). Of course, receiver units including all three of these options are the most versatile because they can be used in conjunction with all types of maps and charts and in both nautical and land-based situations.

We will look next at the practical application of a land-based coordinate system. Finally, after you have had the opportunity to plot and read positions using a coordinate system, we will more closely examine the theories and structures behind each of these three coordinate strategies, beginning with True Geographic Coordinates. Although the use of LAT/LON is not the most advantageous positioning strategy for use on land, it is presented first because it is fitted to our spherically-shaped world and forms the basis for the multitude of other coordinate systems (including UTM/MGRS) that have since been devised to apply perpendicular grids to the flat drawings of the earth's surface we call maps.

Coordinates determined through the use of latitude and longitude are referred to as "true" because the position measurements are not based upon the distortions incumbent with the already flattened earth's surface and square grids. For this same reason, we refer to UTM/MGRS coordinates as being "false eastings" and "false northings", as, by definition, they cannot be precisely true. However, make no mistake about it, lines of latitude and longitude are also quite distorted on flat maps, just as is the portrayal of the earth's surface. It simply can't be avoided. Incidentally, this is what map projections and datums are all about; and these, too, will be explained later in this chapter.

MAP COORDINATE SYSTEMS:

A PRACTICAL APPLICATION

Our experience in teaching people to understand various map coordinate systems has revealed that it is most effective to first show them how to read and apply any one system and, after that, assist them to more fully examine the structures and theories behind them. Therefore, we will begin by learning how to locate and report a position on Alexis Publishing's new road maps using its easy-to-understand Universal GPS (UGPS) Grid™. In addition to these maps being excellent guides for highway travel while using GPS (see Chapter 6), they are designed to be useful teaching aids for introducing the concepts underlying the various grid coordinate systems.

By way of introduction, Alexis' UGPS™ Grid actually consists of UTM grid lines labeled with both MGRS and UTM coordinate values. Don't forget, the MGRS is actually a modified form of the UTM--not a completely separate grid coordinate system.

Because of the several datums used as the basis for drawing the various maps in service over the years, the MGRS has evolved into two versions, both very much in use today. These so-called "old" and "new" versions of the MGRS will be explained later in the chapter, but, for now, let us just say that the Alexis Road Maps utilize grid lines and labels from the "old" version. This is the one designated for use with maps utilizing the North American Datum-1927 (NAD-27).

Without question, the MGRS modification to the UTM grid is the easiest to understand and use land-based position location system ever devised. The best analogy for understanding its use is to compare it to a telephone number; but more importantly, it assigns a unique identifier (worldwide position address) to each and every pinpoint location anywhere on earth.

(Note: The GPS manufacturing company, Eagle/Lowrance, refers to the "old" version of the MGRS as "ALT MGRS;" whereas Magellan calls it "MGRS-1." Conversely, Eagle refers to the "new" version of MGRS as "STANDARD MGRS", whereas, Magellan calls it "MGRS-2". Garmin receivers automatically utilize the correct version of MGRS when you select the correct map datum for the map.)

EMPLOYING THE UNIVERSAL GPS GRID™ USING ITS MGRS LABELS (PREFERRED METHOD)

When using these maps, your GPS unit's MGRS coordinates locate a position by identifying a large region (similar to a telephone AREA CODE), a smaller locality found within that region (analogous to the local area covered by a particular exchange), and a set of unique map coordinate numbers pinpointing a specific location (as in identifying a unique telephone using the last four digits of its number). For example, if you wished to call the main switchboard at the Lehigh Valley International (LVI) Airport near Allentown, Pennsylvania, you would check a directory to obtain the number which is (610) 266-6000. In thinking geographically for a moment, the AREA CODE map found in any phone book will tell you that LVI is located somewhere in central, eastern Pennsylvania (Area Code 610). Furthermore, EXCHANGE 266 within AREA CODE 610 is assigned to Catasauqua, one of Allentown's northeast suburbs located adjacent to the airport.

We will now apply this same thinking to reading and reporting positions on an Alexis highway map (see the segment of the Pennsylvania road map found in **Figure 3-5**). While standing on the north shoulder of U.S. Highway 22 just south of the LVI Airport terminal building, we read our position coordinates on a GPS receiver in "old MGRS" (MGRS-1 or Alt. MGRS) values as being <18T V V 63 99>.

When reading coordinates from a map using any UTM-based system, such as the Alexis road maps or U.S. Geological Survey (USGS) topographic quadrangles, the rule is always to **read right first** (the easting value) and then **up** (the northing value). **Figure 3-6A** illustrates the "regional layout" for the United States on Alexis' maps. Our position adjacent to the LVI Airport is located in REGION 18T-**read right** to Grid Zone 18 and **up** to row T. On the Alexis road maps (**Figure 3-5**), all regional boundaries are marked and labeled in dark green. Next, **Figure 3-6B** depicts the 100 x 100 kilometer square LOCALITIES included within the region named 18T. Our position along US Rt. 22 is found in LOCALITY V V--east (**right**) to column V and north (**up**) to row V. LOCALITY boundaries and labels are shown in purple (**Figure 3-5**). Finally, **Figure 3-6C** depicts a hypothetical map sheet displaying a grid with lines spaced every ten kilometers, just as they are shown on the actual map. In

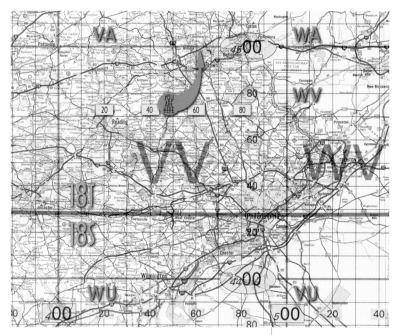

FIGURE 3-5
STATE OF PENNSYLVANIA ROAD MAP
FEATURING: UNIVERSAL GPS GRID™
ALEXIS PUBLISHING, DIVISION OF ALEXIS USA, INC.

fact, let's now shift our full attention to the map segment in **Figure 3-5**.

First, notice the dark green boundary (with labels) separating regions 18S and 18T, which runs along the southern (lower) portion of the map segment. We are, of course, located north of (above) that line in REGION 18T. Next, find the 100 x 100 kilometer square LOCALITY labeled V V outlined and labeled in purple. Finally, reading first to the **right** and then **up**, make use of our four-digit map coordinate 63 99.

Proceeding from west to east (from the left boundary moving to the right) in LOCALITY V V, locate the grid line labeled 60 and then continue to the **right** by estimating 3 tenths of the distance eastward toward grid line 70, thereby, establishing the location of an estimated grid line with a value of 63. Next, proceeding from south to north (**up** from the lower boundary) in LOCALITY V V, locate the grid line labeled 90 and estimate 9 tenths of the distance northward **up** toward the grid line labeled 00 (also considered to be 100), which forms the boundary between LOCALITIES V V and VA. Finally, by determining the intersection of these two estimated grid lines (63 and 99), you have located our position on the state map to within an accuracy of 1 kilometer (approximately 0.6 miles).

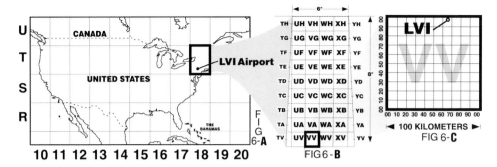

FIGURE 3-6
A: REGIONS
B: LOCALITIES
C: MAP GRID
FROM ALEXIS USA ROAD MAP SERIES

When using the larger scale inset map of the Allentown-Bethlehem area, one of several contained on the reverse side of the Pennsylvania map sheet, shown here in **Figure 3-7**, you should set your GPS receiver unit to report a six-digit coordinate. This allows you to determine your position on the map to within an accuracy of 100 meters (approximately one football field). For our roadside location just south of the airport terminal, the six-digit coordinate would read on the GPS receiver as <18T V V 630 992>. You will notice that the grid lines on this larger scale inset map are spaced at only 1 kilometer. Thus, by estimating values between them in terms of tenths, you are pinpointing a position to within 100 meters. You will note that the airport's runways, located only a few hundred meters to the north fall within the next locality labeled VA. The sequence of upper case letters used to label these localities run vertically (first letter) and horizontally (second letter) from A through V, but exclude the letters I and O because they can easily be confused with numerals.

EMPLOYING THE UNIVERSAL GPS GRID USING ITS UTM LABELS

You will notice that Alexis Publishing's road maps (**Figure 3-5**) carry the special small-digit UTM grid™ values on each of its "00" labeled lines. However, when using the UTM labels, you are to interpret them as being part of every grid line label appearing on the map.

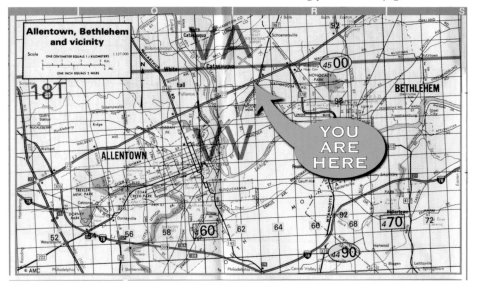

Without right now delving into a full explanation of the worldwide construct of the UTM system (which will be explained later), it is sufficient to say that the position reading on a GPS receiver unit set to report coordinates in UTM values appears a bit different, yet very similar to coordinates reported in MGRS values. The common characteristics are that the larger numerals are identical to those numbers reported in a four-digit MGRS coordinate and subsequent numbers included in the six (or more) digit MGRS coordinates match those small numerals to the right of the large ones in the UTM readout. Returning to our example, a GPS unit reporting our position along the shoulder of the highway in UTM values would read:

FIGURE 3-7
INSET MAP OF LEHIGH VALLEY, PENNSYLVANIA
FEATURING: UNIVERSAL GPS GRID™
ALEXIS PUBLISHING, DIVISION OF ALEXIS USA, INC.

UTM reading	as compared with	MGRS readings
(accurate to 1 m.)		(you select number of digits to be used)

18   4**63**000mE   18T VV 63 99

(accurate to 1000 m./ 1k.)

44**99**200mN   VV 630 992

(accurate to 100 m.)

18T VV 6300 9920

(accurate to 10 m.)

18T VV 63000 99200

(accurate to 1 m.)

Note: With SA, civilian GPS units can be considered to be accurate to within about 100 to 125 meters.

18 (Grid Zone 18)   4**63**000mE--- (463,000 meters easting / 463.0 kilometers easting)

Note: The central (index) vertical grid line within each grid zone is labeled 5**00**000mE (500,000 meters or 500 kilometers of easting). Therefore, for grid lines located to the west (left) of center, their label values decrease from 500,000m and to the east (right), they increase. Each of the 60 UTM grid zones around the globe have a width of six degrees of longitude ($6° \times 60° = 360°$).

44**99**200mN (4,499,200 meters northing / 4,499.2 kilometers of northing)

Note: The central (index) horizontal grid line within each grid zone is synonymous with the equator and for the northern hemisphere is labeled as 0**00**000mN. For the southern hemisphere, the grid line at the equator is labeled as 100**00**000mN (10,000 kilometers north). Each of the 60 grid zones stretch vertically from 80 degrees south latitude to 84 degrees north latitude, thereby, covering most inhabited areas of the globe.

In summary, our position along the shoulder of the highway near Allentown is 37,000 meters (37 kilometers) west of the center of UTM Grid Zone 18 (500,000m - 463,000m = 37,000m) and 4,499,200 meters (4,499.2 kilometers) north of the equator.

In conclusion, it is obvious that the regions, localities, and specific map coordinates defined by the MGRS labels are easier to understand and use than those defined by the UTM labels. Nevertheless, by including both sets of labels on the UGPS Grid™, these maps will meet the needs of all land navigators by accommodating the reporting formats of all GPS receivers. Furthermore, the Universal GPS Grid™ is fully compatible with the USGS's large- and intermediate-scale topographic maps which utilize UTM grid labels and are commonly used by hikers, hunters, and other outdoor enthusiasts who frequently navigate with GPS.

Hint: You might even find it easier to navigate with a USGS topographic map quadrangle while using an MGRS readout on your GPS receiver because when hiking in a localized area, you are only concerned about the large-digit UTM grid values which, if you ignore the REGION & LOCALITY, are identical to an MGRS reading.

MAP COORDINATE SYSTEMS:

THEORY AND STRUCTURE

Now, let's take a closer look at the three most commonly used map coordinate systems used here in the United States to gain a conceptual understanding of their construction.

GEOGRAPHIC COORDINATES

Reporting positions in terms of their **latitude** and **longitude** has been the fundamental method for defining a point on the earth's surface since it was developed by the ancient Greeks. The positional values for this coordinate system are defined within the context of the network of lines formed by: (1) **Parallels** - horizontal lines drawn east and west around the globe, equidistant from each other and parallell to the equator (**Figure 3-8**), and (2) **Meridians** - vertical lines drawn north and south on the globe perpendicular to the parallels and converging at the poles (**Figure 3-9**).

Figure 3-10 puts them together to form a complete geographic coordinate framework. The **latitude** of a point on the earth's surface is its distance north or south of the equator, as measured by the horizontal parallels encircling the globe. You simply count the values of the lines found between the **equator** (0° parallel) and the point you wish to define either in the northern or southern hemisphere. (For example, the latitude of Schweinfurt, Germany, is 50° N. Lat. and of Osorio, Brazil, is 30° S. Lat.)

On the other hand, the **longitude** of a point on the earth's surface is its distance east or west of the **prime meridian** (0° meridian), as measured by counting the values of the meridians running between the poles from the prime meridian to the point being considered either in the eastern or western hemisphere. Most nations recognize the meridian passing through Greenwich, England, as their **prime meridian.** (For example, the

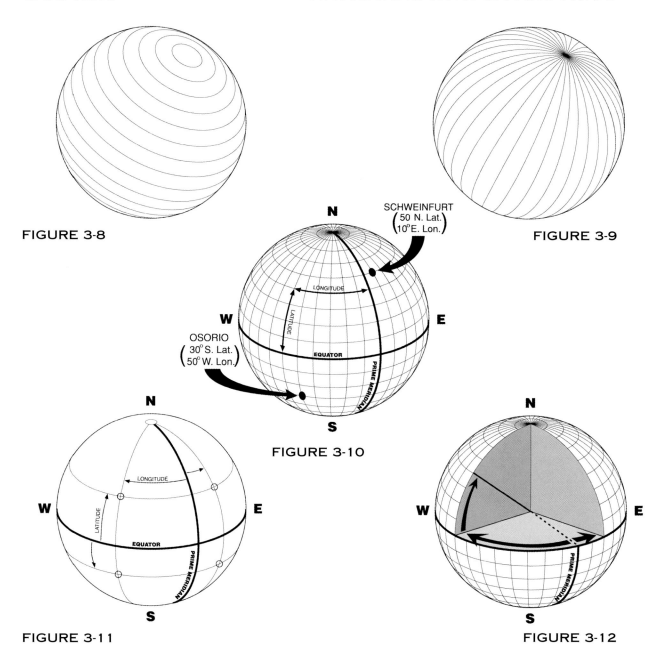

FIGURE 3-8

FIGURE 3-9

SCHWEINFURT
50 N. Lat.
10° E. Lon.

OSORIO
30° S. Lat.
50° W. Lon.

FIGURE 3-10

FIGURE 3-11

FIGURE 3-12

longitude of Schweinfurt, Germany, is 10° E. Lon. and of Osorio, Brazil, is 50° W. Lon.)

Figure 3-11 clearly illustrates that, when using geographic coordinates, locations anywhere on the earth's surface are reported as either **north** or **south** latitude and **east** or **west** longitude. **Figure 3-12** gives us a better conceptual look at this coordinate framework and conveys the angular nature of the geographic coordinate system.

As illustrated in **Figure 3-12**, latitude is measured in degrees north or south of the equator as if you were to read the angular measurement to any point on the earth's surface from its center. The equator would be level with your horizontally outstretched arm and considered to be 0° (0 degrees) latitude, while the north pole would be vertically straight up at a 90° angle. Thus, the north pole would have a latitude of 90° north. Of course, the same would be true south of the equator where latitude has values ranging from 0° to 90° south. Using this same concept of measuring angles to locations horizontally around the earth's surface from a perspective in the center, longitude ranges from 0° at the prime meridian (Greenwich, England) to 180° both east and west—depending in which hemisphere you are located. **The International Dateline** is located at 180° of longitude. (This imaginary line establishes the beginning of a new calendar day when the sun is directly over the prime meridian.)

It's easy to see that every point on the globe can be defined and reported in terms of north or south

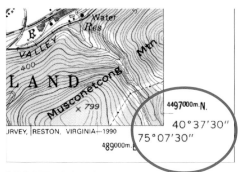

FIGURE 3-13

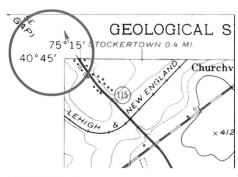

FIGURE 3-14

latitude and east or west longitude. However, when using only full degrees of arc to define a position, this system is not very precise. One degree (1°) of latitude anywhere on the earth's surface and one degree (1°) of longitude only along the equator are equal to a distance of 69.17 miles (111.32 kilometers).

If we are going to use latitude and longitude as a means for locating or reporting our positions precisely on a map, we must divide these measurements into smaller units. Therefore, each degree of latitude and longitude is broken into 60 minutes (60') and each minute into 60 seconds (60"). This has nothing to do with time—they are units of angular measurement. Therefore, 1 minute (1') of latitude anywhere on the earth's surface and 1 minute (1') of longitude only along the equator are both equal to 1.15 miles (1.86 kilometers) of linear distance. And finally, 1 second (1") of latitude anywhere on earth's surface and 1 second (1") of longitude at the equator are equal to a linear distance of 33.82 yards (30.33 meters). Most GPS units can report the latitude and longitude of positions in degrees, minutes, and seconds or in degrees and minutes (down to hundredths of a minute). **Note to Nautical Navigators: 1 minute of latitude anywhere or longitude at the equator equals 1 nautical mile along the earth's surface.**

On most large-scale civilian and military topographic maps, the latitude and longitude of the maps' four corners appear in the margins. For example, the southeast (lower right) corner of the Easton, PA, NJ, USA, 1:24,000-scale U.S. Geological Survey (USGS) topographic map sheet is located at 40°37'30" N Lat. and 75°07'30" W Lon. (**Figure 3-13**). The entire sheet covers an area equal to 7.5' of Lat. x 7.5' of Lon.; therefore, the northwest (upper left) corner of the map is located at 40°45' N Lat. and 75°15' W Lon. (**Figure 3-14**). Graticule marks (a network of lines and ticks representing latitude & longitude) are also shown and labeled at prescribed intervals in many maps' margins (**Figure 3-15**).

Using **Figure 3-16**, what is the latitude and longitude of the dot representing the location of that old ship (to the nearest degree)?

Your answer should be 48° N. Lat. and 27° W. Lon. Now, using the large-scale topographic map found in **Figure 3-17**, determine the latitude and longitude of the black circle to the nearest minute .

FIGURE 3-15

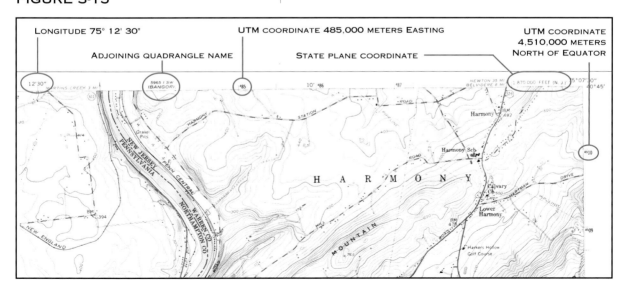

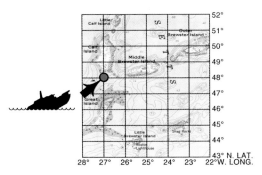

FIGURE 3-16

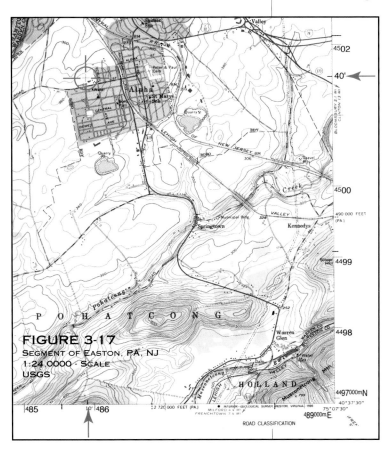

FIGURE 3-17
SEGMENT OF EASTON, PA, NJ
1:24,0000 - SCALE
USGS

Your answer should be 40° 40' N Lat. and 75° 10' W. Lon. Unless you wish to construct or purchase a properly scaled measuring device, you can simply estimate the distances to various locations falling between the parallels and meridians shown on your map or chart.

One disadvantage of using geographic coordinates in land navigation is that 1 degree, minute, or second of **longitude** does not represent the same linear distance along the earth's surface in all locations. They become increasingly shorter as your position moves farther from the equator (both north and south). Remember, the meridians used to measure longitude converge at the poles (**Figure 3-18**). Since we have already stated that 1° of longitude ONLY ALONG the equator is approximately 69 statute miles or 111 kilometers, then 20° of longitude (distance of A1) would equal approximately 1380 statute miles or 2220 kilometers. At 50° North latitude, 1° of longitude represents approximately only 44.6 statute miles or 71.7 kilometers; therefore, 20° of longitude (distance of A2) would equal approximately 892 statute miles or 1434 kilometers of linear distance. On the other hand, linear distances for latitude anywhere on the earth remain unchanged (note B2 and B1). Both are 20° of latitude and both are aproximately 1380 statute miles or 2220 kilometers of linear distance.

Now that you fully understand how to locate any position on a map displaying geographic coordinates, we will proceed to examine a coordinate system that was specifically designed for use on land.

UNIVERSAL TRANSVERSE MERCATOR (UTM) GRID COORDINATES

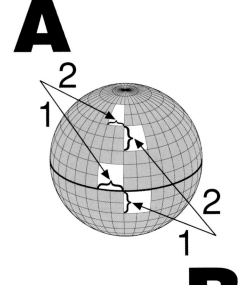

FIGURE 3-18
LONGITUDINAL SECTIONS (A) DO NOT SWEEP OUT EQUAL DISTANCES AT DIFFERENT LOCATIONS ON THE EARTH, WHILE LATITUDINAL SECTIONS (B) DO.

As has been already stated, cartographers must always introduce distortion errors into their maps because they are representing the surface of our spherically-shaped planet on a flat piece of paper. Thus, the only decisions facing any map maker become how much distortion error the maps will have and what type. Over the centuries, a multitude of mathematical schemes, called map projections and coordinate systems, have been developed. The coordinate system used most commonly on medium- and large-scale maps produced by the U.S. and many other governments is the **Universal Transverse Mercator** (UTM) **Grid**. The Transverse Mercator Projection induces the least amount of distortion on a series of large-scale maps covering sizable land areas and the UTM Grid Coordinate System provides a perpendicular grid with constant linear surface distance values between each of its grid lines in all directions.

To understand how this projection works, imagine the earth as an orange with parallels and meridians drawn upon it. Now, using a knife and after slicing off small circles at the poles, make a series of straight north-south cuts in the peel at equal intervals of 6° completely around the orange until 60 identical strips have been detached (**Figure 3-19**).

Each of these segments forms the basis of a separate map projection. Because each zone is relatively narrow (only 6° of longitude), its flattening results in a minimal distortion of the features shown on the surface.

The UTM Projection has been designed to cover that portion of the earth's surface located between the latitudes of 80° South to 84° North in a wide band running around the globe. This includes most of the world's inhabited lands. There is another grid system designed for the circular areas cut out of the two polar regions (Universal Polar Stereographic UPS Grid).

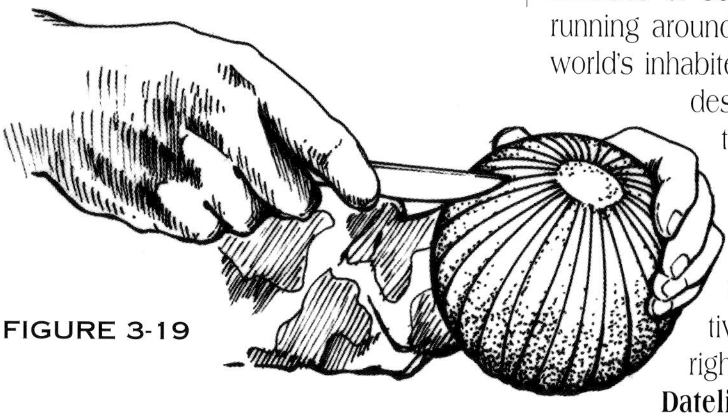

By international usage, all of the UTM grid zones have been consecutively numbered from west to east (left to right) 1 to 60, beginning at the **International Dateline** (180° Lon.). **UTM grid zone 1** is a vertical area running between the meridians located at 180° W and 174° W Lon. (6 degrees in width), with its central meridian being located at 177° W Lon. The Easton, PA, NJ, USA, map sheet discussed earlier is located within UTM grid zone 18 (**Figure 3-20**).

FIGURE 3-19

52

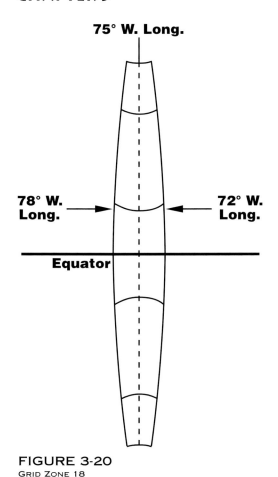

FIGURE 3-20
GRID ZONE 18

Since the pattern of UTM grid lines were superimposed on the "orange peel strips" (grid zones) **after** they were flattened, these grid lines are straight, undistorted, and perpendicular. However, all meridians and parallels, with the exception of the central meridian and the equator (central parallel) within each of these grid zones, were slightly distorted by the flattening process (**Figure 3-20**). This means that only the **central meridian** and **equator** can serve concurrently as lines of latitude and longitude and as perpendicular UTM grid lines. Therefore, these two lines have become the basis for numbering the grid lines within each of the 60 grid zones. In addition, they obviously serve to link the UTM Grid Coordinate System to the True Geographic Coordinate System.

To briefly summarize what you have just learned about the UTM Grid Coordinate System, each of the UTM grid zones (orange peel slices) is 6° wide. The central meridian and the equator serve as the origins for labeling the false easting and false northing values represented by the grid lines superimposed on each of the 60 UTM grid zones which together encircle the globe. Each central meridian is labeled 500,000mE. (500 kilometers E). The equator serves as 000,000mN (0 kilometers N). for the northern hemisphere and 1000,000mN (10,000 kilometers N). for the southern hemisphere. Grid values increase as you proceed from west to east and from south to north (Figure 3-21). Therefore, you read UTM grid coordinates to the **right and up**.

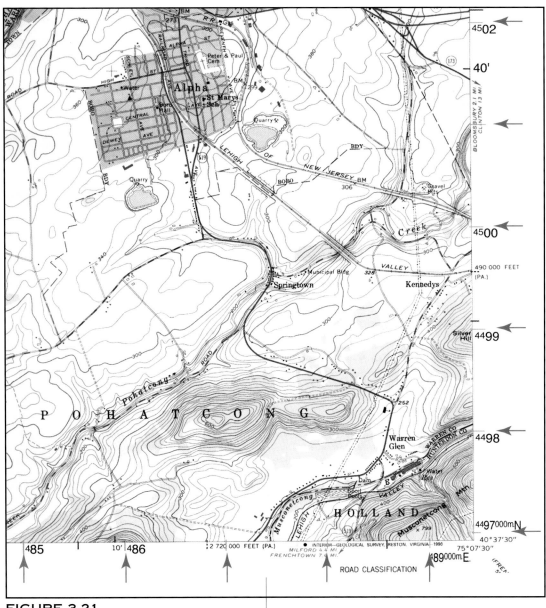

FIGURE 3-21
SEGMENT OF EASTON, PA, NJ
1:24,000 SCALE MAP SHEET
USGS

Use of the UTM grid coordinate system is much easier for the land navigator to adapt to than is latitude and longitude. The grid is made up of perpendicular lines with equal ground distances from one to the next. They are also clearly labeled on most large-scale and many intermediate-scale maps.

For example, take another look at the segment of the southeast (lower right) corner of the Easton, PA, NJ, USA 1:24,000-scale USGS topographic map sheet shown in **Figure 3-21**. The UTM grid system is represented by small blue tick marks and some black numerical labels in the margins outside the frame (neatline) of the map. (Note the arrows in the illustration pointing to these tick marks.) These tick marks can easily be connected using a pencil and straight edge to form the UTM grid pattern on the map as in **Figure 3-48**. The newer large scale (1:25,000 or 1:50,000-scale) and many of the smaller scale USGS map sheets (but larger than a 1:1,000,000-scale) carry a full printed UTM grid. All large- and intermediate-scale military topographic maps produced by the U.S. Department of Defense Mapping Agency (DMA) and its successor, the National Imagery and Mapping Agency (NIMA), have full UTM grid lines printed on them, as well.

Please note that the UTM grid line closest to the east (right) edge of the Easton, PA, NJ, USA, map (**Figure 3-21**) is labeled 489000mE (489,000 meters of false easting). Since the central meridian of each grid zone is arbitrarily labeled 500,000mE, we know that this grid line is only 11,000 meters (11 kilometers) from the central meridian. Because its value is less than

FIGURE 3-22
EAGLE EXPEDITION™ REPORTING A POSITION AS AN
MGRS COORDINATE

MILITARY GRID REFERENCE SYSTEM (MGRS)

500,000mE, we also know that it lies 11,000 meters (11 kilometers) west of (short of) the central meridian. You will recall that UTM grid values increase from west to east. On the other hand, the UTM grid line closest to the bottom of the map sheet is named 4497000mN (4,497,000 meters of false northing). For the areas covered in the northern hemisphere within each grid zone, the equator is the 00 starting point. Thus, this grid line is 4,497,000 meters (4,497 kilometers) north of the equator.

Just as a point of clarification, if your GPS receiver had given you a northing value of 4497700mN, this would mean you would have been located 7 tenths of a grid square north of grid line 4497000mN or 4,497,700 meters (4,497.7 kilometers) north of the equator.

Virtually everything you have learned about the UTM grid applies to MGRS. The general concept is that MGRS divides the world into large geographic areas, each of which is given a unique alphanumeric label called the **Grid Zone Designation** (Alexis calls them **Regions** on their road maps.) Each of these Grid Zone Designations, in turn, is covered by a pattern of 100,000-meter (100 kilometer x 100 kilometer) squares—each being labeled by two letters called the **100,000-Meter Square Identification** (**Locality** on Alexis' road maps). Finally, each 100,000-Meter Square Identification is further subdivided by the regular UTM grid lines with which you are familiar.

Figure 3-22 shows a GPS receiver reporting a position in MGRS coordinates. It should be noted that the Eagle GPS units always report 5-digit easting and northing values on different lines. You may use as many digits as you require, depending on the spacing of the grid lines on the map.

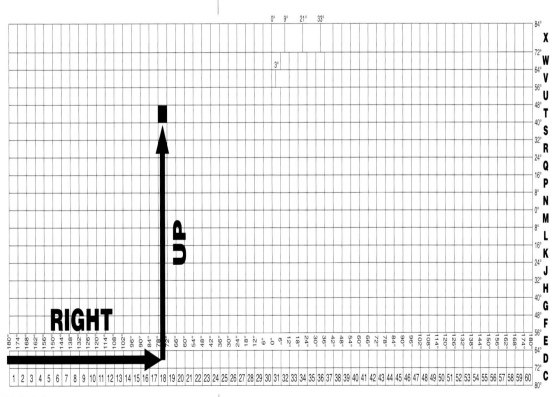

FIGURE 3-23
WORLD-WIDE MGRS GRID ZONE DESIGNATIONS

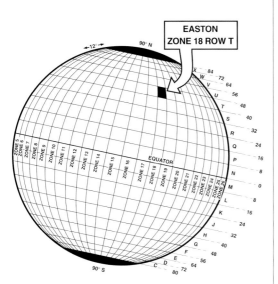

EASTON
ZONE 18 ROW T

FIGURE 3-24
MGRS GRID ZONE DESIGNATIONS

More specifically, the sixty 6° wide UTM grid zones (orange peel strips) are divided in the MGRS from south to north (bottom to top) into 20 lettered horizontal rows, each having a height of 8° of latitude (excepting the most northern row, which is 12°). These then are the building blocks of the MGRS called **Grid Zone Designations**. In **Figure 3-23**, you see the relationship of Grid Zone Designation 18T to those of the rest of the world. **Figure 3-24** shows a number of the 60 vertical grid zones and the 20 horizontal rows as they appear superimposed on a globe. This particular illustration shows us that the Easton, PA, USA, map sheet falls within the area covered by **MGRS Grid Zone Designation 18T** (west to east to UTM grid zone 18 and then south to north to row T). Finally, **Figure 3-25** depicts MGRS grid zone designations superimposed on a map showing most of North America with Easton, of course, being located in Grid Zone 18T.

The basic MGRS pattern of perpendicular grid lines are placed 100,000 meters (100 kilometers) apart and superimposed on each of the 6 degrees of longitude by 8 degrees of latitude (6° x 8°) Grid Zone Designations. This pattern of lines breaks each of these geographic areas into 100,000 x 100,000 meter (100 x 100 kilometer) squares identified by two letters. **Figure 3-26** shows us Grid Zone Designation 18T, the one in which Easton, PA, USA, is located, subdivided into several full and some pleat-shaped dual-letter labeled **100,000-Meter Square Identifications**. These partial

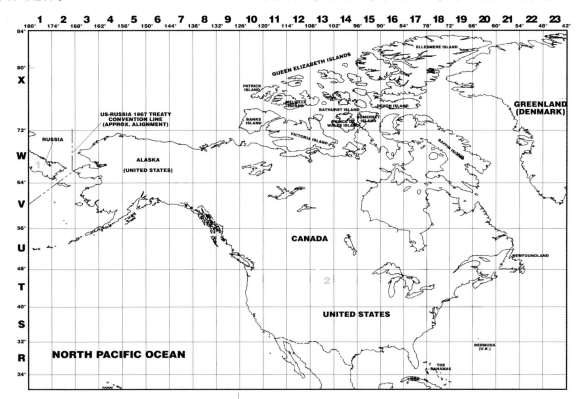

FIGURE 3-25
MGRS GRID ZONE DESIGNATIONS

identifications are created along the pleats of the 6° wide UTM grid zones because the linear widths of the grid zones (orange peel strips) decrease as you proceed north or south from the equator. The illustration highlights the fact that the Easton, PA, NJ, USA, map sheet is located in the 100,000-Meter Square Identification labeled VA.

Finally, these **100,000-Meter Square Identifications** are further subdivided by the regular numbered UTM grid lines spaced either 10 or 1 kilometer (s) apart on most large-scale topographic maps. Remember, the MGRS requires **only** that you read the large numerals (**e.g., 00** through **99**) on the UTM grid line labels. When the map scale is smaller than 1:100,000, these grid lines **may** be placed every 10 kilometers and numbered with a single large-size numeral **0** through **9** (**Figure 3-27**). When a grid line is labeled by a single large-size numeral, such as **4**, it has the same value (and is the same grid line) as when it is labeled on a larger scale map of the same area as **40**. In other words, grid lines labeled with a single large numeral are spaced every 10 kilometers, while grid lines labeled with two large numerals have a spacing of one kilometer.

You will recall that on the Alexis Road Maps using the Universal GPS Grid™ there are large numeral double-digit MGRS labels on grid lines spaced at ten kilometer intervals. This was done in order to remain consistent with the larger scale metropolitan area inset maps showing grid lines spaced at 1 kilometer intervals and to avoid confusion within the series; however, you should know this practice is not followed by the USGS on their intermediate-scale topographic map quadrangles displaying MGRS labels (e.g., 1:250,000-scale map sheets-**Figure 3-31**) or by NIMA on those sheets produced for the military (**Figure 3-27**). References to NIMA's military maps have been included in this book because many are available

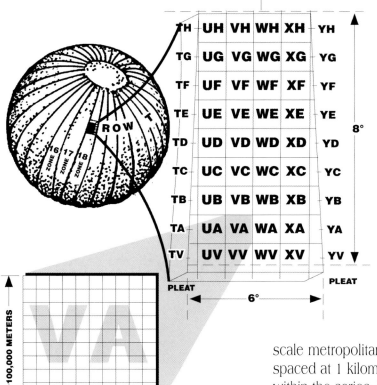

FIGURE 3-26
OLD MGRS (MGRS1 (MAGELLAN),
ALT. MGRS (EAGLE))

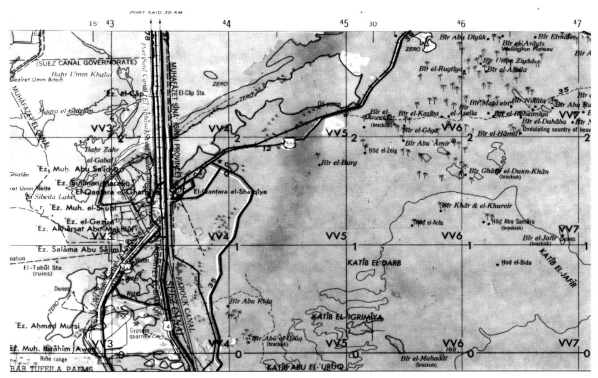

FIGURE 3-27
Suez Canal, Egypt, Map Sheet
1:250,000 Scale
DMA

to the public through sale by the USGS; but, map procurement is a topic we will discuss later.

Maps produced by the U.S. Department of Defense, some maps published by the US Geological Survey and those produced by numerous other mapping agencies around the world include a **grid reference box** in their margins. **Figure 3-28** was taken from the margin of the Evans Mills (Fort Drum), NY, USA, 1:50,000-scale map sheet, **Figure 3-29** from the Al Jumum, Kingdom of Saudi Arabia, 1:50,000-scale map sheet, and **Figure 3-30** from the Newark, NJ, PA, USA, 1:250,000-scale map sheet (USGS.). The medium-scale

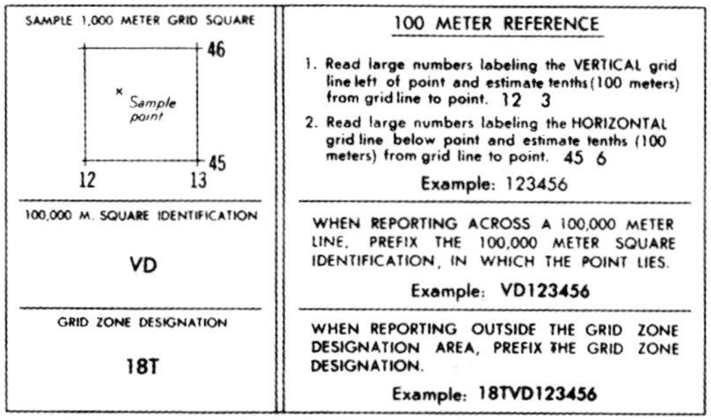

FIGURE 3-28
EVANS MILLS, NY
1:50,000 SCALE MAP SHEET
NIMA (OLD MGRS - NAD 27 CONUS)

TWO MGRS FORMATS

FIGURE 3-29
AL JUMUM, KSA
1:50,000 SCALE MAP SHEET
(OLD MGRS - INTL SPHEROID 1967)

Newark map sheet encompasses the Easton, PA, NJ, USA, area used in previous illustrations.

You will note that the area covered by the Evans Mills (Fort Drum) map sheet is located within the Grid Zone Designation **18T** and 100,000-Meter Identification **VD**. The area covered by the Al Jumum map sheet is located within the Grid Zone Designation **37Q** and the 100,000-Meter Identifications **EE** and **ED**. And, the area covered by the Newark 1:250,000-scale map sheet is located within the Grid Zone Designation **18T** and the four 100,000-Meter Square Idetifications: **VA**, **WA**, **VV**, and **WV**. Please note that the grid line labels on the 1:250,000-scale map sheet have only one large numeral because the grid lines are spaced every 10,000 meters (10 kilometers), rather than every 1000 meters (1 kilometer), as on larger scale maps (**Figure 3-31**).

You will recall that all maps and GPS receiver units utilizing the MGRS position coordinate system refer to either of the two MGRS formats in existence today. They are commonly referred to as "old" and "new" MGRS; but Eagle calls them "ALT. MGRS" and "MGRS" respectively and Magellan "MGRS-1" and "MGRS-2." The primary differences between them being that there are different dual-letter labels for the 100,000 Meter-Square Identifications (Alexis' LOCALITIES) and some differences in grid line placements on the maps within each of the two formats.

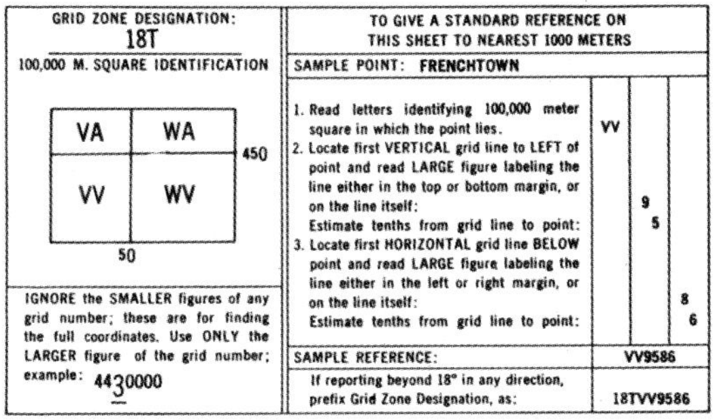
GRID ZONE DESIGNATION:
18T
100,000 M. SQUARE IDENTIFICATION
VA
WA
VV
WV
450
50
IGNORE the SMALLER figures of any grid number; these are for finding the full coordinates. Use ONLY the LARGER figure of the grid number; example: 4430000
TO GIVE A STANDARD REFERENCE ON THIS SHEET TO NEAREST 1000 METERS
SAMPLE POINT: FRENCHTOWN
1. Read letters identifying 100,000 meter square in which the point lies.
2. Locate first VERTICAL grid line to LEFT of point and read LARGE figure labeling the line either in the top or bottom margin, or on the line itself:
Estimate tenths from grid line to point:
3. Locate first HORIZONTAL grid line BELOW point and read LARGE figure labeling the line either in the left or right margin, or on the line itself:
Estimate tenths from grid line to point:
VV
9
5
8
6
SAMPLE REFERENCE:
VV9586
If reporting beyond 18° in any direction, prefix Grid Zone Designation, as:
18TVV9586

FIGURE 3-30
NEWARK, NJ, PA
1:250,000 SCALE MAP SHEET
USGS (OLD MGRS - NAD 27 CONUS)

According to the Defense Mapping School, the "old MGRS" format (Eagle's "ALT. MGRS" & Magellan's "MGRS-1") is applied to maps constructed utilizing datums based upon the following three ellipsoids (theoretical earth shapes): Bessel 1841, Clarke 1866 and Clarke 1880. Furthermore, the School stated that the "new MGRS" format (Eagle's "ALT MGRS" & Magellan's "MGRS-2") is used on maps constructed using datums based upon the following seven ellipsoids: WGS 84, GRS 80, WGS 72, Australian Natl., Everest South Amer., International, and Clarke 1866 only for UTM Grid Zones 47-50. The name of the datum and/or ellipsoid used as the basis for constructing a map is often included in the map's margin, and, if not, it can sometimes be determined by being familiar with the cartographic practices employed by mappers located within various countries.

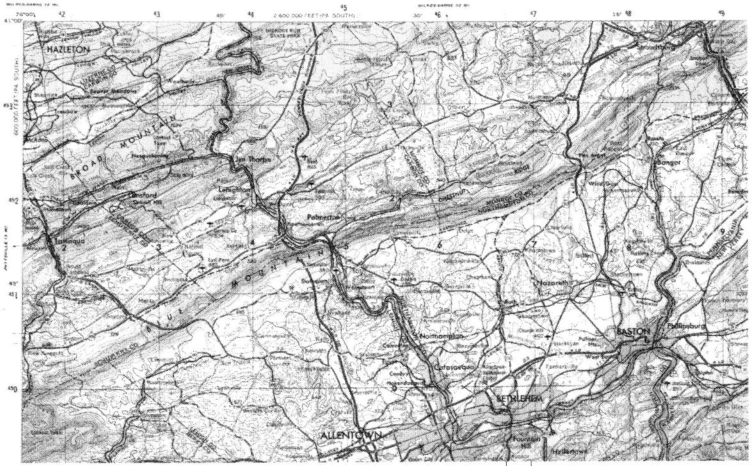
HAZLETON
ALLENTOWN
BETHLEHEM
EASTON
Palmerton

FIGURE 3-31
NEWARK, NJ, PA
1:250,000 SCALE
USGS

For example, most U.S. military maps and USGS topographic map quadrangles for locations within the continental United States (CONUS) were constructed using the North American Datum-1927 (NAD-27), which was derived from earth-based surveys using the Clarke 1866 ellipsoid. Therefore, most existing maps utilizing information contained on USGS quadrangles (including Alexis Publishing's road map series, virtually all other commercial street and highway maps produced within this country, and the vast majority of military maps cover-

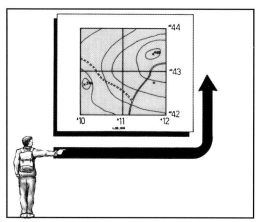

FIGURE 3-32
ALWAYS READ RIGHT FIRST AND THEN UP
(EASTING VALUE FIRST AND THEN NORTHING VALUE)

MORE SPECIFICALLY, WHERE AM I?

ing CONUS) either do or should apply the "old MGRS" grid format when achieving GPS compatibility. Some of the latest military maps, as well other new satellite-based maps, are now just beginning to be constructed on the WGS-84 datum, which utilizes actual gravitational measurements taken from space in deriving the World Geodetic System-1984 (WGS-84) geoid.

Obviously, for a number of years to come, the most commonly used format of the MGRS will continue to be "old MGRS." Nevertheless, NIMA maps covering the largest military installations are presently being revised and based upon the WGS-84 datum. They, of course, utilize the "new MGRS" format. One such example is the Fort Drum, NY, map sheet, a segment of which will be seen later (**Figure 3-36**) as an illustration to demonstrate the importance of entering the correct map datum into your GPS receiver when working with a large-scale map. You will find this discussion at the end of this section on understanding map coordinates.

Now, let's get down to the most useful details. When using a large-scale civilian or military topographic map showing a MGRS/UTM grid every 1000 meters (1 kilometer), we begin to pinpoint locations by first locating the grid square in which the position falls. For example, the "X" marking the top of hill 450 on the map segment in **Figure 3-32** is located in the 1,000-meter grid square "named" 1143 (not 4311) because you must **read right first and then up**. The first two digits,11XX, naming this grid square represent the false easting grid label (read from left to right), and the last two digits, XX43, represent the false northing label (read from bottom to top).

To be even more precise in your position reporting, you can subdivide the 1000 meter square in each direction into tenths (100 meter segments), either by measurement or estimate, and specify the position reading in greater detail. Hill 450 is located .6 of the distance between grid lines 11 and 12 (going east) and .3 of the way between grid lines 43 and 44 (going north). Thus, the coordinates of "X" to the nearest hundred meters, by **reading right first and then up**, are reported as 116433 .

If this position were located in New Jersey some distance northeast of Easton, PA, USA, its full designation in the MGRS (old version) would be 18T WA 116433. By including the Grid Zone Designation (**18T**), 100,000-Meter Square Designation (**WA**), and six-digit numerical coordinates (116433), you have given the "X" on hilltop 450 a unique worldwide address to a degree of accuracy of 100 meters. The MGRS readout on the screen of the GPS receiver would be (18TWA116 433). It would also report its elevation as being 450 feet or 137 meters above sea level, depending upon which units are used to report elevations on the map and were set on the receiver. You certainly should have no difficulty reading and understanding this information. When you go to pinpoint your location on the map, you simply use the two (2) large numerals in the grid line labels and interpolate the number of tenths between them for the third and sixth digits of the six-digit coordinate reading.

Incidentally, 116433 is referred to as a six-digit coordinate for obvious reasons. As a land navigator, you are generally required to work with and report positions on a map in six-digit coordinates (to within a 100-meter square area), but MGRS/UTM coordinates can be further refined.

Some MGRS units display MGRS positions as a single entity without spaces, parentheses, dashes, or decimal points. For example:

18T	Locates a point within the 6° x 8° Grid Zone Designation.
18TVA	Locates a point within a 100,000-meter square.
18TVA80	Locates a point within a 10,000-meter square.
18TVA8205	Locates a point within a 1,000-meter square.
18TVA825052	Locates a point within a 100-meter square.
	(If you are a surveyor, rather than a navigator, you might wish to continue.)
18TVA82500527	Locates a point within a 10-meter square.
18TVA8250105270	Locates a point within a 1-meter square.
	(And so forth.)

Note 1: MGRS grid coordinate 18TVA825052 is the location of the newly constructed Farinon Student Center on the campus of Lafayette College in Easton, PA, USA, (see **Figure 3-33**). Also, please note that its UTM Grid Coordinate is Grid Zone 18 482500mE 4505200mN. Finally, its true geographic coordinate is approximately 40° 41' 51" N. Lat., 75°12'26" W. Lon.

Note 2: Although MGRS grid coordinates are written without punctuation or spaces, GPS units often report them with a space separating the false easting from the false northing values (e.g., the Farinon Center is located at grid coordinates **18TVA825 052**).

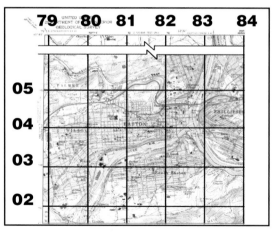

FIGURE 3-33
SEGMENT OF EASTON, PA, NJ
1:50,000 SCALE MAP SHEET
USGS

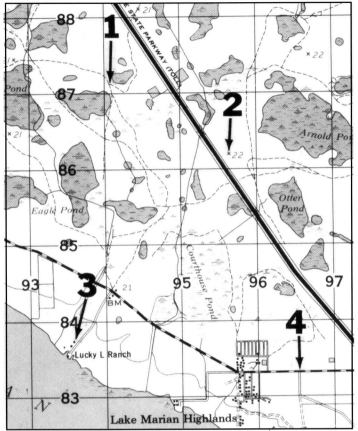

FIGURE 3-34

MAP DATUMS

Using the segment of the Lake Marian, FL, USA, map sheet found in **Figure 3-34**, estimate the six-digit coordinates of the features located at points 1 through 4. Remember, to **read right first and then up**. The Grid Zone Designation of this area of Florida is **17R** and the 100,000-Meter Square Identification for the area shown on the map is **MA**.

The solution to the above exercise is as follows: The position of Pt. 1 = 17RMA941871, Pt. 2 = 17RMA957862, Pt. 3 = 17RMA936838, and Pt. 4 = 17RMA965833. When navigating within a local area, the MGRS grid coordinates can be read and reported by using only the 100,000-Meter Square Identification (MA) or only the six final digits of the position's coordinates (e.g., Pt. 4 may be reported as MA965833 or as 965833).

While it is important when navigating with a large-scale map to select on your GPS receiver the corresponding horizontal map datum, it is not crucial to delve into the somewhat complicated mathematical calculations behind each of them. Nevertheless, the general concepts related to map datums are really quite simple and will be explained here.

For many centuries, educated men understood that our world was round and it was assumed to be in the shape of a nearly perfect sphere. The only question remaining seemed to be its exact size. Then, during the early 18th century, people like Isaac Newton and others began to determine that the earth was slightly flattened at the poles, which was later proven true by the numerous meridian measurements undertaken between 1799 and 1951. Thus, rather than being a sphere, the earth was proven to be an oblate ellipsoid that rotates on its shorter axis. Next, there were questions about its exact shape as well as its size.

In the case of small scale maps and globes, it is safe to assume that the earth is a perfect sphere, but when it comes to intermediate and large scale maps, the coordinate system or systems being placed on them must be fitted to a more accurate approximation of the earth's shape and size. These approximations, or theoretical mathematical models, are what datums are all about. As you can imagine, the comparatively small variations that exist among the configurations and dimensions of the various mathematical models used as the basis for drawing maps do affect both the vertical and horizontal datums associated with them.

Elevation is measured in relationship to a theoretical mean sea level (vertical datum). Linear dimensions (horizontal datums), as delineated on maps by the various coordinate systems, are affected by the amount of earth surface area presumed to exist. Each of these horizontal datums are then tied through a series of surveys to some arbitrary point of origin on the earth's surface. For nearly all intermediate and large scale maps produced by the U.S. Government, and, subsequently, by commercial mapping organizations that nearly always took their base information from the Government's maps, the mathematical model used is the one developed in 1866 by British geodesist Alexander Ross Clarke. The Clarke 1866 ellipsoid has an equatorial radius of 6,378,204.4 meters and a polar radius of 6,356,583.8 meters. In other words, Clarke determined that the earth was 43,241.2 meters (just over fourhundred football fields) "wider" than it is "tall".

For many decades, existing surveys in this country were converted and new surveys and various points of horizontal control were established and tied to the Clarke 1866 ellipsoid. Then, in 1927, the point of origin was moved from Maryland to the horizontal control point at Meades Ranch in Kansas, which, in a sense, became the "center of the earth's surface" for U.S. maps. Certainly, it was near the center of North America. Thus, we have the establishment of the North American Datum-1927 for the continental United States (CONUS), more frequently referred to as NAD-27 (CONUS).

Further study with our vastly improved scientific capabilities revealed that the earth is not really an exact oblate ellipsoid, either. Its theoretical mean sea level shape, called the geoid, actually undulates slightly based upon gravitational variations carefully measured from space. Nevertheless, the shape of the geoid varies no more than about 100 meters above or below the surface shape of an appropriately sized ellipsoid.

Today, the most accurate datum is called the World Geodetic System-1984, most commonly referred to as WGS-84. Unlike the NAD-27 datum, which is tied to a surveyed horizontal control point on the earth's surface in Kansas, the WGS-84 is actually tied to the center of the earth and reflects the true shape of the geoid as determined by gravitational measurements. Surprisingly, the greatest variations anywhere on the earth's surface between various coordinate systems, such as Lat./Lon., UTM/MGRS, and so forth, built on the NAD-27 (based upon the Clarke-1866 ellipsoid) and those same coordinate systems based upon the WGS-84 geoid are never greater than about 300 meters and are frequently far less. Lacking space satellites and today's precision measuring capabilities, Clarke really didn't do too badly in the middle of the 19th century.

As the result of all this study, we now have three different types of surface shapes to consider in regard to maps: 1) the topography of the earth's surface (not associated with datums), 2) the theoretical ellipsoids (mean sea levels) established by geodesists like Clarke and others, and 3) the more accurate geoid determined by gravitational measurements taken from space. See **Figure 3-35** for a graphic illustration.

To learn how significant errors can be induced into a position fix when using a GPS receiver having the wrong horizontal map datum selected for use, examine the MGRS/UTM grid labels found on the small segment taken from the southwest corner of the recently published Fort Drum, New York, Military Installation Map shown in **Figure 3-36**. The figure also includes mapping information taken from the sheet's bottom margin.

You will note that the MGRS/UTM grid based upon the WGS-84 horizontal datum is printed across the face of the map and labeled in black, while black tick marks inside the neatline of the map and occasional blue labels outside the neatline represent the MGRS/UTM grid based upon the NAD-27 (CONUS) horizontal datum (see blue arrows). As compared with the NAD-27, the WGS (1984)-based grid lines are located 33 meters west and 217 meters south of the NAD (1927)-based grid. The graticule used for latitude and longitude also reflects similar differences.

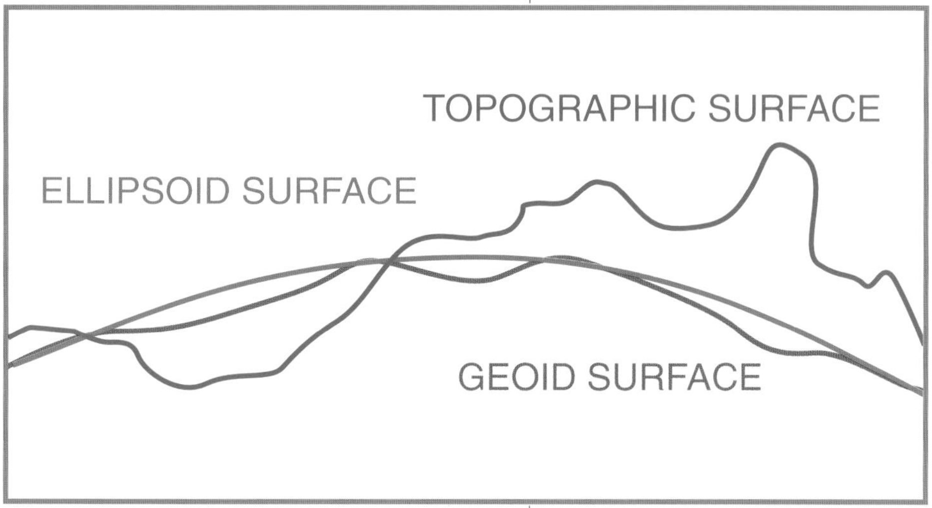

FIGURE 3-35
THREE EARTH SURFACE SHAPES

In order to convert WGS-84 UTM/MGRS coordinates to NAD-27 UTM/MGRS coordinates on the Fort Drum map, you must subtract 33 meters from the easting value and subtract 217 meters from the northing value. Just as important and as was discussed earlier in the section on the MGRS coordinate system, the two existing versions of MGRS (the "old MGRS" based upon the NAD-27 and the "new MGRS" based upon the WGS-

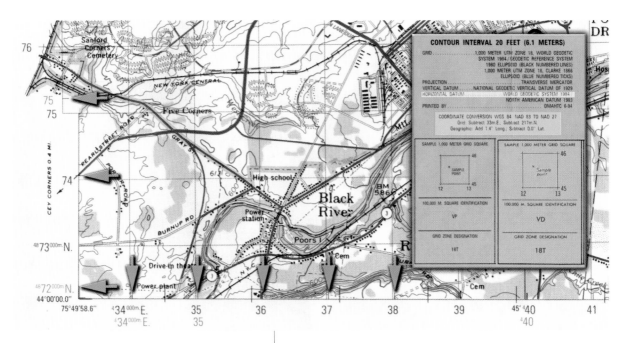

FIGURE 3-36
FORT DRUM, NY
1:50,000 SCALE MAP SHEET
NIMA
BLACK GRID LABELS AND GRID REF. BOX = WGS-84
BLUE GRID LABELS/ARROWS AND GRID REF. BOX =
NAD-27

84) use different labels for the 100,000 Meter-Square Identifications. Nevertheless, the Grid Zone Designations remain unchanged. As you can see from the grid reference boxes in **Figure 3-36**, in the WGS-84 version of the MGRS "new version", Fort Drum, NY, falls within the 100,000 Meter-Square Identification labeled **VP**; whereas, in the NAD-27 version of the MGRS "old version", it is located within the 100,000 Meter-Square Identification labeled **VD**. In either case, Fort Drum falls within Grid Zone Designation **18T**.

Before concluding this short discussion on map datums, you should be aware of the following facts:

• The map datums referred to in the GPS unit user manuals are horizontal map datums.

• GPS receiver units are nearly always set to the WGS-84 datum as the default, which does not match most maps.

• The vast majority of U.S. maps (commercial, USGS, and NIMA (military)) are still based upon the NAD-27.

• For GPS navigation and cartographic purposes, GRS-80, NAD-83 and WGS-84 datums are identical.

• The U.S. Government is now just beginning to produce maps based on datum WGS-84 and very few maps were ever produced using NAD-83 (based upon the GRS-80 geoid).

• Using the wrong horizontal datum on your GPS receiver might cause significant errors in your position fix.

• Between NAD-27 and WGS-84, the additional error (beyond natural GPS errors and those induced by SA) can be up to 300 meters and with other commonly used datums from around the world, the error range can stretch upward to a kilometer (e.g., the difference between the UTM/MGRS grid based upon the Tokyo datum and that based upon the WGS-84 is +156 meters of easting and -712 meters of northing).

Finally, lists of datums included on the various GPS receiver units and used in various places around the world are listed in the user manuals. Virtually all GPS receivers incorporate NAD-27, WGS-84, GRB-36 (Ordinance Survey of Great Britain-1936), EUR-79,

ALASK, OHAWA (Old Hawaiian), and many dozens of others from around the world.

Always knowing where you are in every possible way (relative to a locational grid, the map, and the real world) is imperative for success in land navigation. You now understand how to locate any position on a map using latitude and longitude (Geographic Coordinates) and UTM or MGRS grid coordinates (false easting and false northing). Now, when your GPS unit reports your position, you can easily find it on the map and then quickly relate it to the many features portrayed there and actually found on the ground in the area surrounding you. These features, whether they are natural or man-made, can be used to guide and channel your movements over functional routes to your destination.

Now that you are able to use coordinate systems to locate and report your position on a map, you are ready to consider the many other aspects of map using to assist you in navigating over the land.

SELECTING A GOOD MAP

A good map must include as much useful information as possible to help guide your movements without being cluttered and difficult to read. When selecting a map, you should consider the following: (1) its scale, (2) the amount of detail shown, (3) the quality of its portrayal (accuracy and legibility), (4) the reputation of its publisher, (5) its compilation date, and (6) whether it displays a coordinate system you understand and is compatible with your GPS equipment.

With regard to **map scale**, it should be as large as is practical depending upon the types of movements you are planning to make. You will recall that map scales are reported as a fraction or proportion (e.g., 1/50,000 or 1:50,000). The numerator represents the number of units measured on the map as compared to the number of those same units found in the denominator and out on the ground. Understand that a 1:50,000-scale map is larger in scale than one of 1:100,000-scale (1/2 pie is more than 1/4 pie). It will show more features and in much greater detail, but it will cover less ground area (**Figure 3-37**).

Dismounted navigators prefer to use large-scale topographic maps of 1:25,000- or 1:50,000-scale (**Figures 3-38 & 3-39**), while vehicular-mounted navigators, who are required to cover greater distances, may choose to use a smaller scale map. This might be a 1:75,000- or 1:100,000-scale county topographic or highway map (**Figure 3-40**). Finally, long-distance turnpike or freeway drivers may select a 1:250,000-scale topographic map (**Figure 3-41**) or a 1:1,000,000-scale state highway map (**Figure 3-42**) because a high degree of precision in pinpointing their locations is less important. Ultimately, scale can become so small that the map (or in the case of **Figure 3-43** - the photograph) has little value to the navigator.

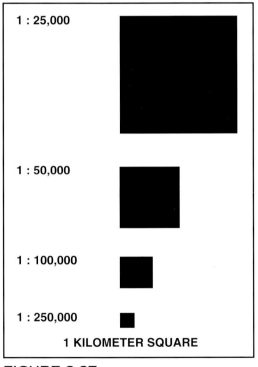

1 : 25,000

1 : 50,000

1 : 100,000

1 : 250,000

1 KILOMETER SQUARE

FIGURE 3-37

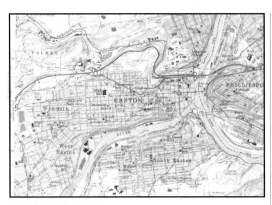

FIGURE 3-38
SEGMENT OF EASTON, PA, NJ
1:24,000 SCALE MAP SHEET
USGS

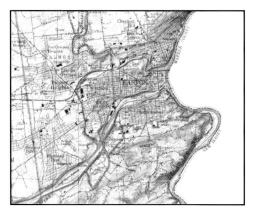

FIGURE 3-39
SEGMENT OF NORTHHAMPTON COUNTY, PA
1:50,000 SCALE MAP SHEET
USGS

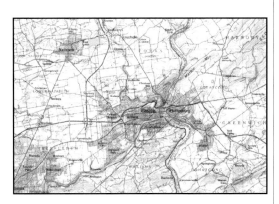

FIGURE 3-40
SEGMENT OF ALLENTOWN, PA
1:100,000 SCALE MAP SHEET
USGS

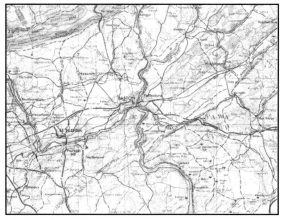

FIGURE 3-41
SEGMENT OF NEWARK, NJ, PA
1:250,000 SCALE MAP SHEET
USGS

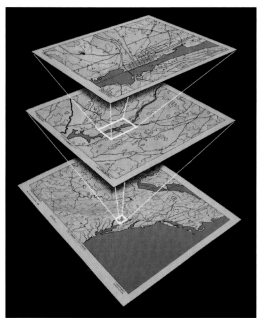

FIGURE 3-42
LARGEST SCALE MAP ON TOP
USGS

Generally, the more **detail of navigational significance** included on your map, the more useful it will become in helping you to select your route and guide your movements. The cross-country navigator must have information relative to terrain, water, vegetation and cultural (man-made) features. Those following trail and road networks can also benefit from this same type of information. However, those moving at a rate of 55 to 65 miles per hour or 90 to 100 kilometers per hour over well-marked thoroughfares can manage with far less detail. Nevertheless, the more information provided by the map, the easier it is to make good routing decisions (in terms of both actual as well as "functional" distances) and to follow that route.

The **quality of a map's portrayal of real world features**, including both legibility and accuracy, is not too difficult to judge by closely examining it. Too much information, inclusion of details not related to LN, and poor choices in the use of colors and symbology all contribute to the degree of difficulty encountered when reading a map. Accuracy is a bit more difficult to judge, but there are also several items you can check quickly to determine a map's quality in this regard.

Whenever the scale of the map is relatively large, look to see if the roads, streams, shorelines, and the edges of any forested areas portrayed seem to show frequent and somewhat irregular ripples and bends. Nature produces few straight lines or sweeping curves. In other words, the appearances of the many details included should be in relatively sharp focus rather than appearing to be highly generalized. Examine the map

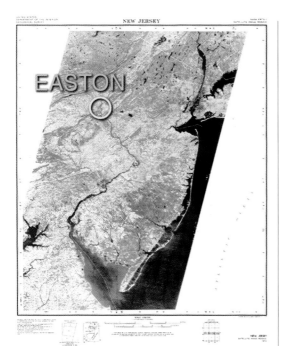

FIGURE 3-43
SEGMENT OF SATELLITE IMAGE MOSAIC
NJ, PA
1:1,700,000 SCALE
USGS

FIGURE 3-44
SEGMENT OF TWENTYNINE PALMS, CA
1:50,000 SCALE MAP SHEET
USDMA

closely to determine if there is a fair amount of detail shown as compared with the amount of space available in which to portray it. Large open areas on the map are an obvious warning sign regarding its comprehensiveness. Finally, closely examine any portion of the map covering an area with which you are familiar and compare its accuracy against your own knowledge of the area. If the map meets these quick tests with rather high marks, its accuracy can generally be relied upon to guide your movements.

Without question, the **reputation of the map's producer** for high quality cartography work can also serve as a guide to the map's potential accuracy. Today, most maps produced by governmental agencies are highly accurate. Do not trust any map that does not carry a credit line somewhere in its margin. If the producer doesn't want you to know who did the work, you probably should not rely upon it either.

Although a map's **compilation date** is not related to the quality of work done in its preparation, it is, nevertheless, directly related to the accuracy you might expect from the map. This is especially true in regard to its portrayal of cultural features, such as buildings and highways, as well as to any information detailing vegetation. Both culture and vegetation are frequently and significantly changed over time. On the other hand, terrain and water features (hydrography) are only rarely changed in any significant way over lengthy periods of time.

When using GPS, the **inclusion of a compatible coordinate system on the map** is of paramount importance.

PREPARING ANY MAP FOR USE WITH GPS

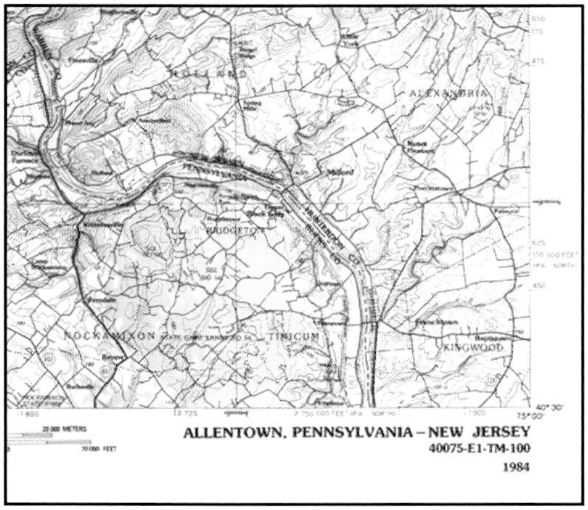

FIGURE 3-45
SEGMENT OF ALLENTOWN, PA, NJ
1:100,000 SCALE MAP SHEET
USGS

Government-produced civilian or military topographic maps (particularly those produced by the USGS or DMA/NIMA), will frequently have the MGRS/UTM grid lines printed across the face of the maps (**Figures 3-44, 3-45, & 3-46**). But when they are represented only by blue tick marks in the margins outside the neatlines of the maps, as indicated by the arrows in **Figure 3-47** on USGS 1:24,000- and 1:62,500-scale quadrangles, you can simply take a straight edge and connect the opposing tick marks to form the familiar grid pattern. You may also wish to label each with larger, more legible numbers using only the two large print numerals found as part of the MGRS/UTM grid labels that are already printed in the map's margins (**Figure 3-48**).

To prepare a localized area street or any other type of map for use with a GPS receiver, refer to large-scale base maps of the area covered by the map. These base maps may be USGS or NIMA quadrangle map sheets. You then add the MGRS/UTM grid lines every kilometer (1000 meters) by "copying" the grid lines found on the reference base maps in their relationships to the various features portrayed on both maps. Draw each of these grid lines on your street map as straight

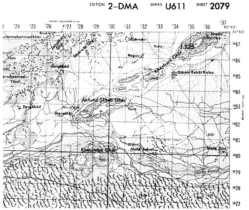

FIGURE 3-46
SEGMENT OF DO AB, AFGHANISTAN
1:100,000 SCALE MAP SHEET
USDMA (NIMA)

FIGURE 3-47

lines connecting three or four points you have identified along the path of the matching grid line displayed on the reference map. These reference points must be identified on both maps and the common points carefully located on your new map in relation to selected features shown on both maps. For example, you may use a unique curve along a road, power transmission line, stream course, or shoreline; a highway or some other type of intersection; or a man-made structure, such as a building or bridge (**Figure 3-49**). If you wish to use geographic coordinates rather than the MGRS/UTM, lines of latitude and longitude can be added to your map in precisely the same manner.

To prepare highway maps or strip trip maps covering an entire state or region, obtain smaller scale government reference base map sheets, (e.g., USGS

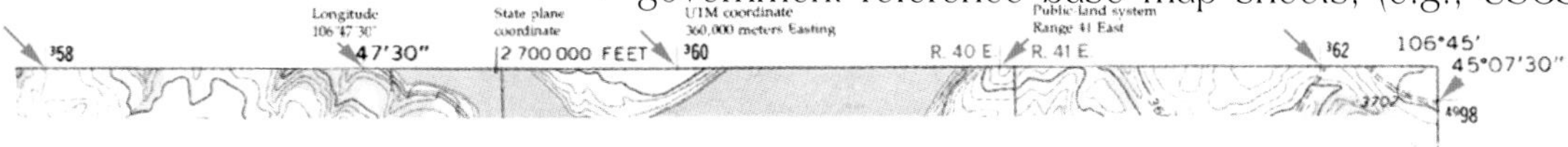

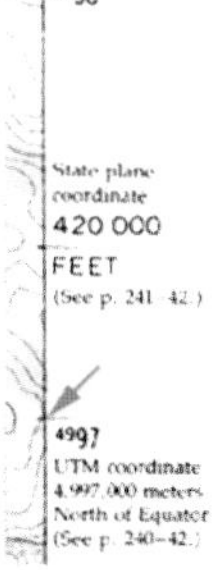

1:100,000-, 1:250,000-, or 1:1,000,000-scale maps or Alexis Publishing's Road Maps covering the same area) and add the UTM/MGRS grid lines every 10 kilometers (10,000 meters), just as they appear on the reference map using the "common points" technique described above (**Figure 3-50**). Use care in drawing these lines to insure as much accuracy as possible. But remember, we are not going to use them as part of a legal survey—we plan to use them to help us find our way. Minor imprecisions should not cause us to become lost. However, it would be much easier and more accurate to use Alexis

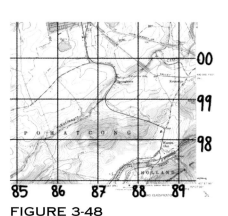

FIGURE 3-48
SEGMENT OF EASTON, PA, NJ 1:50,000 SCALE MAP
SHEET USGS

FIGURE 3-49
SEGMENT OF FAIRFAX, VA
1:50,000 SCALE MAP SHEET
USGS

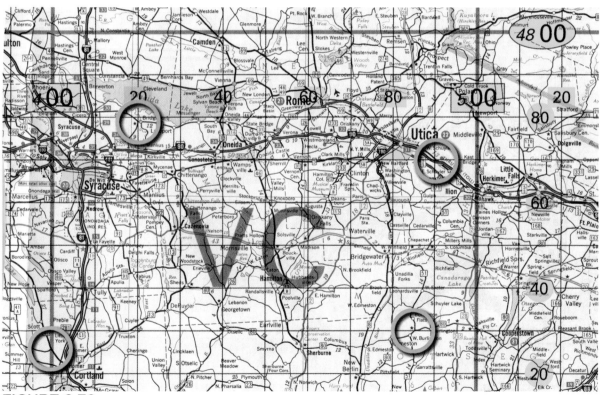

FIGURE 3-50
SEGMENT OF NEW YORK STATE ROAD MAP
1:710,000 SCALE
ALEXIS PUBLISHING

Publishing's new road map series of the United States that already have these lines printed on the face of the maps.

Municipal and county street and road maps can be prepared in this same fashion by local governmental and volunteer public safety and emergency response organizations.

The necessary base maps for accomplishing this map preparation work and for outdoor recreation purposes can be obtained in many local book and map stores or by contacting the appropriate governmental agency. For example, large-, medium-, and small-scale topographic maps, as well as free map indexes and catalogs for each state in the U.S.A. (**Figure 3-51**) and an index to those numerous military map sheets produced by the NIMA and made available to the general public, are available from the National Cartographic Information Center (NCIC),U.S. Geological Survey, 507 National Center, Reston, VA, 22092 (1-800-USA-MAPS). Many states have map production and information units, as well. Finally, several libraries throughout the USA have been designated as **Map Depository Libraries** (e.g., The Lafayette College Geology Library in Easton, PA, USA) for many of the published maps of the USGS and each is listed in the **Catalog of Published Maps** for each state.

For maps of areas within Canada, contact the Canada Map Office, 615 Booth Street, Ottawa, Ontario K1A 0E9 (613-952-7000). One of the best single sources for information on obtaining maps worldwide is the third

FIGURE 3-51

edition of **The Map Catalog: Every Kind of Map and Chart On Earth and Even Some Above It**, by Joel Makower, editor. It was published in 1992 by Vintage Books, a division of Random House, Inc., New York.

Finally, you can position new features and correct mistakes on existing maps by accurately determining a location using your GPS receiver. For example, a new trail or highway can be mapped by obtaining a series of position fixes along its course, plotting these points on the map, and then connecting the dots with the line being added to represent it. Point features, such as the newly constructed Farinon Center at Lafayette College, can simply be added to the Easton, PA, NJ, USA, map using the coordinates determined by standing there with the GPS unit (18TVA825 052).

After any necessary preparation work is completed, the map you have selected is ready for use with your GPS equipment.

THE LANGUAGE OF MAPS

No one knows who first drew, molded, laced together or scratched out in the dirt the first map. A map useful for navigation is a graphic representation of a portion of the earth's surface drawn to scale, generally as seen from directly above. It portrays two types of features: (1) **natural features**, which may include water (hydrography), vegetation, and relief (topography), and (2) those **cultural features** erected by man. Depending upon the map's scale and intended purpose, those cultural features included may be streets and highways, bridges, railroads, power or communication transmission lines, and buildings. Also, the various political boundaries that exist within the portrayed area may be included.

Now it's time to begin the task of reading the map. Maps convey information to you in four ways: (1) marginal information, (2) colors, (3) symbols, and (4) descriptive labels.

MARGINAL INFORMATION

Items of marginal information are generally classified into three categories: (1) map identifications, (2) map interpretation and use, and (3) other miscellaneous data. **Map identifications data**, such as sheet names and edition numbers, series names and numbers, grid reference boxes, scale notes, credit notes, adjoining sheets diagrams, and stock numbers all help you to determine the location and amount of area covered by a map and to identify the specific sheet you are examining. **Interpretation and use data**, such as compilation dates, legends showing the meanings of the colors and symbols used on the map, magnetic declination diagrams, contour intervals, and graphic distance scales, all assist the reader to fully understand and utilize the map. Finally, **miscellaneous data** might include such ancillary information as an index to boundaries, mileage chart between cities, map datums and so forth.

It should be noted that not every map includes all the marginal information discussed here. Civilian and military topographic maps, however, will include much of this information.

COLORS AND SYMBOLS

In the development of the language of maps, there has been an attempt over the centuries to apply logic to the process. This is true for the use of both colors and symbols.

By the fifteenth century, most European maps were carefully colored. Profile drawings of mountains and hills were shown in brown, rivers and lakes in blue, vegetation in green, roads in black or yellow, and special information in red. As we can see, the use of colors hasn't changed much since that time. A quick check of the map's **legend** will help you to confirm whether or not the map you are using conforms rather closely to the age-old color scheme described above. Most likely it does.

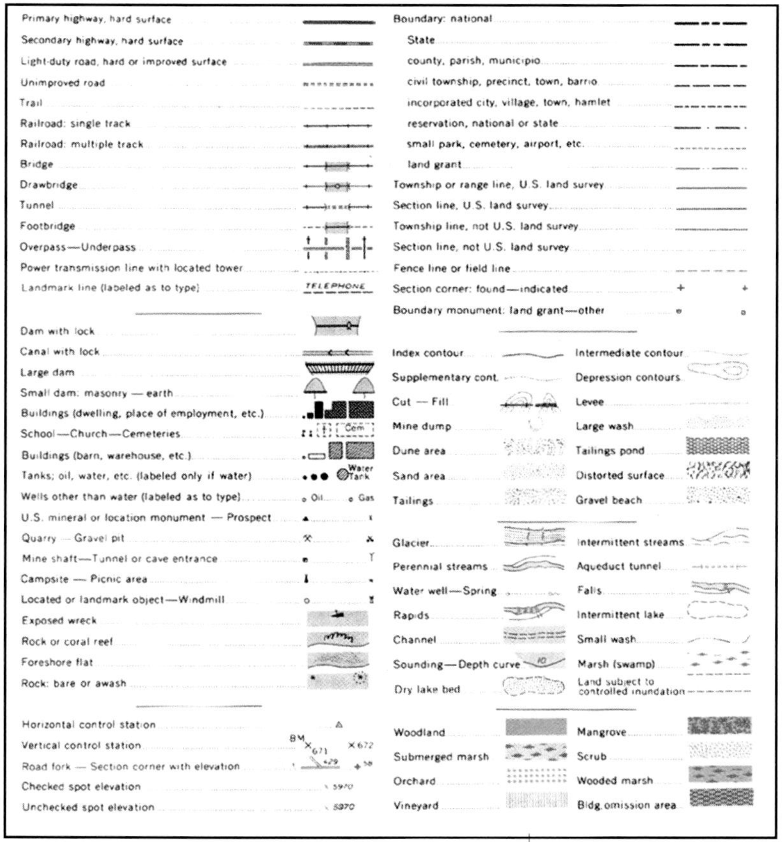

One difference may be that major highways are shown in reddish brown on U.S. topographic maps and are generally shown in

Primary highway, hard surface
Secondary highway, hard surface
Light-duty road, hard or improved surface
Unimproved road
Trail
Railroad: single track
Railroad: multiple track
Bridge
Drawbridge
Tunnel
Footbridge
Overpass—Underpass
Power transmission line with located tower
Landmark line (labeled as to type)   TELEPHONE

Dam with lock
Canal with lock
Large dam
Small dam: masonry — earth
Buildings (dwelling, place of employment, etc.)
School—Church—Cemeteries   Cem
Buildings (barn, warehouse, etc.)
Tanks; oil, water, etc. (labeled only if water)   Water Tank
Wells other than water (labeled as to type)   Oil   Gas
U.S. mineral or location monument — Prospect
Quarry — Gravel pit
Mine shaft—Tunnel or cave entrance
Campsite — Picnic area
Located or landmark object—Windmill
Exposed wreck
Rock or coral reef
Foreshore flat
Rock: bare or awash

Horizontal control station
Vertical control station   BM   671   672
Road fork — Section corner with elevation   429   58
Checked spot elevation   5970
Unchecked spot elevation   5970

Boundary: national
State
county, parish, municipio
civil township, precinct, town, barrio
incorporated city, village, town, hamlet
reservation, national or state
small park, cemetery, airport, etc.
land grant
Township or range line, U.S. land survey
Section line, U.S. land survey
Township line, not U.S. land survey
Section line, not U.S. land survey
Fence line or field line
Section corner: found—indicated
Boundary monument: land grant—other

Index contour   Intermediate contour
Supplementary cont.   Depression contours
Cut — Fill   Levee
Mine dump   Large wash
Dune area   Tailings pond
Sand area   Distorted surface
Tailings   Gravel beach

Glacier   Intermittent streams
Perennial streams   Aqueduct tunnel
Water well—Spring   Falls
Rapids   Intermittent lake
Channel   Small wash
Sounding—Depth curve   Marsh (swamp)
Dry lake bed   Land subject to controlled inundation

Woodland   Mangrove
Submerged marsh   Scrub
Orchard   Wooded marsh
Vineyard   Bldg omission area

FIGURE 3-52 MAP LEGEND, USGS

red and black on U.S. commercial highway maps. On the other hand, Michelin highway maps of Europe, for example, show them in red, yellow, and black—in order of their importance.

The legend, again, is the place to look when searching for the meanings of various colors and symbols found on any particular map (**Figure 3-52**). This is true whether you are using a civilian or military topographic map produced by a government agency or a commercially produced street or highway map. Most symbols are obvious, but some may be somewhat difficult to associate with the features they represent. Due to maps' scale restrictions and legibility considerations, symbols placed on them are often greatly exaggerated in size. For example, a road 20 meters wide may be shown on a 1:50,000-scale topographic map as a line that would, according to the map's scale, measure 60 meters in width. As a result, some features must also be displaced in order to depict them (e.g., a highway running parallel to a

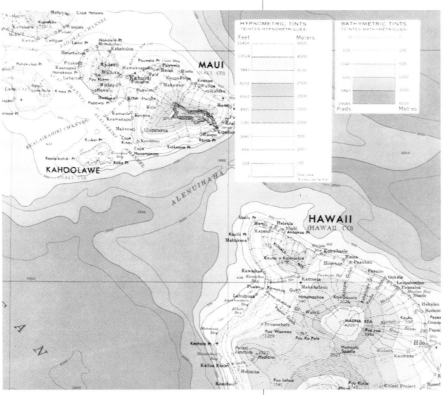

FIGURE 3-53
SEGMENT OF HAWAII
1:1,000,000 SCALE MAP SHEET
INTERNATIONAL MAP OF THE WORLD

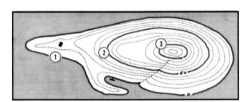

FIGURE 3-54

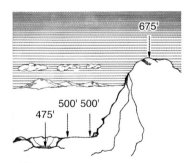

FIGURE 3-55
LOCAL RELIEF

stream and railroad track) and some may be left out (e.g., some buildings within a cluster or along streets within a heavily built-up urban place) because these symbols are exaggerated in size. This is why the user must interpret the map—not just read it.

If you have a physical map, it may use elevation tints (various colors or shades of black and white) to identify the various elevation intervals set for that sheet (**Figure 3-53**). Or, it may use line symbols, called contour lines (lines connecting points of equal elevation), to convey specific elevation information as well as portray local relief (**Figure 3-54**). Relief is the shape (topography) of the local surface area being portrayed (**Figure 3-55**). Contour lines were first used on a map to portray elevation changes in 1749.

The vertical interval (elevation difference) between contour lines on the map is referred to as the map's **contour interval**, which is reported as a marginal note. Generally, areas with pronounced relief differences (i.e., mountains) have larger contour intervals than relatively flat areas. However, the greater the contour interval used on a map, the less specific will be the portrayal of the physical shape of the land in its relatively flat areas. Thus, more interpretation will be required by you, the reader. There will be some hints about how to do this later in the chapter.

Today's topographic maps generally use only four types of brown contour lines to depict the infinite number of configurations the land can take. They are:

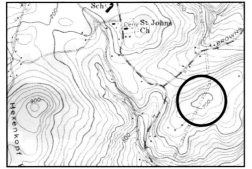

FIGURE 3-56 INDEX AND INTERMEDIATE CONTOUR LINES

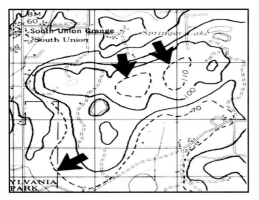

FIGURE 3-57 NUMBER TOPS USUALLY POINT UPGRADE

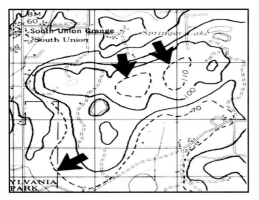

FIGURE 3-58 SUPPLEMENTARY CONTOUR LINES

Index Contour Lines - Every fifth contour line, which is drawn a bit heavier than the four lighter ones in-between, is called an index contour line. These lines are periodically broken so their elevations can be printed on the map (**Figure 3-56**). Incidentally, the top of this elevation number (**Figure 3-57**) is **usually** (see circle) – but not always pointing upgrade .

Intermediate Contour Lines - The four lighter contour lines located between any two index contours are called intermediate contour lines (**Figure 3-56**). Remember, the vertical distance between individual contour lines (either between an index and intermediate or between intermediate contour lines) is always equal to the contour interval. Elevation values are generally not printed on intermediate contour lines.

Supplementary Contour Lines - On some maps, particularly in those specific areas of the map where there is little local relief, there may appear either very light or broken contour lines. They are placed there to portray the shape of the land which might not otherwise be perceivable because its contour interval is too large to effectively portray the topography of these areas (**Figure 3-58**). They generally, but not always, represent half the map's contour interval and their elevations are frequently labeled.

Depression Contour Lines - An area such as a gravel pit, a man-made cut to accommodate a highway, or some form of natural depression that is of lower elevation than all the immediate surrounding terrain is portrayed by use of depression contour lines. They

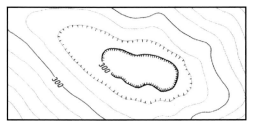

FIGURE 3-59 DEPRESSION CONTOUR LINES

FIGURE 3-60
STEEP SLOPE

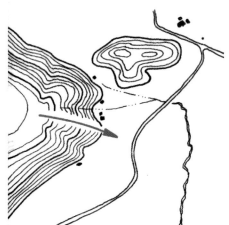

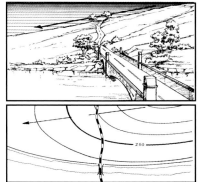

FIGURE 3-61
GENTLE SLOPE

have small hachures (short dash lines) pointing down slope, and each may be labeled with its elevation (**Figure 3-59**).

Every wiggle (twist or turn) in your map's contour lines, no matter what size, signals what is to be encountered while traveling across the space that falls between them. Relatively wide spaces between contour lines are rarely flat places or areas of uniform slope, but the only way to tell for sure is to look for minute bends or wiggles in the contour lines found on either side. In fact, it is wise to look at the next two or three lines to help you determine just what you will encounter there on the ground.

As you will recall, the closer the contour lines are placed together (the less horizontal distance falling between them), the greater is the slope being por-

**FIGURE
3-62**
CONCAVE
SLOPE

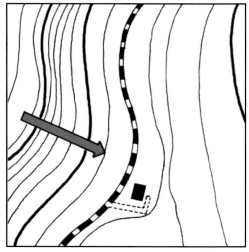

trayed (**Figures 3-60 & 3-61**). Also, when a slope is steeper at the top (contour lines are closer together) than at the bottom (where the lines are further apart), the slope is **concave** in shape (**Figure 3-62**). Conversely, when the slope is more gentle on the top (contour lines are further apart) and steeper at the bottom (contour lines are closer together), the slope is **convex** in shape

FIGURE 3-63
CONVEX SLOPE

(**Figure 3-63**). Finally, when the contour lines are evenly spaced, the slope is **uniform** in shape (**Figure 3-64**). To better understand these fundamental concepts for interpreting the shapes of slopes using contour lines on a map, see **Figure 3-65**.

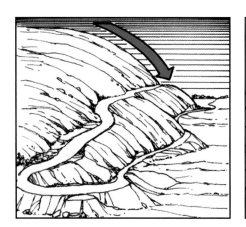

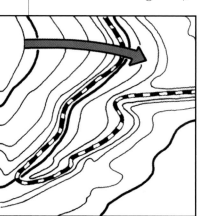

FIGURE 3-64
UNIFORM SLOPE

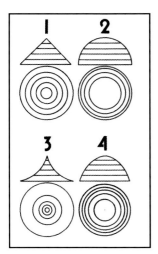

FIGURE 3-65

Geologists and geographers have developed thousands of terms to define and describe the various landforms found out in the real world, but we are simply trying to observe, interpret, and recognize what nature displays as a guide to our movements. Therefore, our classification list of five **major terrain features**, two **minor terrain features**, three **supplementary terrain features**, and the concept referred to as a **complex terrain feature**, is quite sufficient for our purposes. **Figure 3-66** illustrates how each of these terrain features might appear in the real world.

The **five major terrain features** are (1) hill, (2) ridge, (3) saddle, (4) valley, and (5) depression. A **hill** tends to be round (although not perfectly) and slopes downward in all directions. A **ridge** is an elongated piece of high ground, generally with three downward and one upward slope along its crest. **Saddles** are either wide or narrow and deep or shallow dips between hilltops or along the crest of a ridge. A **valley** slopes rather steeply upward in two directions and gently upward and downward in the other two directions. Finally, a **depression** is either a natural or artificial hole in the ground (e.g., a sand or gravel pit) with the ground sloping downward in all directions toward its generally wet center.

The two **minor terrain features** are (6) spur and (7) draw. Basically, a **spur** is a small ridge and a **draw** a small valley. Often, they are proportionately steeper than their larger counterparts.

FIGURE 3-66
1. Hill 2. Ridge 3. Saddle 4. Valley
5. Depression 6. Spur 7. Draw 8. Cliff
9. Cut 10. Fill

The three **supplementary terrain features** are (8) cliff, (9) cut, and (10) fill. A **cliff** can be nearly vertical. Its portrayal on the map features contour lines placed either very close together or merging into a single line denoting a sheer, perpendicular slope. **Cuts** and **fills** are created by man to prepare the ground for the bed of a highway or railroad in order to reduce the slope or keep the roadway dry through low, swampy areas.

Figure 3-67 helps you to see how contour lines are used on a map to represent various slopes, shapes, and features found on the earth's surface. And, finally, **Figure 3-68** presents a USGS illustration of how the

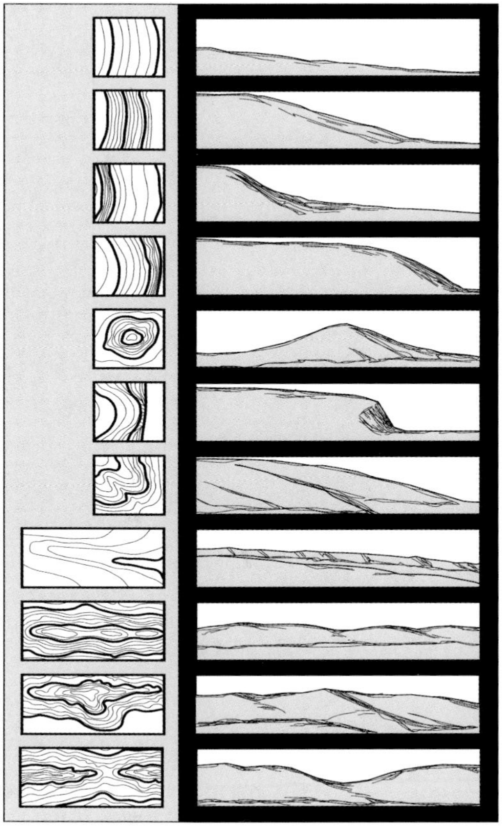

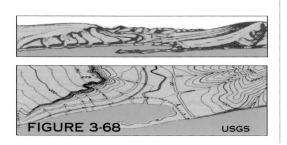

FIGURE 3-67

DESCRIPTIVE LABELS

FIGURE 3-68   USGS

terrain of a hypothetical area would appear as contour lines on a large-scale topographic map.

You may have noticed that you will generally not find terrain features standing alone. They are most often part of a larger, more **complex terrain feature** that stands out as a single observable entity.

Ken White, who served for several years as the Land Navigation Instruction Chief at the Committee Group, U.S. Army Armor School, Fort Knox, KY, USA, developed a strategy that is quite useful for interpreting contour lines on a topographic map. When interpreting microrelief - those features not shown directly by contour lines due to the size of a map's contour interval - you can make use of the <u>implications</u> made by the presence of their small wiggles and larger curves. He believes that map interpretation is a matter of learning to "read between the lines." **Figures 3-69 A.-D.** explain much with few words. **Figures 3-70A & 3-70B** also illustrate how to read between the contour lines by closely observing either their pronounced curves or more subtle "wiggle" patterns.

Colors and symbols are the two most fundamental tools used by cartographers to convey information on their maps. However, reading **descriptive labels** can add much to your understanding of what is portrayed. They are used to identify the names of cities, towns, roads, mountains, rivers, and so forth; but they are also used to more specifically describe general symbols found on the map. For example they may identify oil tanks, post office buildings, apple orchards, fire towers, rice paddies, and so forth.

SELECTING
A GOOD ROUTE

Much of your success or failure may be determined before you ever take that first step or roll over that first mile or kilometer toward your destination. As for any type of activity, the foundation for success in navigation rests upon the quality of thought and effort you devote to planning and preparing for your move.

When selecting a route, it should be done in conjunction with a study of the map. Simply asking your GPS unit to give you the direction and distance from your starting point through several intermediate checkpoints and on to the final objective can lead to many serious problems. This approach completely ignores the realities presented by the time available, terrain, weather-related ground conditions, and the numerous special considerations placed upon the move by the task at hand.

Don't forget Forest Ranger Hagedorn's caution that we consider the terrain from one point to another in terms of the time and effort to be expended while moving over it (functional distance), rather than only in terms of linear distance. Thus, you must carefully study your map and expect this study to result often in the planning of complex multi-segmented routes. It should

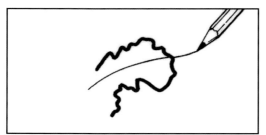

FIGURE 3-69A CREST OF SMALL SPUR

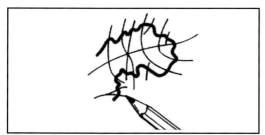

FIGURE 3-69B MINOR CRESTS ADDED

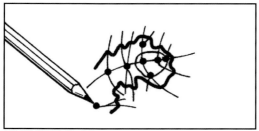

FIGURE 3-69C SMALL HILLS
WHERE CRESTS CONVERGE

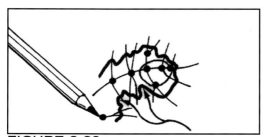

FIGURE 3-69D SMALL DRAWS
BETWEEN MINOR CRESTS

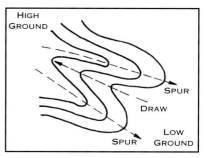

FIGURE 3-70A

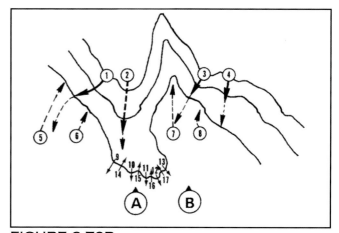

FIGURE 3-70B
A. SPUR   B. DRAW
1 - 4, SMALL SPURS; 5 - 8, SMALL DRAWS;
9 - 13, MICRO SPURS; 14 - 17, MICRO DRAWS

now be obvious that the GPS unit's capability for storing and helping you to navigate over a preprogrammed route consisting of multiple legs will be quite beneficial.

A map study focused on the trail, street, and highway networks of an area to be traversed is just as important to the success of highway travel as it is to cross-country movement. Many of the same considerations must be reviewed prior to making routing decisions in either case. For example, heavy rains often wash out dirt roads and trails in hilly and mountainous areas, bridges on secondary roads often do not support heavy loads, and travel times on level roads over greater distances may be less than those over steep, twisting "shortcuts." A new chapter, Chapter 6, on highway navigation has been added to this third edition of the book.

KEEPING TO THE ROUTE

After having selected a good route to your destination, effective use of your map and GPS can keep you on it with little difficulty. Periodic position checks will tell you if or when you stray from the route and the map will encourage you to use the terrain and other natural and man-made features to help direct and guide your movement between these checks.

Position information from your GPS receiver is not useful until it is placed within the context of the reality confronting you on the ground. After all we are not really interested in going to a set of coordinates; we wish to proceed to a real world place represented by those coordinates (e.g., base camp, a fishing hole, the place we plan to meet for lunch or Wayne's house for a party).

As we have already stated, straight line travel over moderate and long distances is impractical because the terrain, highways, and numerous other factors preclude it. For example, the terrain will channel and guide both your route selections and movements. Therefore, being able to positively identify the terrain and other features you encounter is of great importance to your navigational success; and it makes any walk or drive more enjoyable, as well.

It is a fact that the ability to identify specific terrain features simultaneously on the ground and on a topographic map can be extremely helpful as you proceed over the land. Then, by using an association between the terrain and the map, you can mentally "hand-off" your position from feature to feature as they guide you almost effortlessly along the route toward your destination. Whenever the level of uncertainty about your position mounts, you can confirm it with GPS and make any necessary correction. In other words, use of a GPS receiver in conjunction with map-terrain referencing skills cause this movement technique to become what we call **"fail-safe terrain association"**.

Here is a simple strategy you might employ for recognizing and identifying specific terrain features encountered on the ground and portrayed on the map. It was first developed by the U.S. Navy Personnel Research and Development Center (NPRDC) for the U.S. Marine Corps and was later refined by the U.S. Army Research Institute for the Behavioral and Social Sciences (ARI). A modified **Map Interpretation Terrain Association Course (MITAC)**, by Jennifer N. Drescher, was developed by Alexis USA, Inc. and is presently in use for training military personnel on the techniques of movement by terrain association in the Kingdom of

ROUND HILL
FIGURE 3-71

ELONGATED RIDGE
FIGURE 3-72

FIGURE 3-73
IN LINE SPUR

Saudi Arabia. Soldiers attending both the "Light Fighter School," 10th Mountain Division (Light Infantry) at Fort Drum, NY, and the U.S. Army Infantry School at Ft. Benning, GA are also using this technique.

First, this terrain association technique requires that you be able to name and identify the ten classifications of terrain features presented earlier. They are **hill, ridge, saddle, valley, depression, spur, draw, cliff, cut,** and **fill.** Once a particular feature has been classified, it can then be identified both on the map and in the real world by analyzing it in terms of up to five of its physical characteristics known by the acronym SOSES. These physical characteristics include: (1) shape, (2) orientation, (3) size, (4) elevation, and (5) slope.

Identifying Specific Terrain Features Using Five Physical Characteristics (SOSES)

Shape - the general form or outline of the feature at its base. It may be (1) **round (Figure 3-71)**or (2) **elongated (Figure 3-72)**.

Orientation - the general trend or direction of an elongated feature from your viewpoint. A feature can be (1) **in line**, (2) **across**, or (3) **at an angle** to your viewpoint. You will note that the center portion of the ridgeline shown in **Figure 3-72** lies oriented generally <u>across</u> your viewpoint, while the segments on both the left and right are at an <u>angle</u> to your viewpoint. **Figure 3-73** shows a spur <u>in line</u> with your viewpoint.

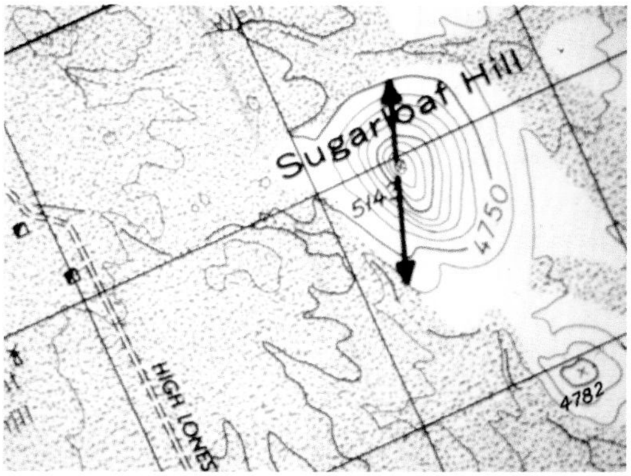

FIGURE 3-74
SIZE MEASURED ACROSS BASE

FIGURE 3-75A
DEEP SADDLE

FIGURE 3-75B
SHALLOW SADDLE

Size - the length or width of a feature horizontally across its base. For example, one landform might be referred to as being (1) **larger** or (2) **smaller** than another, or it might actually be measured across its base (**Figure 3-74**).

Elevation - the height of a landform. This can be described either in absolute terms or as compared to other features in the area or to your own position. One landform may be (1) **higher**, (2) **lower**, (3) **deeper**, or (4) **shallower** than another. In **Figure 3-74**, SUGARLOAF HILL is higher than hill 4782 by 361 meters; and in **Figure 3-75**, the SADDLE on the top is much <u>deeper</u> than the <u>shallow</u> SADDLE on the bottom.

Slope - the type and steepness of the slope on either side of the landform (left or right). These slopes may be (1) **uniform**, (2) **convex**, or (**3**) **concave** and they may be (1) **steep** or (2) **gentle**. SUGAR LOAF HILL, as shown with a photograph and portrayed by contour lines in **Figure 3-76** (camera position indicated by the black triangle on the correctly oriented map segment), has a relatively steep yet nearly uniform left slope. You will note that the contour lines are relatively close together but nearly evenly spaced along the entire left slope. On the other hand, the right slope begins as a gentle convex slope along the top, but suddenly falls off into a steep concave slope as it drops sharply away toward the more gently sloping ground located near the bottom. The contour lines depicting this right slope are spaced some distance apart

FIGURE 3-76A

FIGURE 3-76B

just to the right of the peak, then quite closely together down most of the right slope, and, finally, spaced apart at a greater distance near the bottom.

It may not be necessary or even possible to use all five physical characteristics in identifying all landforms. You are to use only as many of them as may be useful or necessary in allowing you to make positive identifications. You will find this technique invaluable in generally keeping track of your position on the map between more precise position fixes with the GPS receiver and as a means for guiding you along the route over and around the various features being encountered.

MAP INTERPRETATION AND TERRAIN ASSOCIATION COURSE STRATEGIES (MITAC)

The following five examples will enable you to better understand how to employ the MITAC strategy in positively identifying specific terrain features encountered in the real world through a close examination of their portrayals with contour lines on topographic maps. Once you have grasped the simple concepts involved, you can easily improve your skill with additional practice. What a great excuse to get some exercise and enjoy nature.

FIGURE 3-77A

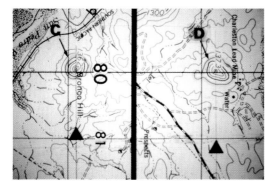

FIGURE 3-77B

There may be a number of similar appearing landforms out there, but, just as with human fingerprints and DNA, no two are exactly alike. Once you fully develop this skill, you won't need to use a written worksheet (as we have in the first three examples) while navigating in the field. You can mentally run through the procedure while making the comparisons in your head. Finally, you will soon discover that it will rarely be necessary or even possible to use all five SOSES characteristics each time you attempt to identify a terrain feature on a map.

Now, let's examine the five examples.

Example 1: Does the terrain feature pictured in **Figure 3-77** match the landform labeled C or that labeled D on the accompanying map segment? For these examples, a black triangle locates the position (or supposed position) of the camera when the real world scene was photographed.

MITAC Worksheet for Example 1
(See Figure 3-77)

Landform	Real World Feature	Terrain Feature C	Terrain Feature D
Name:	hill	hill	hill
Shape:	elongated	round	elongated
Orientation:	across	not applicable	across
Size:	?	?	?
Elevation:	?	?	?
Slope:(of crest)	uniform/convex	concave/concave	uniform/convex

Discussion: The landform pictured here is obviously a somewhat elongated hill oriented across our front. The closed concentric contour patterns portraying both mapped terrain features C and D also represent hills, but only D is elongated and oriented across our front. Thus, we know that when making a choice between C and D, terrain feature D represents the correct selection for this example. Obviously, actual navigational situations often present more than two alternatives; consequently, you must proceed further with your analysis in order to confirm your selection. In this case, both features are nearly the same size across the base and of approximately equal elevations; so, in this example, the physical characteristics of size and elevation provide little assistance. Finally, the hill pictured in the real world scene has a nearly uniform and rather steep left slope and a convex right slope, which places the peak to the left of center on the terrain feature. This is yet another match for hill D. On the other hand, hill C has concave slopes on both the left and right, which obviously places the peak close to the center of the feature. Note on hill C that the contour lines portraying all slopes are closer together (steeper) at the top than at the bottom, denoting its concave silhouette. In summary, there is no question that the real world landform pictured here is portrayed as hill D on the map.

Example 2: Does the terrain feature pictured in **Figure 3-78** match the landform labeled G or that labeled H on the accompanying map segment?

FIGURE 3-78A

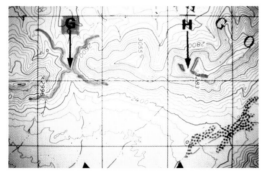

FIGURE 3-78B

MITAC Worksheet for Example 2
(See Figure 3-78)

Landform	Real World Feature	Terrain Feature G	Terrain Feature H
Name:	saddle	saddle	saddle
Shape:	elongated	elongated	elongated
Orientation:	across	across	across
Size:	large	800 meters	250 meters
Elevation:	Deep	Deep	Shallow
Slope:(of crest)	concave/concave	concave/concave	?/uniform

Discussion: The landform pictured here is obviously a saddle oriented across our front, as are both mapped terrain features G and H. Furthermore, the saddle in the photograph is fairly wide across (size) and deep (elevation). Without question, this definitely results in a match with the contour pattern shown for mapped feature G. Conversely, the contour lines portraying feature H indicate a saddle that is both much narrower and shallower. Finally, both the right and left slopes of the real world saddle are concave (steeper at the top and more gentle at the bottom). This completes a perfect match to mapped terrain feature G. It must be noted that there is only one contour line forming the left slope of saddle H, thereby making it impossible to determine its shape. On the other hand, the contour pattern for the right slope indicates that it is nearly uniform (contour lines evenly spaced). Once again, there is no question that the real world landform pictured here is represented on the map as saddle G.

FIGURE 3-79A

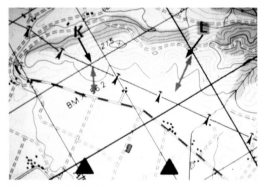

FIGURE 3-79B

Example 3: Does the terrain feature pictured in **Figure 3-79** match the landform labeled K or that labeled L on the accompanying map segment?

MITAC Worksheet for Example 3
(See Figure 3-79)

Landform	Real World Feature	Terrain Feature K	Terrain Feature L
Name:	ridge	ridge	ridge
Shape:	elongated	elongated	elongated
Orientation:	angle	in line	angle
Size:	?	500 meters	200 meters
Elevation:	?	?	?
Slope: (of crest)	concave	uniform	concave

Discussion: The real world landform identified here (see arrow) as well as the mapped terrain features K and L are ridges. Some might argue that they are actually large spurs sloping down from the crest of a large ridge running perpendicular to them across our viewpoint, but there is no reason to argue the issue. As you will recall, spurs are simply small ridges. Regardless of the name used, you will note that the landform marked by the arrow in the photograph is located at an angle to your viewpoint. A line drawn along its crest line would extend significantly to the left of the camera's position, which is also true for the map portrayal of terrain feature L. But, the map portrayal of terrain feature K (especially at the bottom) shows the crest pointed nearly directly at (in line with) the purported camera's location. Size is difficult to determine from the photograph, but L certainly is the smaller of the two ridges clearly shown; and, at about 200 meters in width, landform L has the least size of any of the ridges included on the map segment. Finally, you see that the slope of the crest of the photographed ridge is significantly steeper at the top than at the bottom; therefore, making it concave in shape. The contour portrayal of feature L displays the same concave-shaped crest with contour lines near the top of the crest being closer together than at the bottom. On the other hand, an examination of the terrain feature portrayed as K indicates its crest has a nearly uniform slope. The contour lines here are quite evenly spaced. Consequently, both the real world landform and that portrayed as L on the map segment appear to be a match. Should you require further confirmation, you might undertake a SOSES analysis of the ridge pictured to the right of the indicated feature and the map portrayal of that ridge located to the right of L on the map. They, too, form a perfect match confirming our choice of L. As compared with L, the ridge to its right is more in line with our viewpoint, much larger in size and higher in elevation, it leads to a well defined peak, and it has a somewhat convex slope along the line of its crest. In summary, it would seem that this should provide enough confirmation for the selection of L to satisfy anyone.

Some landforms can be so large and complex that it is impractical to analyze them in their entirety. **Figures 3-80** and **3-81**, which are part of Jennifer Drescher's modified MITAC for Saudi Arabia, illustrate this point and present some additional insights for confirming terrain-map associations.

FIGURE 3-80A

FIGURE 3-80A
UPSIDE DOWN TO ALLOW FOR ORIENTATION OF THE
MAP

Example 4: In **Figure 3-80**, you see a real world scene showing the northwest face of a large, complex landform we suspect might be Jabal (Mountain) Sidr, just southwest of the village of Al Jumum, KSA. We think this is Sidr for two reasons. First, we know that we have been heading southeast on a dirt trail down the rather broad wadi (valley) labeled on the map segment as "Fajj ar Rimaythi" and, second, Jabal Sidr is, without question, the most prominent feature in our immediate area and along the mountain range running parallel to our movement on the left (east). Go ahead; turn the map around as you have been instructed so it is properly oriented to the picture before you rotate the book. Unfortunately, the picture rotates as you attempt to orient the map. We left this one map segment oriented to the north so you could initially read the labels as well as better appreciate the value of orienting it.

Discussion: To confirm that the massive landform we are viewing out to our left front is, in fact, Jabal Sidr, we need only focus on the uniquely shaped peak visible to us in the photograph atop the mountain. A close examination of the landform as it is portrayed on the map reveals that it has two major peaks and several lesser (lower) ones. First, the 556 meter-high "saddle peak" closest to the English label "Jabal Sidr" (grid square 6987) cannot be seen from our position (far off down the valley to the northwest) because the taller approximately 650 meter-high peak we see in the photograph and near the Arabic label on the map (grid square 6888) is closer to us and blocks it from view. Therefore, it is this uncommonly shaped singular peak in the foreground (grid square 6888) that easily confirms

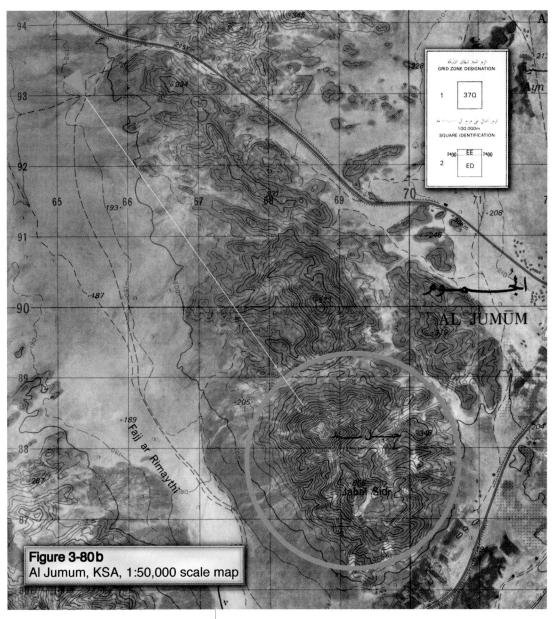

Figure 3-80b
Al Jumum, KSA, 1:50,000 scale map

FIGURE 3-80B

Sidr's identity on the map. From our perspective nearly 5.5 kilometers to the northwest, we see it as being very angular with a distinctly convex right slope (almost knob-like) near the top. A match is quickly confirmed by examining the unique contour patterns on the map. Finally, once we confirm that this landform is, indeed, Jabal Sidr, we can easily locate our position on the map at the intersection of the dry stream bed and the dirt road seen in the foreground of the photograph at MGRS map coordinates 37Q ED 654 930. Of course, a quick check of the GPS receiver will confirm this position estimation in an instant. In this case, our terrain association position fix may well be more precise than that of the GPS unit because we are in such close proximity to easily identified mapped features and our use of the terrain association technique is not subject to the U.S. Government's imposition of Selective Availability (SA). In conclusion, if we were to continue to proceed up the valley toward the southeast, it would be a simple matter to guide ourselves by "fail-safe terrain referencing" (terrain association with periodic GPS confirmation checks), keeping the range of hills to our left and using the towering Jabal Sidr as a landmark "beacon" out toward the front to help us maintain both a sense of direction and position. Anytime we needed reassurance, we could check one of the graphic navigation screens or the position screen on our GPS receiver (described in Chapter 5).

Example 5: In the final example, we will examine a fairly large but somewhat isolated landform standing out in a relatively flat area. Jabal al Qurayn can be seen for miles from nearly every direction and is located just

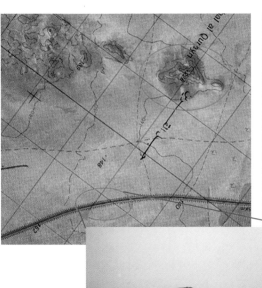

FIGURE 3-81

west of the major highway running between Mecca and Medina. It was included in our discussion because it is an example of a landform that requires only a "quick and dirty" SOSES analysis to confirm its identification on a map. This small mountain and its contour portrayal are included as **Figure 3-81**. Can you confirm it?

Discussion: Unlike the landforms used in the first four examples, this terrain feature has little competition with other formations within its immediate area. Just to be certain you have a match, you might notice that unique little hill mass attached to its right side which, by the way, causes the landform to appear elongated and oriented across our viewpoint. The contour lines shown on the map obviously match this cursory description, and, under the circumstances, this should be enough to confirm the identity of this rather isolated feature. If you wish to proceed further, the main hill mass certainly claims title to the greatest elevation in the immediate area and its left slope is quite gradual with numerous shallow saddles appearing along its crest. The right slope is obviously quite different. Up near the peak, it is concave, rather steep, and devoid of saddles. The contour lines shown on the map easily confirm its identification for us. Remember, a detailed examination of all five of the physical characteristics need not be accomplished in all cases before determining that you have a match.

This concludes our brief discussion of map interpretation and terrain association techniques using the five physical (SOSES) characteristics. Hopefully, it will provide you with that secondary means of navigation that GPS manufacturers always encourage us to employ when using their products. Of course, when darkness falls or weather severely limits visibility and where there are few terrain features to serve as guides, casual use of the compass and the measurement of distance (dead reckoning) replaces terrain association as the preferred backup during GPS navigation

Also remember, while the GPS unit will get you to within a few dozen meters of your intended destination, associated use of a good topographic map and map-terrain association skills allow you to be very precise. If you placed your deer stand in a tree growing on a small spur, don't expect to find it later a few dozen or so meters away down in a little draw just because your GPS unit led you there. Your stand didn't move, but the coordinates for the tree in which you placed it did change a bit on the GPS receiver due to errors caused, in part, by a different geometry resulting from the ever-changing positions of the satellite vehicles (SVs) relative to the earth's surface. However, most of the error encountered (up to 50 meters or more) is directly attributable to the Government's policy of Selective Availability.

Some additional facets of the full MITAC program that were not presented here include a review of the five terrain association factors and four map design guidelines. Having knowledge about these terrain association factors enables you to more fully comprehend how (1) various **map scales**, (2) **contour intervals**, (3) **map dates**, and (4) **differing regions** and (5) **seasons** affect your ability to interpret maps. Also, knowing some of the conventions (rules) followed by cartographers when producing their maps (map design guidelines) can greatly enhance the quality of one's map interpretation capabilities. These guidelines fall under the headings of (1) **selection** (what will and will not to be portrayed), (2) **classification** (which types of features are grouped for portrayal using the same symbols), (3) **simplification** (when and where heavy concentrations of the same types of features, such as buildings, streets, streams, etc., are to be generalized in their portrayal), and (4) **magnitude** (the guideline governing the exaggerations used in order to make various symbolizations stand out for readability).

As you can see, a more comprehensive discussion of the MITAC could easily call for another book. Hopefully, we can soon look forward to writing and publishing it.

Other terrain referencing techniques that you might find helpful in guiding your movements are the use of (1) **handrails**, (2) **catching features**, and (3) **navigational attack points**. Navigational **handrails** are linear features, like roads, highways, railroads, power transmission lines, ridgelines, streams, or the line of hills discussed in MITAC example 4 that run roughly parallel to your direction of travel. Instead of paying close attention to compass readings and position fixes, you can proceed quickly using the "handrail" as a guide to your movement.

When you reach the point where your route and the handrail are to part company, you can make use of a prominent feature located nearby to serve as a warning. This feature is now being used as a **catching feature**. You may also use your GPS unit's navigation capability along each route segment to notify you when you have arrived at the next checkpoint, which you have pre-planned to also serve as a catching feature. A similar terrain feature may also serve as your **navigational attack point**, but that discussion fits better under the next heading.

RECOGNIZING THE DESTINATION

A **navigational attack point** is a readily-identified feature located near your destination when it is rather obscure or difficult to recognize. From this attack point, a short precision movement, carefully negotiated with a compass and monitored with your GPS receiver, will then easily bring you to your final objective or destination. By using the map and the terrain, referring to your compass (next chapter), and employing the navigational capabilities of your GPS receiver (Chapter 5), you will have no difficulty either in keeping to the route or recognizing the objective.

IN SUMMARY

You should now be able to read and interpret maps to the extent necessary for you to use them effectively as you navigate with GPS. With a map in hand, you can know any area as if it were part of your own neighborhood. You can grasp the complex interrelationships among the several places, various routes, numerous features, and the positional grid found printed on it. Thus, with GPS, you will always know where you are and where you are going in relation to: (1) the map's grid, (2) the map's feature portrayal, and (3) the complete inventory of real world features to be encountered on the ground. In summary, with the marriage of the map and GPS, your mental navigational and locational perceptions will now very closely match reality.

When using maps, such as topographical maps showing a great number of natural and cultural features, you should recall that it is the terrain and hydrographic (water) features that serve as the most reliable movement guides because they change least over time. Both vegetation and those features constructed by man are frequently changing. In addition, map scale, compilation date, and contour interval have a great impact upon what is and is not shown on a map. Maps are not photographs or comprehensive portraits of what is found on the ground—they are only partially complete graphic tools for the navigator. Remember, too, the numerous pieces of information contained in the map's margin, especially the legend, and the labels included along with the map's symbolic portrayal can add greatly to your level of understanding, if you take the time to study them in detail.

Where few features of any type exist, most will be included on the map (e.g., buildings, water, vegetation, and trails in the desert). And, where many exist, several will be omitted (e.g., stream courses in well-watered areas and buildings and streets in urban settings). You must also recall that many feature symbols are exaggerated in size on the map to insure legibility. Also, vegetation on the ground may mask more than it reveals.

Finally, you must orient your map to the ground to effectively use it. Techniques for orienting the map will be explained in the next chapter.

FIGURE 4-1

4

GPS NAVIGATION WITH AND WITHOUT A COMPASS

(SPATIAL RELATIONSHIPS: DIRECTION & DISTANCE)

This chapter will explain how to integrate to maximum advantage the use of a magnetic compass along with the GPS receiver and a map as you proceed to find your way. Even during this age of GPS technology, your compass remains the most useful tool for determining direction out on the ground and for orienting your map.

Whenever you think about determining direction, you must also consider the measurement of distance because of their common spatial link. All features and positions on the earth's surface are held in a unique spatial relationship—each has a specific direction and distance to and from all the others. In other words, when moving from here to there, you must know which way to go and how far. Thus, a discussion of both direction and distance will be included in this chapter.

BACKGROUND

Although you can use the navigational feature on a GPS unit to determine what direction you are moving and keep correcting yourself through trial and error, it is the magnetic compass that will most quickly and easily point you in the right direction out on the ground. You can then use the GPS unit to help keep track of your progress and suggest steering corrections as you proceed along your route.

The lensatic compass will report directional azimuth readings in either degrees (360 parts of a circle) or mils (6400 parts of a circle), but it is suggested that you use degrees for LN purposes.

Although nearly every type of magnetic compass will work, your best choice is use of the lensatic compass meeting current U.S. military specifications (**Figure 4-1**). It is designed to withstand rugged field conditions, uses copper induction damping, is most accurate in sighting directions for navigational purposes, and contains vials of tritium gas that continuously illuminate its nighttime features. The military style lensatic compass is manufactured by Stocker & Yale, Inc. in Salem, New Hampshire, U.S.A.

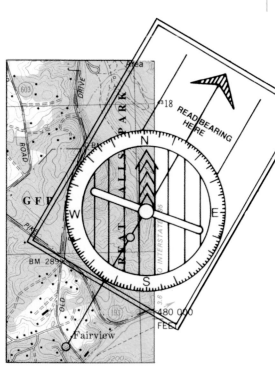

FIGURE 4-2
SOME PREFER TO USE A PROTRACTOR-
STYLE COMPASS

In comparison, popular liquid damped protractor-base style compasses have an upper temperature range of only 120° F before their capsules begin to fail (crack and leak) due to expansion. However, some hunters and hikers find them easier to read and use (**Figure 4-2**). For more information regarding the advantages of using the military lensatic compass, see "In Defense of the Lensatic Compass," by N.J. Hotchkiss, on pages 31-34 of the November-December 1991 issue of **Infantry**, a bimonthly professional military publication of the U.S. Army Infantry School at Fort Benning, GA, USA, 31905-5593.

HOW MANY NORTH'S ARE THERE?

Before we embark on a discussion about determining direction on both a map and on the ground, you should understand that map and compass norths are generally not the same direction. The difference between the two is a condition known as **magnetic declination** (sometimes called **compass variation**).

There are, in fact, three norths on any map (**Figure 4-3**): true north (★), grid north (**GN**), and magnetic north (*I*). **True north** is the direction you would take to travel to the North Pole and **grid north** is the direction represented by going straight up a grid line toward the top of a map. Land navigators need not concern themselves with the small difference between true and grid norths, which results when map makers represent a part of the spherically shaped earth on a flat piece of paper. However, they must consider the difference between **grid north** (map north) and **magnetic north**, the direction in which the compass needle points. The variation between them is called the **grid-magnetic (G-M) angle.**

Magnetic declination results from the fact that the compass needle is attracted by the earth's magnetic force patterns that presently converge in the northern hemisphere at a location near Bathurst Island in northern Canada (**Figure 4-4**). In the contiguous United States, the G-M angle presently varies from 20° west of grid north in parts of Maine to 20° east in parts of the State of Washington. There are, of course, places in the world where there is little or no declination. For example, there is a line, called the Agonic line, in the U.S.A. along which there is no magnetic declination. It lies just off the west coast of Florida; runs up through Georgia, Tennessee, and Kentucky; on along the western shore of Lake Michigan; and into Canada. The Middle East, too, is an area with little magnetic declination.

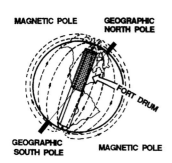

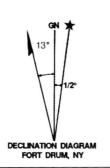

DECLINATION DIAGRAM
FORT DRUM, NY

TRUE NORTH

THE DIRECTION FROM ANY POSITION ON THE EARTH'S SURFACE TO THE NORTH POLE. ALL LINES OF LONGITUDE ARE TRUE NORTH LINES. THIS REFERENCE POINT IS SYMBOLIZED BY A STAR.

GRID NORTH

THE NORTH THAT IS ESTABLISHED BY THE VERTICAL GRID LINES ON THE MAP. THIS REFERENCE POINT IS SYMBOLIZED BY THE LETTERS GN.

MAGNETIC NORTH

THE DIRECTION OF THE NORTH MAGNETIC POLE IS INDICATED BY A COMPASS. THIS REFERENCE POINT IS SYMBOLIZED BY A HALF ARROWHEAD.

FIGURE 4-3

Although GPS receivers can be set to report already converted magnetic azimuths among stored positions (waypoints), you must consider this mathematical conversion requirement between grid and magnetic azimuths when measuring directional values with a protractor directly on a map.

ORIENTING THE MAP

Don't forget the paramount rule for LN: **Always navigate with a correctly oriented map.** Use of a lensatic compass is the quickest and easiest method for accomplishing this task, but inspection (terrain referencing) can also work in the absence of a compass.

ORIENTING THE MAP USING A LENSATIC COMPASS

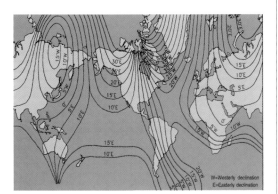

FIGURE 4-4
ISOGONIC LINES SHOWING MAGNETIC DECLINATION

Just follow this simple two-step method:

1. With the map laying flat, place the compass on it parallel to a north-south UTM/MGRS grid line with the cover end of the compass pointing toward the top of the map.

2. Rotate the map (and compass) until the declination angle formed by the black index line and the compass needle match the declination diagram (or note) printed in the margin of the map. The map is now oriented (**Figure 4-5**).

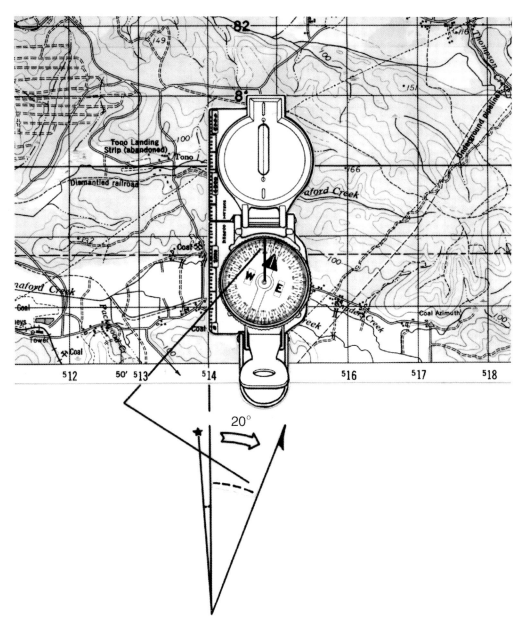

FIGURE 4-5

Be certain the magnetic arrow is resting on the correct side (right or left) of the index line, as compared to the declination diagram that may be found in the margin of your large-scale topographic map. You should be able to accomplish this task to an accuracy of within 3°, but the map should never be misoriented to the ground more than 30° in order to avoid almost certain confusion.

When the map you are using has no diagram or marginal note describing the area's magnetic declination, you can obtain that information for any geographic

FIGURE 4-6

area by consulting the appropriate large- or medium-scale topographic map (e.g., USGS' quadrangle sheets). When this is not practical, better than 30° accuracy can normally be achieved by laying the compass along the edge of any map and orienting it to magnetic north. If more accuracy is desired, you can stand on or near a linear feature, such as a road, facing in the direction which is known from its portrayal on the map. After taking a compass reading, the magnetic declination for the area in which you are located will become apparent as you compare the reading to the measured directional azimuth taken by using a protractor on the map.

ORIENTING THE MAP USING INSPECTION (TERRAIN REFERENCING)

Follow these three steps to orient the map to the ground by map-terrain referencing:

1. Find your position using the GPS.

2. Using the SOSES and other terrain-referencing techniques, identify three or four features on the ground in common with the portrayal on the map, such as hilltops, saddles, valleys, ridges, highways, buildings, bridges, or rivers and streams.

3. Rotate the map as you inspect it for these features until its portrayal is aligned with these same features in the real world (**Figure 4-6**).

DETERMINING DIRECTION AMONG POINTS ON A MAP

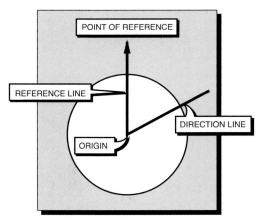

FIGURE 4-7

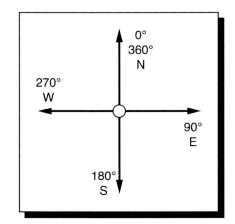

FIGURE 4-8

The **best** method for determining the direction (and distance) between any two positions is to save as landmarks (waypoints) their coordinates and elevations from a map into the memory of the GPS receiver and then let the unit calculate these values from one to the other. GPS units can be set to report these azimuth directions either in magnetic or true values. For navigational purposes, it is best to have the unit set to give you magnetic azimuth values so they can be used in conjunction with your lensatic compass without first making conversion calculations.

An azimuth is any directional value being measured as an angle that is read in a clockwise direction from a north (0°) reference line (**Figure 4-7**). For example, north is at a 0° or 360° azimuth, east at a 90° azimuth, south at 180°, and west at 270° (**Figure 4-8**).

There are times when you may wish to measure directional values directly on a map. For example, you may be required to make some short, finely tuned directional changes along a route between major checkpoints when an obstacle or some other unexpected difficulty is encountered on the ground in order to make the movement safer or easier.

Determining direction from a map is best accomplished through use of a 360° protractor with 0° oriented toward grid (map) north. When using this method, the next illustration, **Figure 4-9**, shows the correct method for placing a protractor on the map and measuring directional values. Note that the center of the protractor is placed over the position from which the azimuth is to be measured and the index lines on the protractor are oriented parallel to the grid lines on the map.

When measuring a directional azimuth directly on the map, don't forget to convert the grid azimuth values being read on your map before applying them to your compass. Many large-scale topographic maps include conversion notes in their margins that are quite useful when making these conversion calculations. **Figure 4-10** contains the conversion notes from the (A) TENINO Washington, USA, 1:50,000-scale map sheet and (B) the Watertown, New York, USA, 1:50,000-scale map sheet.

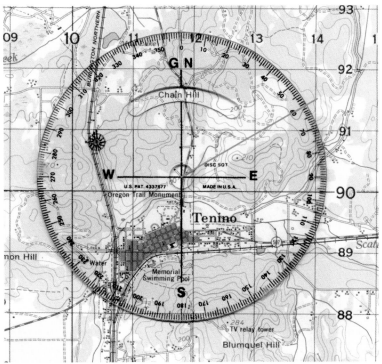

FIGURE 4-9

THE MAP PROTRACTOR MEASURES THE GRID AZIMUTH OF THE RED LINE ON THE TENINO MAP AS BEING 60 DEGREES

DETERMINING DIRECTION ON THE GROUND

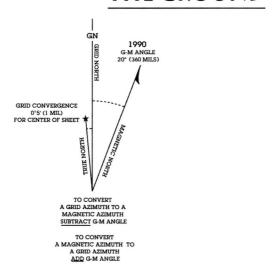

GN

1990
G-M ANGLE
20° (360 MILS)

GRID CONVERGENCE
0°5' (1 MIL)
FOR CENTER OF SHEET ★

GRID NORTH

MAGNETIC NORTH

TRUE NORTH

TO CONVERT
A GRID AZIMUTH TO A
MAGNETIC AZIMUTH
<u>SUBTRACT</u> G-M ANGLE

TO CONVERT
A MAGNETIC AZIMUTH TO
A GRID AZIMUTH
<u>ADD</u> G-M ANGLE

FIGURE 4-10A
TENINO, WA

GN

1990
G-M ANGLE
13° (230 MILS)

GRID NORTH

MAGNETIC NORTH

TRUE NORTH

★ GRID CONVERGENCE
0°26' (8 MILS)
FOR CENTER OF SHEET

TO CONVERT
A GRID AZIMUTH TO A
MAGNETIC AZIMUTH
<u>ADD</u> G-M ANGLE

TO CONVERT
A MAGNETIC AZIMUTH
TO A GRID AZIMUTH
<u>SUBTRACT</u> G-M ANGLE

FIGURE 4-10B
WATERTOWN, NY

The lensatic compass (**Figure 4-11**) is the best instrument for determining direction on the ground. It contains a "floating" protractor scale with a mounted (magnetic) north-seeking arrow that measures the angular values for any direction (azimuth) in the real world.

You will note that the dial of the compass, known as the compass card, has an inner (red) protractor scale printed on it with the north-pointing arrow being defined as 0° or 360° (**Figure 4-12**). Just as on the map protractor, north on the compass is at a 0° or 360° azimuth, east at 90°, south at 180°, and west at 270°. Note that a black mil scale is located on the outer edge of the compass card. Remember, it is the red (inner) degrees scale, marked off in 5° increments, that is used in LN.

When using a lensatic compass, you read directional azimuth values from the protractor scale directly under the black index line printed on the cover glass. There are two methods for holding the compass for daylight use: (1) the center-hold technique (**Figures 4-13 & 4-14**) and (2) the compass-to-cheek method (**Figures 4-15 & 4-16**), which is the most accurate.

For night use, the luminous line and bezel ring serration and clicking device are invaluable. Starting with the luminous line oriented right over the black index line, for every counterclockwise click of the bezel

127

FIGURE 4-11

ring, the luminous line is moved +3°. To set the compass for use at a particular azimuth at night (for example 30°), the luminous line is set over the black index line and then rotated 10 clicks (30° / 3 = 10 clicks) counterclockwise. Now, holding your open compass so that it is pointing directly out in front of you, rotate yourself until the luminous north arrow is lined up with the luminous line. You are facing at an azimuth direction of 30° (**Figure 4-17**).

There is a quick method for presetting the compass during daylight for night use. Place your open compass in the center-hold position and face in the desired direction for the preset (i.e., 275°). While holding the compass steady with a reading of 275° under your black index line, rotate the bezel ring so that the luminous line aligns with the luminous north-seeking arrow. Later, when you open the compass and rotate yourself to again align the north arrow with the luminous line, you are facing in the desired azimuth direction of 275°.

Before using a lensatic compass, be certain all the parts are there and functioning properly. Also, do not use your compass near high tension power lines (55 meters), truck (20 meters), telephone or barbed wires (10 meters), or a rifle (.5 meters). Metal eyeglass frames may also affect the accuracy of a compass reading when using the compass-to-cheek method.

Yes, the lensatic compass can and should be used during vehicular mounted navigation as well.

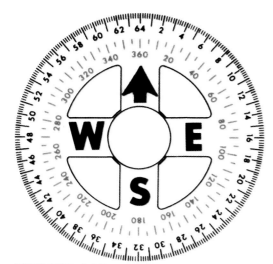

FIGURE 4-12 LENSATIC COMPASS CARD

There is a five-step method for using it on a vehicle (**Figure 4-18**):

   1.   Dismount and move at least 25 meters forward of the vehicle.
   2.   Locate a distant sighting point and take a directional reading with your compass.
   3.   Remount the vehicle and move slowly forward toward the distant sighting point and take another reading.
   4.   Determine the difference between the two readings, which is the error (compass deviation) caused by the metal and electrical system within the vehicle. This deviation is generally less than + or - 10°.

FIGURE 4-13

FIGURE 4-15

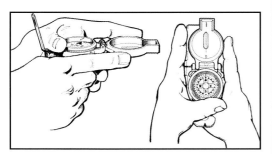

FIGURE 4-14 CENTER HOLD TECHNIQUE

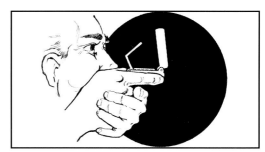

FIGURE 4-16 COMPASS-TO-CHEEK TECHNIQUE

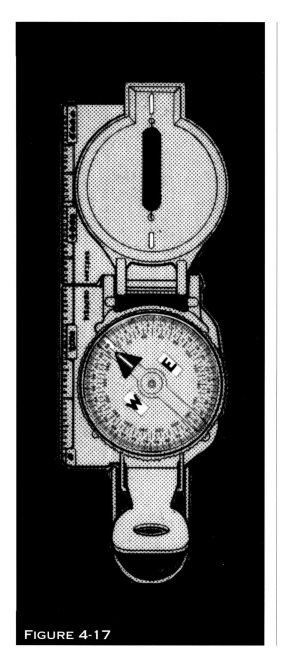

FIGURE 4-17

5. Apply that deviation (add or subtract) to every subsequent reading you take from this vehicle using that compass.

FIGURE 4-18

In summary, whenever you navigate over the land, you should have a magnetic compass to use in conjunction with your GPS receiver and map. The GPS receiver locates your position by coordinates, the map relates this position to your surroundings through its grid and feature portrayal, and the compass orients both you and the map to these surroundings by reporting real world directions. These are the three vital ingredients needed for that first important step in LN – **know where you are** in every possible way: (1) on the map, (2) on the ground, and (3) in relation to all features and positions in your area.

On a number of their navigation screens, GPS receiver manufacturers assign specific terms when referring to various directional concepts, which can be reported in either grid or magnetic values.

For example:

course	= the directional azimuth from any starting point to destination (waypoint to waypoint)
track	= the directional azimuth of your present heading
bearing	= the directional azimuth from your present position to the destination (next waypoint)

FIELD EXPEDIENT METHODS FOR DETERMINING DIRECTION ON THE GROUND

When you don't have a compass, there are some techniques you can employ for determining direction. Here are just a few.

USE OF GPS

You can use your receiver's graphic steering feature to determine direction at any time. Establish a route from your present position to some other point on the map after having already saved both as waypoints. Set out in any direction and, using the navigation feature, the unit will determine the direction you are actually moving (track). With that accurate directional information, you can then estimate any real world direction from your position. Be certain to move several dozen meters in a straight line before trusting the directional reading due to the effects of SA.

Just be careful you don't face in a different direction during a halt because the unit shows your direction of travel in relation to your forward progress. **It is not a compass**. If you turn your body while standing in place, you will misorient the graphic display.

DAYTIME EXPEDIENT TECHNIQUES

1.   At noon (standard time), the sun is nearly due south for most of the northern hemisphere and due north for most of the southern hemisphere. Remember that this will not apply in tropical areas.

2.   The sun melts snow more quickly on south-facing slopes in the northern hemisphere and on north-

facing slopes in the southern hemisphere. This may be obvious during winter months, but it may also be determined during the summer because these sun-facing slopes experience more erosion due to water runoff during the winter when vegetation is less able to hold the soil in place.

3. Sunflowers face east.

4. Blue sky over large bodies of water may appear darker than sky over land. At times, you may be able to guide your movement by this darker sky along a coastline or large lakeshore.

5. An oasis may develop a cloud that can serve as a locational and directional guide.

6. Certain areas have prevailing winds, such as the "westerlies" over much of the continental United States. They may be helpful in roughly judging direction, especially over short periods of time if the wind direction was checked before starting the movement.

7. A quick look at a map reveals prevailing drainage patterns or directions in which ridgelines or hill or mountain chains are generally oriented in an area. These natural cues can be useful if attention is paid to them during the map study prior to the start of a movement.

NIGHTTIME EXPEDIENT TECHNIQUES

1.   You can tell direction from the stars.

a.   In the **northern hemisphere**, locate the Big Dipper constellation in the sky (**Figure 4-19**). The two front stars of the "soup ladle" point almost directly toward the North Star (Polaris), which is about five times the distance between these two front pointer stars above the open top of the dipper. When you face the North Star, you are always facing to within 5° of true north. To select your NORTHERN LANDMARK on the horizon that is directly below this point in the sky, hold a string, rope, shoestring, ruler, or straight stick in front and above you that is in line with the NORTH STAR and is long enough to extend vertically down to the horizon. The spot on the horizon that your makeshift "plumb line" indicates is your NORTHERN LANDMARK.

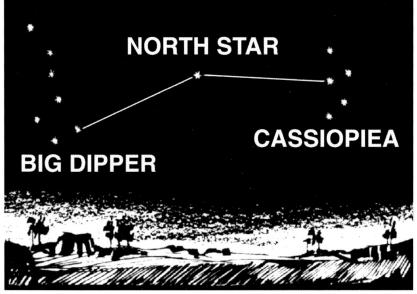

FIGURE 4-19

b. In the **southern hemisphere**, locate the Southern Cross star pattern in the sky (**Figure 4-20**). Although there is no star located in the sky directly above the South Pole, this projected south point in the

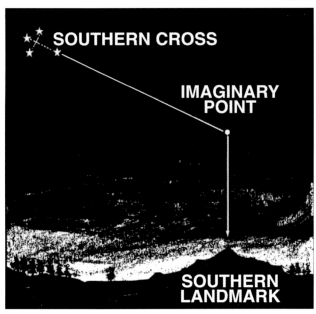

SOUTHERN CROSS

IMAGINARY POINT

SOUTHERN LANDMARK

FIGURE 4-20

sky can be easily determined. It is 4 1/2 times the distance from the top to the bottom of the Southern Cross and below it. You should then select a landmark directly below this imaginary "south spot" in the sky and face toward it to estimate any other direction on the ground, as in 1-a above.

2. You can sometimes tell direction by observing the moon. An imaginary line drawn through the "horn-tips" of a crescent moon will run approximately north and south.

3. A nighttime rural sky is dark, but an urban sky is bright and will serve as a navigational beacon that can be seen for many miles. Notice the bright "blink" in the sky above even small urban places.

4. Smells and sounds can also help you keep track of direction as you navigate— especially when it is relatively quiet and the winds are nearly calm, as they often are at night. Some examples of sounds might be traffic on a main highway or the pounding surf, and helpful smells might be a freshly plowed field or some stench from a polluted site.

ESTIMATING DIRECTIONS

Once you have determined a direction (such as from the GPS unit or the stars), the "clock method" for estimating directions may be very useful to you (**Figure 4-21**). Just envision north (0°) as being represented by

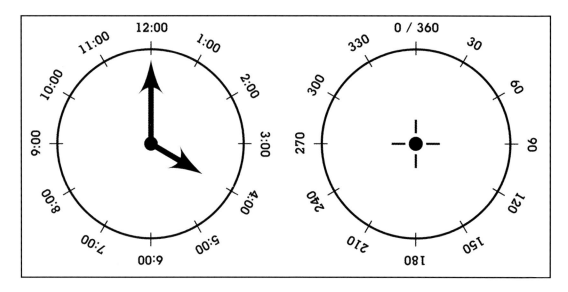

FIGURE 4-21

noon on the clock face and each of the succeeding eleven hours as being 30° greater than the previous one. Of course, it is also easy to interpolate azimuth directions that fall between each of the hours. You might be surprised how accurately you can estimate directions using this method.

DETERMINING DISTANCE

Distances between any two stored positions (waypoints) are calculated and reported by the GPS receiver at the same time as direction through use of the navigation function. These distances can also be measured on the map using a piece of scrap paper and the graphic scales found in the margins (**Figure 4-22**).

GPS receivers report only straight line distances—not irregular ones. Thus, it is more practical to measure irregular distances, such as road or trail distances between locations, directly on the map.

To measure irregular distances along a winding road, or stream, a scrap of paper is again used. In doing so, the paper is placed along the edge of the road at the starting point. Tick marks are made both on the map and on the paper at the starting point and at the point where the road curves away from the edge of the paper. Keeping the second set of tick marks aligned, the paper is pivoted until its edge is again running along the same edge of the road. A third set of tick marks is made where the paper's edge and the route again separate. This process is repeated as many times as is necessary until the entire route has been marked off in this manner (**Figure 4-23**). Finally, the paper's edge is placed along the graphic scale to read the measured distance. Also, chenille stems (pipe cleaners) from craft stores can be bent along irregular routes and small map measuring wheels can be rolled over mapped roadways to measure the same distances.

As was the case prior to the development of GPS technology, ground distances can be measured by an odometer, pacing (the average hiker takes 120 steps for every 100 meters), or elapsed time (using time-distance formulas). However, the GPS unit can keep track of your movement progress and report distances yet to be

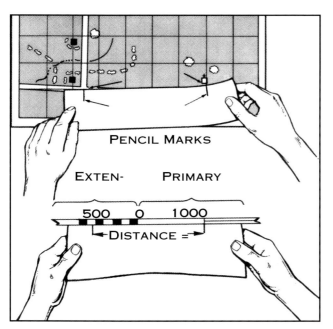

PENCIL MARKS

EXTEN-   PRIMARY

500   0   1000

◄DISTANCE ►

FIGURE 4-22

traveled in moving from your current position to the next waypoint (landmark) along your selected route.

You are cautioned that ground distances calculated mathematically through use of the grid (as are those accomplished by a GPS receiver), as well as those actually measured over the flat surface of a map, fail to account for the discrepancies actually encoun-

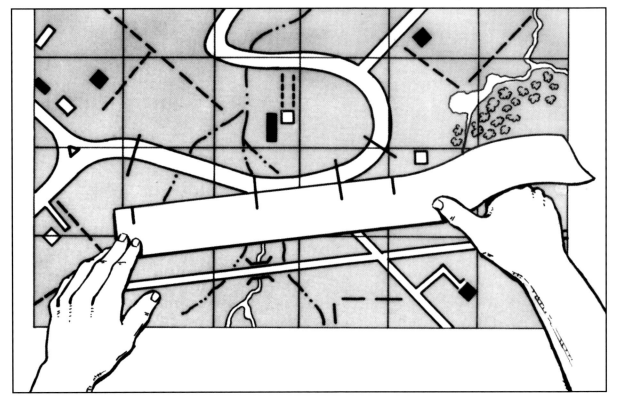

FIGURE 4-23

tered out on the ground. Some of these discrepancies are caused by the unevenness of the terrain, which adds more surface distance to any horizontal calculations or measurements taken from the map. Other discrepancies are the result of the many slippages and small detours caused by slopes, soil types, mud, snow, the presence of rocks and boulders, wet areas, trees, depressions, small escarpments, and so forth. Therefore, there is a table of factors to be added to measured horizontal map distances before they are applied to your odometer readings, pace counts, or elapsed time distance calculations out on the ground.

**FACTORS TO BE ADDED TO MEASURED
HORIZONTAL MAP DISTANCES**

Flat, scrub desert or temperate terrain ....add 10%
Rolling temperate wooded terrain ....add 20%
Any loose surface material or snow ....add 20%
(for wheel, track, and foot slippage)
Jungle or hilly temperate terrain ....add 30%
Sandy desert...add 30%
Mountainous terrain ....add 40%

Source: U.S. Army Research Institute.

IN SUMMARY

We said earlier that in order to get there from here, you must know which way to go and how far. You should now be able to determine both.

This chapter explained how to integrate use of the magnetic compass with GPS equipment and a map while navigating over the land. This included how to orient the map using a compass and terrain referencing and how to determine directions with a compass, the

GPS receiver, and several field expedient techniques. It also reviewed techniques for using the GPS unit to calculate both directions and distances among various positions saved as waypoints. And, finally, it reviewed the technique used to measure distances on a map and how to factor those measurements for a more accurate application out on the ground.

EMPLOYING GPS

Now that you have acquired map and compass using skills and become familiar with the many applications and advantages of today's highly reliable GPS equipment, it's time to learn how to integrate and routinely employ them as you move from place to place.

BACKGROUND

FIGURE 5-1
MAGELLAN GPS NAV 1000M

Since 1989, when the Magellan Systems Corporation introduced the world's first hand-held GPS receiver, a host of manufacturers and models have entered and exited the market. In fact, several Magellan GPS NAV 1000M™ units were purchased in 1991 by Alexis for use in instructing soldiers in land navigation at the Royal Saudi Air Defense Forces Institute in Jeddah (**Figure 5-1**). The cost of this multiplex receiver at that time was over $5,000.

FIGURE 5-2
TRIMBLE SCOUTMASTER GPS™

FIGURE 5-3
MAGELLAN TRAILBLAZER™

FIGURE 5-4
EAGLE EXPEDITION II™

In those early days, there were basically two manufacturers vieing for the hand-held market: Trimble and Magellan (**Figures 5-2 & 5-3**). Today, both companies remain active in the GPS industry, but Trimble, the larger of the two companies, made a decision to withdraw from the general consumer market and concentrate on the more technical/professional applications of this new technology. In fact, there are still many of the older Magellan and Trimble units in use today and this chapter is as useful to the owners of these older pieces of equipment as it is to those purchasing equipment fresh off the production lines. The principles of wayfinding as well as the applications of GPS for land navigation remain quite constant.

What have been changing and developing are some of the features, characteristics, and capabilities of GPS receiver units. They are getting faster, lighter, and easier to read; becoming equipped with more useful graphics; rendering more varied and useful navigational reports; and demanding less power.

Today, there are primarily three manufacturers producing the vast majority of hand-held products for the general consumer market, which is poised to grow astronomically as people become more aware of the utility these products have in terms of work, play, and safety (**Figures 5-4, 5-5, 5-6, & 5-7**). The reason you have been shown models displaying four different brand names is that Lowrance manufactures under both the Eagle and Lowrance trade names, while Magellan and Garmin round out the trio of companies.

FIGURE 5-5
LOWRANCE GLOBALNAV 212™

FIGURE 5-6
MAGELLAN COLORTRAK™

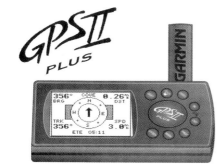

FIGURE 5-7
GARMIN GPS II+™

We are frequently asked by people who are ready to buy a GPS receiver which is best. The problem with answering this question is that neither an "expert" nor a salesperson knows the questioner's particular needs and preferences. When just starting out, he probably doesn't either. Thus, you may find that reading this chapter before making a purchase can be very helpful. Here are a few examples. Is the price or the speed in calculating a position fix and good reception in areas with moderate amounts of foliage most important? Do you care or not about having data ports to interface your equipment with other GPS units, a laptop, or PC? Do you wish to have the capability for utilizing the easy-to-use MGRS coordinate system along with Alexis' Road and other maps? As you can see, not all GPS receivers have the same features, characteristics, and capabilities, nor do all navigators have the same requirements and preferences. First, you need to be able to determine what you want and then select the piece of equipment that comes closest to fitting it at the best price.

We are not in the business of endorsing any particular piece of equipment, but we do have our preferences for accomplishing various tasks. To our knowledge, none of the equipment manufactured by these corporations is of poor quality. Nevertheless, you must remember that you get what you pay for. So, our advice is to be willing to first study the question and then pay for what you want and need.

On the other hand, if you feel your present equipment isn't very useful to you, perhaps you just don't know how to use it to maximum advantage. That's what this chapter is about. The owner's manual that comes with the equipment tells you how to operate a particular receiver, whereas, this chapter explains how to apply it to your navigational efforts most efficiently, effectively, and with a minimum of effort and stress. We have attempted to include and describe practically every feature, characteristic, and capability available on units today; explain what they can do; and suggest how to utilize each of them to meet your needs.

With so many new models continually being released, it is not practical to make unit-by-unit comparisons in a published book such as this. That can best be left to the monthly periodicals, such as *GPSWORLD* and various outdoor magazines. They frequently run these comparisons and generally call them "buyers' guides." For example, a recent article appeared in a summer issue of *Outdoor Life*. In this article, author Charles Plueddeman focused on five hand-held GPS units by comparing their attributes. He featured the EAGLE EXPLORER™ (Lowrance), MAGELLAN 2000XL™, LOWRANCE GLOBALNAV 200™, GARMIN GPS12™, and the PIONEER™ (Magellan) by examining weight, dimensions, power source, battery life, receiver type (12-parallel vs. multiplex), waypoint memory, route memory, waypoints per route, pro/con, and price.

This author said he particularly liked the easy to understand operating system and high responsiveness of the Rockwell 12-channel receiver found in the EAGLE EXPLORER™ and Lowrance GLOBALNAV 200™; the six navigation screens and battery life of the fine 12-

parallel channel receiver found in the Magellan 2000 XL™; the smaller dimensions and ergonomic design of the 12-parallel channel Garmin GPS 12™; and the amazingly low price, size, and battery life of the multiplexing Magellan PIONEER™. Finally, the article included a sidebar discussing some units with additional features that are somewhat more expensive. It included the Lowrance GlobalMap 100™, Magellan ColorTRAK™, and Garmin GPS 48™ (the GPS 45 upgraded to a 12-parallel channel capability). Most manufacturers today also produce models with electronic "moving maps" which do provide a general frame of reference for your movement; however, they offer a limited perspective and lack the detail found on large-scale topographic maps or even small-scale state road maps.

After reading this chapter and before purchasing your next hand-held GPS receiver, you are encouraged to review **Appendix E** which provides a listing of the most important features, functions, and characteristics available on the various GPS units currently found on today's market. Furthermore, you will find brief descriptors for each of these attributes. **Appendix E** serves as a concise review of the chapter and can be quite valuable when used in conjunction with a "buyers' guide" and/or promotional materials distributed by the manufacturers.

In the three years since the first printing of the second edition of this book, a host of improvements have been made in the hand-held portable GPS navigational equipment being offered to consumers. Among these improvements are the introduction of a number of models providing 8- and 12-parallel channel reception; a modest number of new features; some innovative and imaginative graphic presentations; further reductions in unit size, weight, and price; increased battery life; and, not to be overlooked, the development of more readable and understandable user manuals.

Finally, a quick look into the near future tells us that unit price reductions are not the only aspect of GPS development that will slow down. The development of new functions and features will do so as well. Most of the new improvements to come next will be less about what the units can do and more about how well they do it. We can expect to see developments that allow for continued size reduction, improved reception, sharper and more colorful graphics, a bit more accuracy (government SA policy is, of course, the biggest problem), and longer battery life.

One interesting way to assess the progress that has been made in recent years is to compare the new Magellan PIONEER™ (**Figure 5-8**) with the old Magellan GPS NAV 1000M™ (**Figure 5-1**). The PIONEER is about $5000 cheaper, 30% shorter, 40% narrower, only 60% as thick, 70% lighter, uses only one-third the number of batteries, and has three to four times the battery life as the old GPS NAV 1000M™. Yet, it has just about the same navigational capabilities and characteristics (e.g., it has a multiplexing receiver) as the bulky old units we used to train Saudi soldiers back in 1991. When compared with products on today's market, the PIONEER's greatest strengths are its compact size/ weight, battery life, and price; while its limitations are

FIG 5-8
MAGELLAN GPS PIONEER™

mainly the result of its multiplexing (two channel) receiver. Although there are more expensive and superior 12-parallel channel units presently available on the market from all three manufacturers, it is, nevertheless, far better than being lost because you have no equipment. It may not be as quick in calculating a new fix or always have the reception that you might prefer, but it certainly can accomplish the fundamental task being asked of it—knowing where it is located. Certainly, the old GPS NAV 1000M™ was good enough play an important role in the defeat of Iraq's Republican Guard.

THE SITUATION

You have read the first four chapters presenting general navigation skills and now wish to proceed step-by-step with your new GPS receiver in hand in order to achieve maximum advantage from this powerful new tool. Because the majority of our map illustrations are taken from the Easton, PA, area, you are to assume that you are located there for the purposes of learning to initialize and set-up your unit. Also, since no single hand-held GPS unit possesses all the features, characteristics, and capabilities to be discussed here, we will use illustrations showing screens from a variety of makes and models to illustrate the numerous teaching points which follow.

In order to better organize the presentation and make it more understandable, the subject matter has been divided into the following topics: (1) receiver unit characteristics, (2) initialization and set-up procedures, (3) the four GPS navigation functions and their related features, and (4) other features, special characteristics, and GPS unit accessories.

When you have finished this chapter, you will understand and be able to effectively employ virtually any function and feature found on the popular GPS receiver units now available. Furthermore, you will know how to program these sets to better meet your individual needs and preferences.

GPS UNIT CHARACTERISTICS

Most of today's portable receiver units are tough, reliable, resistant to dust and water, fit comfortably into the palm of your hand, and weigh less than a pound. In addition, they operate without difficulty through a wide range of temperatures and weather conditions as they report crucial position and other navigational information clearly through a combination of words, numbers, and innovative, easily understood graphic presentations.

As surprising as it may seem, unit accuracy is not related to price. Instead, price more directly translates into the numbers and types of features and capabilities included with the unit. Some might argue the point that the more expensive 12-parallel channel receivers are more accurate than the cheaper multiplexing models; however, they only win on a technicality. Because 8- or 12-parallel channel receivers can track more satellites, the units are able to calculate positions more rapidly; therefore, they can report "calculated" position fixes more frequently. In order to give the illusion of one per second updates, the multiplexing units often "predict" positions by estimations between actual calculations. Nevertheless, whether a unit is a multiplexing or a parallel channel model, the actual position calculation is just as accurate with either type of set.

Still, there are those who would continue to argue that because parallel channel units track more satellites simultaneously, they are more likely to receive signals in areas with less than a horizon-to-horizon "view" of the sky; therefore, having a reading is much more accurate than not having one at all. Regardless, the point being made here is that, whether you have a $100 multiplexing unit or an $800 model with 12 parallel channels, built-in digital compass, moving maps, and even a compartment to store your lunch, when placed in a position where adequate signals can be received and given the necessary time required for an actual calculation (up to several seconds for multiplexing units), all of these hand-held GPS receivers should yield equally accurate position fixes.

One final note on the subject of accuracy and price, if and when the government allocates more frequencies for civil use and as the technology improves for utilizing a second carrier to help calculate the accuracy of pseudo-ranges from SVs to the receiver, the price paid for a GPS unit will by then more directly reflect its accuracy. However, these improvements are still some years off for the general consumer market. For now, the only way to gain significant accuracy for GPS is through use of DGPS when and where it is made available because the government's SA causes today's greatest inaccuracies (see **Appendix A**).

In regard to the features you might expect to find on the more expensive units; they are often equipped with 12-parallel channel receivers and designed to accept external power sources and active antenna systems; render more and a greater variety of reports; include more elaborate graphics displays; possibly include scrolling electronic maps; hold greater numbers of positions as landmarks or checkpoints (waypoints), preplanned routes, and route segments in memory; and have various electronic interface ports for such equipment as PCs and laptops or other interfacing communications or navigational devices. They are also more likely to have the capacity for taking advantage of a differential DGPS environment, performing position and speed averaging computations, and accomplishing more sophisticated location projection and triangulation functions—both of which are explained later in the chapter. Keen competition, however, is forcing manufacturers to include greater numbers of these features on their more economical models.

Although they are constantly improving, two fundamental characteristics common to all portable GPS receivers are their rather heavy draw on battery power and the need for proper set placement and antenna orientation. You should frequently monitor reserve battery power (generally included on the satellite status screens of most models) and always carry fresh replacements. Rechargeable batteries are now accepted by many units; however, you are warned that they may very rapidly drop to an unusable level often "misleading" the battery indicator, which, in most cases, is designed for use with alkaline batteries.

For maximum performance, you must place the unit so that it has as unobstructed a "view" of as much of the sky as possible and with its antenna facing upward. Make every effort not to have the receiver shielded by your hand, vegetation, structures, or the terrain. Locations in heavily forested areas, steep and narrow canyons, and inside or up against the outer walls of buildings will generally preclude your obtaining either an optimum reading or any reading at all. When this occurs, the best corrective action to take is to move with your receiver to a more favorable location and try again. Of course, the 12-parallel channel units will operate more favorably and more rapidly in less optimal situations than the multiplexing models.

Contrary to what you might expect, the strength of the signals being received from the various SVs has little impact upon the accuracy of a position fix. As long as the information has been received by the unit, it can be used. However, poor signal quality (SQ) messages warn that a particular satellite's incoming data may soon be lost to the unit. Unless there are ample numbers of signals coming to the unit from alternative SVs (a total of four for a 3-dimensional fix and three for a 2-dimensional fix), you may not be able to continue to obtain readings as the result of various obstructions situated close by. On the other hand, the geometric angles resulting from the locations of the satellites being used by the receiver to calculate its position can significantly

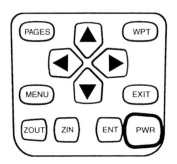

FIGURE 5-9
EAGLE KEYPAD

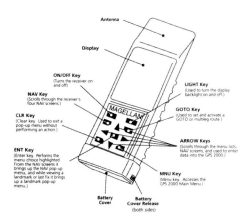

FIGURE 5-10
MAGELLAN 4000 XL KEYPAD

affect its accuracy. Whenever the geometric quality (GQ) is not acceptable, most GPS units will provide an on-screen warning to caution you about the questionable accuracy of the fix. The relative quality of the horizontal fix can be reported in several ways. Some units report (1) **GDOP** (geometric dilution of precision), (2) **values for all DOP components** of GDOP, or other such schemes as (3) **"figures of merit" (1-9)** or (4) **"expected horizontal position error"** (in feet or meters).

A more thorough discussion of position dilution, DGPS, multiplex and parallel channel operation, upcoming improvements in accuracy through use of carrier waves, as well as a better understanding of the operation of the System as a whole can be found in **Appendix A** (How GPS Works: Some Technical Talk for the Layman).

In addition to the warnings about low battery power, weak SQs, and poor GQs, most GPS units employ a variety of logical on-screen messages and icons to convey various warnings and other vital pieces of information. Some units even have audible alarms. Here is a list of the most common examples:

• position information being reported is old (generally in excess of 10 seconds) (blinking data or icon warning)

• position reported is based upon a 2-dimensional calculation (signals from only 3 SVs)

• screen backlighting is turned on and consuming additional battery power

• end leg landmark (waypoint) or final route destination has been reached

• you are off course and the cross track error (XTE) exceeds the margin set for the warning

• up, down, left, right arrows appear to indicate that these keys can be pressed to select menu items, access further information or to input commands or data

• battery power is low (replace soon)

The last general characteristic we will examine is the commonality evolving in unit keypad designs (**Figures 5-9, 5-10, and 5-11**). The keypad is obviously the means by which you interact with the unit. Most functions are accessed by pressing various labeled keys (e.g., **ON/OFF, LIGHT, NAV, MENU, PAGES/MODE, LMK/WPT, ENTER, CLEAR**). Four directional ARROW keys are also generally included. (Some units have what Garmin calls a "rocker key," which is simply a larger button-type key that lets you "rock" it in any of four directions serving the same purposes as the four **AR-ROW** keys found on other sets.) They are used to scroll through lists of menu items or stored data, access additional information reports or graphic displays associated with the screen currently being displayed, or to "type in" alpha and/or numeric data being called for at the cursor (such as naming landmarks or waypoints and/or entering or editing their coordinates manually), and to move the cursor about the screen for menu selections or data input. Any instructions or data you select or "type" into the GPS unit are inputted by press-

FIGURE 5-11
GARMIN 12 XL

ing the **ENTER** key. Conversely, various instructions and data are generally deleted either by pressing the **CLEAR** key or a designated **ARROW** key, as per instructions found on your particular unit's screen. Today's receivers do tend to carefully lead you through the procedures for operating them.

Viewing the three keypad examples found in **Figures 5-9, 5-10,** and **5-11,** we see many similarities as well as some differences. For example, the arrow keys (or rocker key) have similar roles on all three sets with the exception that Eagle (Lowrance) frequently uses the right arrow key to execute various commands; whereas, Magellan and Garmin most often use the **ENTER** key for this purpose. On the other hand, Magellan and Garmin also use the **ENTER** key to input information; while this is the only function of this key for most Eagle / Lowrance units.

MENU keys generally give you access to a variety of options that allow you to both initialize and tailor the unit to your specific needs and preferences. When tailoring your GPS receiver using the setup menu(s), for example, you have the options to select the coordinate system, speed / distance unit (metric or British), and directional value (true / magnetic) you prefer to use; set the map datum and alarm parameters to warn of navigational errors and announce destination arrivals; adjust screen contrast, screen lighting intensity, automatic turn-off delays, and local time (12 or 24 hour clocks); set-up DGPS / NMEA / COM PORT configurations; and, finally, to access the unit's simulator / trainer.

With some units you can access the various screens providing navigation information by pressing the **NAV** and **GO TO** keys, but with others, you use the **PAGES** or **MODE** key. On many sets, repeatedly pressing the **ENTER** key will back you out of a menu to a position or navigation screen, but with the Eagle (Lowrance) unit, a special key labeled **EXIT** will let you escape back to the screen you were using at the time you accessed either the menu/submenu or the various landmark (waypoint) or page screens.

Finally, **ZIN** and **ZOUT** (zoom in / zoom out) keys appear on some sets which allow you to change the scale (zoom) on the plotter screen (graphical display of your track) and, if the unit has the feature, it allows you to do the same with the display of an electronic "moving map."

UNIT INITIALIZATION & SETUP

There are a few steps you're required to take before your GPS receiver is ready to find its position and guide you across the wilderness. You must first initialize it and then tailor its setup specifications to meet your particular preferences. After insuring that your unit has a fresh set of batteries, you are ready to begin.

INITIALIZE

In order to save time in obtaining your first position report, it is necessary to give your set some idea as to where in the world it has been awakened.

This will not be necessary whenever the last position it computed before being powered off was within 300 miles / 482 kilometers of your present position (PP).

Your initial position can be entered as part of the unit's "setup function" (see below) in LAT/LON or any other coordinate system (including UTM or the MGRS format of UTM), depending upon what options are carried in its software and which has been selected by you. Even when you plan to use a coordinate system better suited to land navigation on a USGS topographic map quadrangle (such as UTM or MGRS), it is probably easiest to enter your initial position in LAT/LON coordinates. This information can be read directly from any corner of a USGS topographic quadrangle and many other types of maps. For example, **Figure 5-12** shows the northeast (upper right) corner of the Easton, PA, NJ, USA 1:24,000-scale USGS 7.5-minute Series topographic map

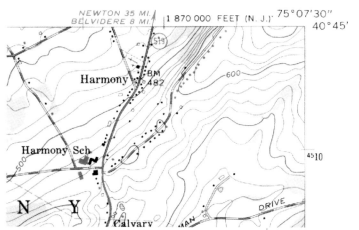

EASTON QUADRANGLE
NEW JERSEY—PENNSYLVANIA
7.5 MINUTE SERIES (TOPOGRAPHIC)

FIGURE 5-12

quadrangle. Since we are planning to navigate using this map, you should input **<40º45' N Lat, ENTER, 075º 07.50' W Lon, ENTER, 680 (feet) ENTER>** as your initial position. (This normally can be accomplished through one of the items found in the setup menu.) On the other hand, whenever you are planning to navigate over the highways with an Alexis Road Map, you are encouraged to first setup your unit to report positions in old MGRS (MGRS-1 or ALT MGRS) and enter the coordinates for any position found on the map sheet as your initial position (e.g., 18T WA 000 000).

When you first purchase your GPS unit or whenever it does not locate appropriate signals from the SVs, the unit may automatically ask you to select and enter the country and state in which you're located in an effort to initialize the set. If it does not have this "easy initialization" feature or if you do not react to the prompts, it will automatically resort to a "cold start." This means that the unit will methodically start searching for signals from the various GPS satellites, update its clock and almanac, and then calculate its position. With multiplex receivers, this may take up to 12 or more minutes, and with 12-parallel channel units, it may take more than five minutes. You may also manually request a "cold start" from the setup menu. When your set has not been used for six or more months, this is a good idea because it allows signals from the SVs to correct the receiver's clock and upgrade its almanac information.

SETUP

Now, let's review the specific selections you can make in tailoring your GPS receiver to best meet your needs relative to the various situations you expect to encounter while navigating with this map of Easton. If you own a GPS unit, after initializing it using the setup menu(s), you are encouraged to practice setting each of following common options on your GPS receiver. While doing so, you should have your owner's manual handy, just in case you wish to refer to it.

The following setup capabilities are included on many hand-held GPS receiver units:

The <u>map coordinate system options</u> available on various GPS receivers offer you a number of choices for your position displays. For example, as a minimum, older units offer LAT/LON and UTM, while the majority of the units coming onto the market today (by late 1998) offer the easy-to-use MGRS option, as well. Also included are coordinate systems matching a variety of maps from around the world. They range from the British, Irish, and Swiss grids to those of Finland, Australia, and New Zealand.

The coordinate system you select during unit setup should, of course, match the one found on your map. However, if both LAT/LON and UTM are included (as is the case when using the EASTON topographic quadrangle map), it is suggested that you opt for the UTM because its perpendicular grid better accommodates navigation on land. This is fully explained in Chapter 3. Most GPS units have LAT/LON set as the default because your initial position is most easily entered from the true geographic coordinates shown at the corners of USGS topographic maps.

If you should find occasion to use LAT/LON, such as when using your hand-held receiver in conjunction with a water navigation chart, you have options within LAT/LON to select your position reports in degrees, minutes, and seconds or in degrees, minutes, and hundredths of minutes. UTM coordinates are always reported with 6-digit easting and 7-digit northing values; and MGRS coordinate values can generally be reported in readings of 2-digits (nearest 10,000 meters), 4-digits (nearest 1000 meters), 6-digits (nearest 100 meters), 8-digits (nearest 10 meters), and 10-digits (nearest meter). Some manufacturers allow you to setup the number of digits preferred in the coordinate readout while reporting both easting and northing values on a single line, while others (including Eagle / Lowrance) give you an entire 5-digit easting and 5-digit northing on separate lines of text. Eagle's approach is slightly more confusing to the novice because of the extra numbers, some of which will be ignored, but it is quite handy when the more experienced navigator is using maps of different scales (i.e., Alexis Road Maps with small scale state maps and large scale urban insets).

Given the fact that the government's SA program degrades GPS accuracy to generally being no better than about 100 meters, 4- and 6-digit coordinates are about all you would be likely to select for navigational purposes (4-digit MGRS coordinates for small scale maps with grid lines spaced at 10 or more kilometers and 6-digit MGRS coordinates for large scale maps with grid lines spaced at 1 kilometer intervals). You will recall that estimates are easy to make down to tenths of a grid square.

When using large scale USGS topographic maps which include UTM grid lines (or tick marks that allow you to draw on the grid lines), it is suggested that you set the unit to report coordinates in 6-digit MGRS coordinates because they are easier to read and use. When hiking over terrain covered by one or a few adjacent USGS topographic quadrangle sheets, you can ignore the grid zone number (region) and the 100,000-meter square designation (locality) and concentrate on the grid label values in your position readout. To better understand which form of MGRS and which datum to use in conjunction with various maps, see the extensive discussion of these topics found in Chapter 3.

There is no question that the MGRS format of the UTM is rapidly becoming the coordinate system of choice in this country. Incidentally, Canadian topographic maps already use MGRS coordinates based upon the UTM grid system and NAD-27 datum. Today, most GPS receivers have LAT/LON and WGS-84 horizontal map datums programmed as defaults. Land navigators are well advised to use neither. LAT/LON doesn't form a square grid and few maps have been produced thus far using the WGS-84 geoid. The MGRS format of UTM based upon the NAD-27 CONUS horizontal datum will for many years to come be the best option for most who navigate using GPS with a map within the continental United States.

It is important to note that some GPS receivers will report a position on one screen in a "primary" coordinate format and on another screen in a "secondary" coordinate format. The Lowrance GlobalNav 212, for example, will even report two coordinate formats on a single screen. You, the user, have the option to designate what your primary and secondary coordinate selections will be during the setup. Of course, these selections can be changed at any time you may wish to do so. Take a few minutes to practice setting the coordinate system of choice on your GPS receiver unit.

You must also select the best <u>map datum</u> to use with any particular map or chart. GPS units available today allow anywhere from a few dozen to nearly a hundred choices from nearly everywhere around the world. See your owner's manual for the listing that applies to your receiver. To determine what datum to use, your best bet is to read the marginal notes on the map to determine what horizontal datum was used in constructing that map. If it is not stated and it's a commercial map produced in the United States, you can bet that it's based on NAD-27 CONUS. Most commercial maps produced here were and are compiled from USGS base maps utilizing the NAD-27 CONUS datum.

When you have no idea which datum was used in developing a map or when the appropriate choice is not available on your GPS receiver, it is suggested that you go to a location about which you are certain both on the ground and on your map (e.g., a bridge, road intersection, or railroad crossing) and then experiment by obtaining position fixes with the unit set with various datums. Then, simply select the one that gives you the most accurate GPS fix for the known location as compared with its coordinates on the map. Nearly all GPS manufacturers designate the WGS-84 datum as the default, but it is presently a poor choice because it's based on the newest (admittedly, most accurate) geoid dimensions and shape of the earth. The problem is that few maps have been produced using this datum. Looking into the more distant future (many years), after substantial numbers of new base maps have been produced, it will undoubtedly become the option of choice. As is stated in its margin, the EASTON map was constructed using the NAD-27 (CONUS) horizontal map datum. So, make that datum selection in your setup.

The <u>north reference</u> option simply allows you to choose between magnetic north and true north for directional reports. When navigating with a map and compass, it is wise to instruct your receiver to report directions that coincide with your compass (magnetic north). Automatic magnetic declination corrections for all areas of the world have been built into the unit's software. Furthermore, most units use magnetic directional values as the default, which is the preferred choice of most navigators.

The <u>time display setup</u> provides two options: (1) Universal Time Coordinated (UT), until recently known as Greenwich Mean Time (GMT), and (2) local time. In most cases, you can choose to have local time reported on either a 24-hour basis or in AM and PM. We suggest you use local time since Easton, PA, is located five hours behind UT (Greenwich, England).

The <u>position elevation mode</u> option often offers three different choices to the user: 2-D, 3-D, and automatic mode. When given a choice, you should always seek the more accurate 3-dimensional reading and be certain to buy a unit that tells you through an icon or warning message when you are not being given a 3-D readout (using signals from 4 SVs) on your position fix.

Distance/speed settings include choices among statute miles/MPH, nautical miles/knots, and kilometers/KPH. While navigating when using topographic or any other types of maps showing the UTM / MGRS grid lines, it is suggested that you set the unit to report distances and speeds in metric units because the grid lines are generally spaced at either 1 or 10 kilometer intervals. However, if you feel more comfortable using miles/MPH in your automobile, you may certainly take this option. Remember, 1 kilometer equals approximately .6 miles and 1 mile equals approximately 1.6 kilometers. Practice setting the receiver to report linear distance and speed first in metric units and then in British units for use in conjunction with the EASTON map.

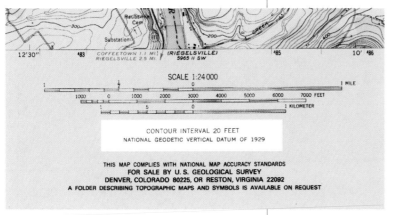

FIGURE 5-13
EASTON, PA, NJ, USA USGS MAP

The elevation setup option offers a simple choice between feet and meters. A check of the marginal information found on the EASTON map (**Figure 5-13**) tells us that elevation values are given in feet. Thus, you should now practice setting your GPS receiver to report elevation in feet.

<u>Warnings</u> about navigational situations and <u>clock alarms</u> are available on many GPS units. You can establish parameters that cause the receiver to warn you, either audibly or through on-screen icons, when you have erred when following a route or when you have arrived at the next landmark (waypoint) or final destination. Those units that possess these features also give you the option of turning the sound on and off. Incidentally, when the sound feature is turned on, each key stroke is confirmed by a "beep."

<u>Screen backlighting brightness</u> and <u>automatic timed light turnoff parameters</u> are generally controlled as setup options, but screen backlighting is generally turned on and off directly from the keypad. Some units have a LIGHT key, while others require a quick touch of the POWER key.

<u>Screen contrast settings</u> are also generally controlled as part of the setup. Ambient temperature has an effect on the display, thus some adjustments may be required as these conditions change. Just as for backlighting brightness, most units display a graphic scale to help you select or change the contrast setting. You are encouraged to stop and practice making these backlighting and contrast adjustments.

<u>Various features, which allow you to monitor and capture or track any number of information pieces</u>, are also included on the setup menu(s) of various makes and models. Some will allow you to determine

FIGURE 5-14
POSITION REPORT - LAT/LON
POSITION REPORT - UTM GRID
POSITION REPORT - MGRS

how frequently your unit makes automatic position saves in what one manufacturer calls a "last fix buffer." Whether they call it following a "breadcrumb" trail or just retracing steps, several receivers have this capability. Some GPS sets also include trip odometers, stop watches that count either up or down, and other such features. Whenever this is the case, the unit's setup menu(s) allow you to use various preset, reset, and units of measure options (i.e., miles or kilometers on a trip odometer).

Finally, foreign language options are available on some units.

FOUR GPS NAVIGATION FUNCTIONS & RELATED FEATURES

Next, we will review in some detail the capabilities and applications of the four primary functions available on virtually all GPS receiver units. They are (1) reporting position, (2) storing landmark (waypoint) names and coordinates, (3) planning and storing single or multi-segment route information, and (4) navigating (following a selected route).

POSITION FUNCTION

By simply powering up most GPS units, they will report positions in the pre-selected map coordinate format. **Figure 5-14** shows three GPS unit screens reporting the same position in (a) LAT/LON, (b) UTM, and (c) MGRS-1 (NAD-27) coordinate formats on a Magellan

FIGURE 5-15
EAGLE EXPEDITION II™ POSITION REPORT
ALT. MGRS COORDINATES (NAD 27 CONUS)

LANDMARK (WAYPOINT) FUNCTION

Trailblazer. **Figure 5-15** pictures an Eagle (Lowrance) Expedition II displaying an ALT MGRS (NAD-27) coordinate readout. It cannot be overemphasized that time spent in finding and/or preparing a good map for use with your GPS will pay rich dividends in terms of the enjoyment, speed, and accuracy you are able to derive from use of your GPS equipment.

Commercial map producers must be encouraged to add the lines and labels of a standard grid coordinate system (preferably MGRS) on their products. It is you, the consumers, who must demand this change. Just as Alexis Publishing has done, other producers of both hiking and highway maps, should include bold UTM grid lines on their maps labeled with the convenient MGRS labels. Until then, you must add them yourselves to your favorite maps.

Now that manufacturers are becoming accustomed to designing GPS receivers for use specifically on land, they are beginning to overcome their nautical roots and drop some unaccustomed terms for land navigators such as "waypoint" and "man overboard" and refer to "landmarks","checkpoints", or just plain "locations". The purpose of the landmark (waypoint) function on any GPS receiver is to either automatically or manually store in the unit's memory the position information for various designated locations. There are a variety of ways this information can be categorized or reported, but the purpose is always the same; so it will be available whenever you wish to use it to define a multi-segmented route or designate a simple "go to" destination from any PP (present position).

Since it is awkward to keep using both terms in the text, we will refer to all saved position coordinates simply as LANDMARKS, although some people refer to them as WAYPOINTS or even CHECKPOINTS.

Whenever you take a position fix, the information defining it—including its horizontal coordinates; vertical position; time/date stamp; and, perhaps, the numbers of the satellites used to compute it, the strengths of their signals and the geometric quality of the fix—can be automatically stored in a library of position saves. Furthermore, they can either be chronologically numbered, beginning with 001, or named by you for easy recognition and later use. Finally, map locations you have not yet visited with your GPS can be manually entered into the landmark library and, again, each can be automatically numbered or named by you. Also, you can delete and edit any of these stored landmarks at any time unless they are being used to help define part of a stored route.

Additionally, some units automatically save your most recent fixes in what is sometimes called a LAST FIX or LAST LOCATION BUFFER. This enables you to retrace your steps. Also, they can generally be added to your LANDMARK "library."

Yet another feature commonly found within the landmark function on most receivers is a provision for scrolling through the list of LANDMARKS stored in the "library" by numerical and/or alphabetical order and, sometimes, even by a chronological order of the saves or according to their proximity to your PP.

Present position coordinates are generally automatically saved as LANDMARKS by twice pressing either the ENTER or LANDMARK keys, depending upon the make and model you are using. After having done so, the unit will save the coordinates of its PP (along with pertinent information such as the date and time of the save) as the next unused numbered LANDMARK. After pressing the appropriate key only once, you will be presented with the option to designate a different number or create a name for the position being stored before entering its coordinates into the "library." Stored LANDMARKS can later be edited in many ways. They can be moved to a different numbered position in the listing, renamed, or have their coordinates changed.

Of course, the coordinates of any location in the world can be entered manually into the list of LANDMARKS and a name assigned. These manually entered positions, too, can be moved on the list edited, and deleted. However, saved LANDMARKS, whether entered automatically or manually, cannot be changed or deleted if they are currently being used to define part of a route (see next section).

Some units also allow you to connect a brief message to each LANDMARK. It could be anything from "caution quicksand" to "trail head." Also, many units allow you to attach a symbolic icon to a saved

SELECT ICON
PRESS ENT KEY

FIGURE 5-16
LOWRANCE LANDMARK (WAYPOINT) ICONS

LANDMARK to aid in identification (see **Figure 5-16**). They are most helpful when used in conjunction with the PLOTTER SCREEN to be explained later.

Finally, all but the most economical models allow you to PROJECT LANDMARKS in either of two ways and in much the same manner as the military projects targets from observation posts. First, you can project a new position from an existing LANDMARK by selecting the LANDMARK from the stored list and indicating a directional azimuth and a distance to the projected location. Or, you can project a new position from two existing LANDMARKS by selecting them from the stored list and indicating a directional azimuth from each as a triangulation computation. These new positions, too, can then be added to your "library."

ROUTE FUNCTION

This function includes features that allow you to develop, store, and select a number of routing options in preparation for navigating over them. First, you can connect several stored LANDMARKS to create a multi-segmented route and then instruct your GPS receiver to navigate over it. For example, you might go from CAMP to BRIDGE, to LNDMK 6, to DEERSTND. Many GPS units will allow you to preplan several routes in advance and activate the one you wish to follow at any time. You can also edit, reverse, and delete any of these routes.

Another route planning function available on most GPS receiver models involves the quick selection of single segment "go to" routes. You simply select the stored LANDMARK to which you wish to proceed and the unit begins to navigate to that location from your PP. Some units access this function from the LANDMARK menu, while others have a special GOTO button on the keypad.

Furthermore, some units have a special routing feature that allows you to navigate back to automatically stored positions at designated time intervals in the "last location buffer." Magellan has referred to this as their "bread crumb" feature.

Finally, some manufacturers that have not yet shed their nautical roots have a "MOB" (man overboard) feature. At the moment someone falls into the sea, you press the MOB key and the unit saves the position and starts to navigate back to that point in order to find the clumsy oaf who tumbled off the deck. It will, however, not ward off sharks.

FIGURE 5-17
MAGELLAN POINTER SCREEN

NAVIGATION FUNCTION

Use of the navigation function enables your GPS unit to "steer" you along a prescribed route; be it over the various legs of a multi-segmented route, a quick GO TO movement from wherever you might be to any selected landmark, an electronic "bread crumb" backtrack, or in REVERSE along a just navigated multi-segmented route. **Figure 5-17** illustrates what is meant by having a GPS unit "steer" you along a route. In this

FIGURE 5-18
LOWRANCE/EAGLE NAV SCREEN

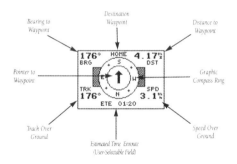

FIGURE 5-19
GARMIN NAV SCREEN

case, you see Magellan's "pointer screen" leading a navigator back to camp. The enlarged screen image from a Trailblazer XL™ at the bottom of the figure tells us that the campfire is on an azimuth of 86° magnetic, 5.37 miles away, and, provided you maintain your current rate of progress, the time to go (TTG) before cooking marshmellows is about 1 hour 49 minutes. The "X" inside the circle represents the direction of the camp relative to North (N) and the direction of travel, which is represented by the arrow pointing toward the top of the screen. You are reminded, however, that a GPS unit is not a compass and if you stop to talk and turn your body to face a fellow hiker, the arrow pointing in your direction of travel will not swing on the screen as you turn, but, will, instead, maintain its position. The set can only orient itself while you are moving and as long as you don't change the orientation of the set. It always assumes that you have the top of the set pointed in the direction of movement (your track).

Figures 5-18 and **5-19** show similar screens from the Eagle (Lowrance) Expedition II™, and Garmin GPS II Plus™, respectively. You will note that the Expedition II™ screen includes a protractor compass rose and, in this case, indicates that the unit is very close to reaching either an intermediate or final destination. When that circle appears in the center of the screen (your position), the unit will have reached its destination.

You may frequently take walks in the woods or drives over highways without first creating a preplanned route. In these cases, the GPS unit will be

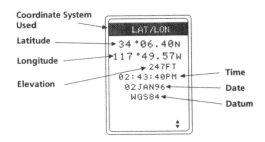

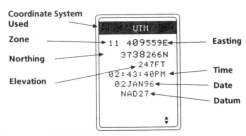

FIGURE 5-21
MAGELLAN POSITION SCREENS

of assistance in telling you at any time precisely where you are located so you can find yourself on the map and proceed over the most convenient route either back to your starting point or to another destination. **Figure 5-20** shows an Eagle (Lowrance) Expedition II™ displaying a position screen using ALT MGRS coordinates, while **Figure 5-21** includes two illustrations showing Magellan GPS 4000 XL™ position screens using LAT/LON and UTM coordinates.

Figures 5-22 through **5-24**, picturing Eagle Expedition II screens, illustrate three uniquely different situations in which the graphic navigation screen may be reporting various types of information to you. **Figure 5-22** displays the screen as it would appear when no route has been set. Regardless, it still shows your position in the center of the screen (arrow), your direction of travel (arrow outside the protractor scale), and various other written data in the small windows, such as your track of 355° (direction of travel) and ground speed (10.0) in units that were determined during the setup.

Figure 5-23 displays a great deal more information because either a multi-segmented route or simple GO TO route is being navigated. This additional information includes the display of a triangle representing the direction of your next intermediate or final destination inside the protractor scale, as well as other data in the small windows. This data includes a bearing of 22° (azimuth from PP to end-of-leg LANDMARK), a course of 22° (azimuth from starting point to end-of-leg LANDMARK), and any cross-track error, called XTE, which is the distance you may have wandered off the course.

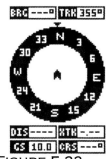

FIGURE 5-22
LOWRANCE/EAGLE NAV SCREEN (NO ROUTE SET)

FIGURE 5-23
LOWRANCE/EAGLE NAV SCREEN (IN ROUTE)

FIGURE 5-24
LOWRANCE/EAGLE NAV SCREEN
(APPROACHING DESTINATION)

Eagle and Lowrance units also include a "road graphic" on this navigation screen. In this case, it shows your position (center arrow) in the middle of the "road" leading directly toward the end-of-leg LANDMARK). As your XTE increases, it may become so great, especially during highway navigation, that you won't be able to see the "road" pictured on the screen. Also, as your track (direction of travel) swings away from the correct bearing (direction from PP to end-of-leg LANDMARK), the triangle representing the relative direction of the LANDMARK moves accordingly inside the protractor scale, which also rotates to accurately report your direction of travel (track). This is particularly useful during highway navigation because roads rarely proceed directly toward a destination. Thus, when you see that your destination is, let's say, approximately 90° to the right, it's time to make a right hand turn onto the next road or street you encounter. Of course, this screen continues to report your track and ground speed in the windows, just as it did when you were not navigating a designated route.

Finally, **Figure 5-24** shows the situation in which you are coming very close to your end-of-leg LANDMARK or final destination. In fact, you're down to a distance of just .21 miles. When you have set your Eagle or Lowrance unit to report distances in miles, more than 100 will be reported in full miles; less than one hundred but more than ten will be reported in miles and tenths of a mile; less than ten in miles and one hundredths of a mile, and, finally, in feet. Of course, similar circumstances are encountered when using metric units. When the center of the small LANDMARK circle ultimately reaches the center of the screen (surrounding your position arrow), you have arrived. If you have arrived at an intermediate destination, the unit will then automatically begin to navigate over the next route segment toward its defining LANDMARK.

It is important to note that whenever you have drifted off the course missing your LANDMARK, as you pass over an imaginary line drawn perpendicular to the intended course and through that end-of-leg LANDMARK, the unit will automatically begin to navigate over the next route segment to its defining LANDMARK. When navigating to a single LANDMARK using a GO TO route, the unit will continue to navigate to that LANDMARK until you instruct it to stop navigating or until you set another GO TO route. This is true even after passing through the LANDMARK location and continuing to proceed directly away and at increasing distances from its location.

The newest GPS units feature a broad array of navigation function screens to assist you in keeping to your route and recognizing when you have reached either an intermediate or final destination. To further assist you, some units provide either or both visual and audible alarms to warn when you have strayed a particular distance from an intended course and/or when you have reached an important decision point along the route or the final destination. Some even sound a warning if your anchor slips and your boat begins to drift. Furthermore, as we discussed earlier, you can set the distance parameters for each these various alarm features.

By reviewing the various screens commonly found on Eagle / Lowrance, Magellan, and Garmin receiver units, you can gain an understanding of the vast majority of the types of reports you might encounter while using most any hand-held GPS receiver unit. The Lowrance units, such as the Eagle Explorer™ and Expedition II™, as well as the Lowrance GlobalNav 210™, offer more screens than most, although many of the items of information carried on them are redundant to other screens for the sake of convenience. Most of the Eagle / Lowrance screens are accessed by pressing the PAGES key (MODE key on older sets), with the notable exceptions being that when you first power up the set you first view the SATELLITE STATUS screen until the initial position fix has been calculated, at which time the set shifts to whatever screen you last activated through use of the PAGES key feature.

After pressing the PAGES key, a small menu appears giving you four options which are convenient to think of as chapters. Each, in turn, holds various numbers of pages within them. After having made your selection with the arrow keys (UP or DOWN to scroll and then RIGHT to select), you must press the EXIT key to clear the screen of the menu listings (see **Figure 5-25**). In fact, pressing the EXIT key will, at all times, clear the screen of any menu or submenu listings, thus allowing you to back out of menu hierarchies and view the navigation "page" last selected. The options (what we just called chapters) accessed by pressing the PAGES key are (1) SATELLITE STATUS screen, having only a single page which you also see when you power the set; (2) NAV screens, of which there are three; (3)

PLOTTER screens, of which there are also three; and (4) GROUP screens, of which there are about a dozen, depending upon the particular model you're using. Many of these GROUP screens can be tailored by the user.

EAGLE / LOWRANCE SCREENS

FIGURE 5-25
LOWRANCE/EAGLE PAGES MENU

The only page in the **STATUS SCREEN** "chapter" is the satellite status screen shown in **Figure 5-26**. This particular page tells you the numbers of satellites "in view" at your location and where they are located in the sky relative to your position. This screen assumes that you are facing north. The center of the two concentric circles is considered to be straight up, the inner circle is at 45° above the horizon, and the outer circle represents the horizon. Signals are being received from SVs when their numbers are highlighted in black on the graphic and their signal strength bar graphs are active beneath it. In this case, the report indicates the weakest signal is coming from SV 17 and the battery indicator tells us that they are either fresh or the set is being operated on external power. Finally, you should notice the "FIX" number in the upper right portion of the screen. Based upon the GDOP, a relative position accuracy is reported as being in the range of 9 (best) to 1 (worst). It's not recommended that you trust position coordinates calculated when the set is reporting less than a 3.

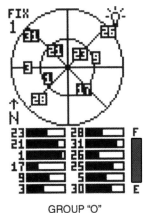

GROUP "O"

FIGURE 5-26
LOWRANCE/EAGLE STATUS SCREEN
(FIX NO. = 1 UNTIL FIRST PP IS CALCULATED)

The two **NAVIGATION SCREENS** are found in **Figure 5-27**. **Nav 1** has already been discussed, but, in this case, you are so far off course following a highway that the "road graphic" does not appear and the triangle inside the compass rose protractor indicates that you must take a left turn and follow a bearing (azimuth from PP to LANDMARK) of 300°. **Nav 2** presents all the navigation information in digital form. Here are some brief definitions of the abbreviations found in the various Eagle / Lowrance windows:

BRG - azimuth from PP to LANDMARK

DIS - distance from PP to LANDMARK

TRK - azimuth direction of travel

GS - ground speed

ETE - estimated time en route

CRS - azimuth from point navigation began to LANDMARK

CDI - course deviation indicator

XTK - cross-track error

Note: XTK tells you the actual measure of your deviation from the intended course, whereas, the CDI graphically indicates the direction you need to steer in order to correct your error. When on course, the line rests in the center, when it moves to the left, you have drifted off to the right, and so forth. Also, you can adjust the range of the CDI (default is .25 mile) and also set the alarm as a warning.

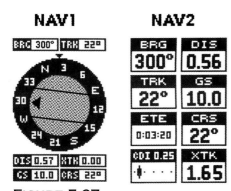

FIGURE 5-27
LOWRANCE/EAGLE NAV SCREENS

The three **PLOTTER SCREENS** are found in **Figure 5-28**. The plotter shows your track as seen from above. **Plot 1** uses a diamond to represent your PP and the line extending

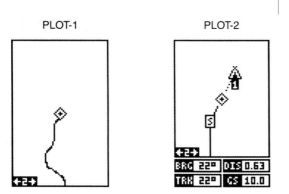

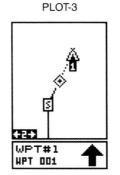

FIGURE 5-28
LOWRANCE/EAGLE PLOT SCREENS

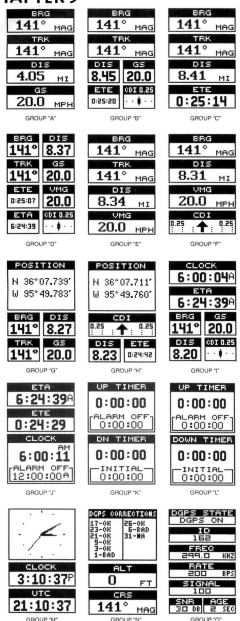

FIGURE 5-29
LOWRANCE/EAGLE "GROUP" SCREENS

from the diamond is your track. The adjustable plotter "range" (controlled by the ZIN & ZOUT keys) is shown in the lower left hand corner (in this case, 2 miles horizontally across the screen). **Plot 2** has navigation data added in windows at the bottom. **Plot 3** presents LANDMARK information at the bottom of the screen. Furthermore, when used in conjunction with the arrow keys, the plotter screens show a cross hair cursor (easting and northing lines) which can be moved to pinpoint position coordinates and save LANDMARKS. Finally, the navigator can use a track on a plotter screen to guide himself back over the same route to the point where he started.

The many **GROUP SCREENS** are found in **Figure 5-29**. Here is a sampling of the various "pages" available under the "GROUP SCREENS" menu on various Eagle and Lowrance GPS units. First, you should review the remaining definitions for abbreviations not yet encountered. Remember, the windows on the various NAV, PLOTTER, and GROUP screens can be reprogrammed to show the report windows preferred by the user. What is shown here are screens presented as factory defaults. Here are some additional definitions:

ETA - estimated time of arrival

UT - universal time coordinated (Greenwich)

VMG - velocity made good
   (rate of approach toward destination)

POSITION - present position
   (various Coords. MGRS, UTM, LAT/LON, etc.)

UPTIMER - stop watch (elapsed time)

DOWNTIMER - stop watch (time to go)

The GROUP N & O screens show DGPS information to include the corrections being made by satellite number. For more detailed information, see the owner's manual.

MAGELLAN SCREENS

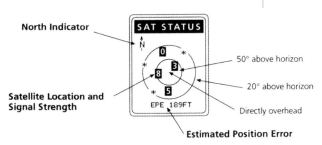

North Indicator

Satellite Location and Signal Strength

50° above horizon

20° above horizon

Directly overhead

Estimated Position Error

SAT STATUS

EPE 189FT

FIGURE 5-30
MAGELLAN SAT SCREEN

Most Magellan GPS units present the following six screens to aid with navigation. These particular samples were taken from the GPS 4000 XL™. The first **POSITION SCREEN** comes up automatically as soon as a fix has been calculated, while the **SATELLITE STATUS SCREEN** is accessed through the MENU key (**Figure 5-30**). Notice that, among other data, it reports the EPE (estimated position error based upon GDOP) in feet. All other navigation screens are accessed through use of the NAV key and they can be scrolled through by using the UP and DOWN ARROW keys. As is common on all units, there are also a number of "working screens," generally accessed through the MENU for unit INITIALIZATION, SETUP, accessing the LANDMARK LIBRARY, ROUTE DEFINITION, and so forth.

The **NAV 1** and **NAV 2** screens can also be customized to show reports desired by the user. Here are Magellan's definitions for on-screen abbreviations:

BRG - azimuth PP to LANDMARK

DST - distance PP to LANDMARK

SPD - speed over ground

HDG - azimuth of track (direction of travel)

VMG - velocity made good toward LMK

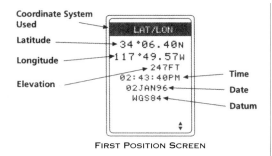

Coordinate System Used
Latitude
Longitude
Elevation
Time
Date
Datum

FIRST POSITION SCREEN

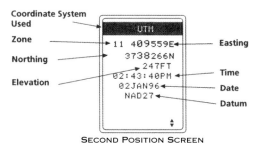

Coordinate System Used
Zone
Northing
Elevation
Easting
Time
Date
Datum

SECOND POSITION SCREEN

FIGURE 5-31
MAGELLAN POSITION SCREENS

CTS - course to steer to get back on course

ETA - estimated time of arrival

TTG - time to go to LANDMARK (present rate)

XTE - cross-track error

The **FIRST POSITION SCREEN** is shown along with a SECOND POSITION SCREEN in **Figure 5-31**. It appears when the unit first acquires a fix, but it can always be accessed at other times by pressing the NAV key and scrolling through the six screens types with ARROWS. The **SECOND POSITION SCREEN** can be added for the purpose of showing positions in a second coordinate system or it can be deleted from the NAV screen sequence through the SETUP. These position screens, which display the date, time, and datum, are most convenient when locating or checking your position on a map. Newer GPS 4000 XL™ and other Magellan models offer MGRS, UTM, LAT/LON and a number of other coordinate system options. Be sure to check the owner's manual when you anticipate foreign travel. When using MGRS, both the new Magellan and Garmin receivers automatically select the correct version of MGRS when you select the correct horizontal map datum to match the map being used. For example, when you set NAD-27 CONUS, the Magellan unit automatically utilizes what it calls MGRS-1 (what the Army calls "old MGRS" and Lowrance has designated as ALT MGRS).

The **NAV 1 SCREEN**, shown in **Figure 5-32**, fills in all the information windows included, provided a route is currently being navigated. When navigating to a LANDMARK, the screen will show the bearing and

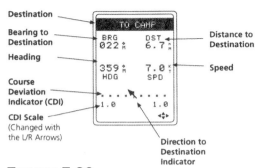

FIGURE 5-32
MAGELLAN NAV 1 SCREEN

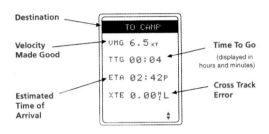

FIGURE 5-33
MAGELLAN NAV 2 SCREEN

distance to the destination and if you are moving, it will display the azimuth of your heading (track) and your ground speed. The **course deviation indicator** at the bottom differs in that it has a small arrow indicating the direction in which you should proceed in order to correct any XTE. Distance units (miles, nautical miles, and kilometers) can be selected from the SETUP menu.

The **NAV 2 SCREEN**, which reports additional navigation information, is shown in **Figure 5-33**. Again, not all information can be shown unless the unit is actively navigating a route and you are moving along it. NAV 1 and NAV 2 screens can be customized to display information selected by the user. The available options include: BRG, DST, SPD, HDG, VMG, CTS, ETA, TTG, XTE (NAV 2 only).

We have already discussed Magellan's **POINTER SCREEN**, which is shown again here in **Figure 5-34**. In order for this screen to function completely, there must be an active GO TO or multi-segment route set for the unit to navigate.

Figure 5-35 presents Magellan's **PLOTTER SCREEN**, which is similar to those on other manufacturer's GPS receivers. It provides you with a record of your movements, as well as other direction and distance information.

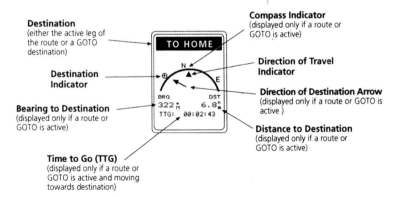

FIGURE 5-34
MAGELLAN POINTER SCREEN

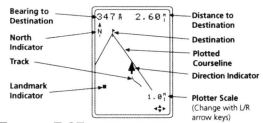

FIGURE 5-35
MAGELLAN PLOTTER SCREEN

Bearing to Destination
North Indicator
Track
Landmark Indicator

Distance to Destination
Destination
Plotted Courseline
Direction Indicator
Plotter Scale
(Change with L/R arrow keys)

Finally, Magellan offers an interesting graphic it calls a **ROAD SCREEN**, which is pictured in **Figure 5-36**. This screen is designed to help you proceed to the next LANDMARK by simply staying on the road. In a sense, it is just another way of illustrating XTE on a CDI.

Although the GPS 4000 XL™ has no audible alarm, it does provide an on-screen bell icon to alert you when any of your preset parameters have been exceeded or when you arrive at a destination. This model also allows you to project LANDMARKS, attach short messages to saved LANDMARKS, and utilize a trip odometer. Finally, it provides you with what Magellan calls "**PAN-N-SCAN** functions." In short, from the PLOTTER screen you can create and save LAND-MARKS using an easting-northing cross-hair cursor.

Destination
(either the active leg of the route or a GO TO destination)
Bearing to Destination
(displayed only if a route or GO TO is active)
Landmark Indicator
Road Scale
(Changed with the L/R Arrows)
Direction to Destination Indicator

Distance to Destination
(displayed only if a route or GO TO is active)
Destination Indicator

FIGURE 5-36
MAGELLAN ROAD SCREEN

GARMIN SCREENS

One of the most unique features of the Garmin II Plus (**Figure 5-37**) is its ability to let you change the orientation of its screen for vehicular dashboard use (left) and hand-held use for hiking (right). Samples of Garmin's navigation screens are included below and taken from the GPS II Plus™, GPS 12XL™, and GPS III™ models. When the set is powered on, the first active screen to be viewed is the **SATELLITE PAGE** (**Figure 5-38**). As you can see, it shows battery status, SV signal strength for up to either eight or twelve SVs (depending upon model), and the EPE (estimated position error) in feet.

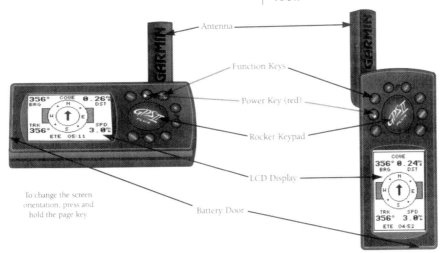

FIGURE 5-37
GARMIN GPS II+

Next, after the initial position fix has been calculated, the unit will display its **POSITION PAGE**, as seen in **Figure 5-39**. This screen tells you where you're located, what direction you're headed, and how fast you're going. It is the most useful screen when you have not set a route for the unit to navigate. The middle field between the compass face and the position/altitude field can be customized by the user. The options are as follows: **TRIP** (trip odometer), **TTIME** (trip timer), **ELPSD** (elapsed time), **AVSPD** (average speed), **MXSPD** (maximum speed), and **ALT** (altitude).

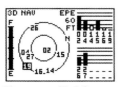

FIGURE 5-38
GARMIN SAT STATUS SCREEN

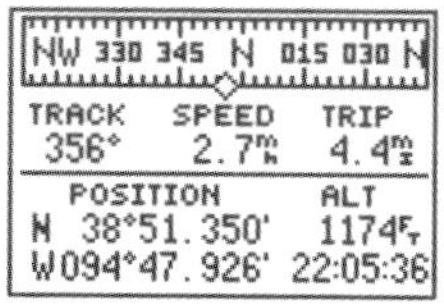

The **MAP PAGE**, found in **Figure 5-40**, is quite similar to the Eagle and Magellan PLOTTER SCREENs. In addition to the track, the four corners of the screen are used to display navigational data. Also, the dedicated ZOOM keys can be used to change the scale of the page, and a pop up window can be called upon that reports the screen scale currently in use.

FIGURE 5-39
GARMIN POSITION SCREEN

Graphic steering guidance is offered by two SCREENS on many Garmin sets. You should by now be familiar enough with both the graphic concepts and the abbreviations to completely understand the use of these screens. **Figure 5-41** illustrates the **COMPASS PAGE** and **Figure 5-42** presents the **HIGHWAY PAGE**. Again, Garmin models include many of the same options, functions, and features found on other GPS receiver units.

Don't lose sight of the purpose of this chapter. It has not been to make a comparison among GPS units; instead, it was written to assist you to more fully understand how to apply the new GPS technology to your navigational needs. Screen samples have been included here that best support and clarify a variety of teaching points using a number of sampled units.

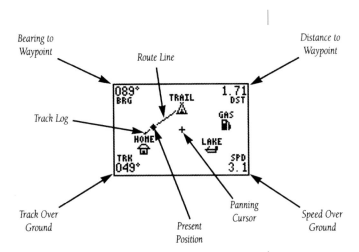

FIGURE 5-40
GARMIN MAP SCREEN

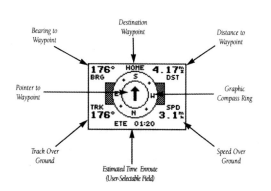

FIGURE 5-41
GARMIN COMPASS SCREEN

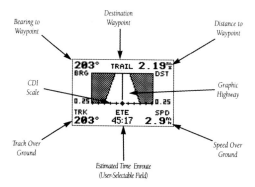

FIGURE 5-42
GARMIN HIGHWAY SCREEN

ELECTRONIC MAP DISPLAYS

FIGURE 5-43
EAGLE ACCUMAP SPORT™

FIGURE 5-44
MAGELLAN NAV 6000™

FIGURE 5-45
GARMIN GPS III™

Most GPS manufacturers now make available some hand-held units featuring electronic map displays (see **Figures 5-43**, **5-44**, and **5-45**). Eagle and Magellan use electronic maps stored on mini-cartridges produced by IMS Smart Maps and C-Map NT, respectively (see **Figure 5-46**), while the Garmin III™, pictured in **Figure 5-45**, holds in its memory maps covering most of North, Central, and South America. As an example of what's available—IMS cartridge coverage chart—are included as **Figure 5-48**.

As with the PLOTTER screens found on most GPS models, you are able to change the scale of the map shown by using the ZIN and ZOUT keys. Also, the maps will scroll, thereby, continually displaying the area surrounding your position. Your PP is displayed on the moving map with or without the cross hair cursor (see **Figure 5-47**). When the easting-northing cross hair cursor is turned on, position coordinates are displayed somewhere on the screen. Furthermore, the dashed lines forming the cross hair cursor can be moved by using the ARROW keys, thereby allowing you to create and save position coordinates as LANDMARKS for use in developing multi-segment routes and GO TO destinations. No question, this is a handy feature. Movement of the cursor will, of course, cause the map display to scroll in any direction.

Most units featuring electronic map capabilities also provide the same types of screens, menus, features, and functions found on other hand-held units.

The interactive atlas
that fits in your pocket.

FIGURE 5-46
ELECTRONIC MAP CARTRIDGES

There are, without question, significant advantages in always having a map available inside the receiver; nevertheless, the units including this feature tend to be larger, heavier, and more expensive (plus the cost for necessary cartridges); and, with screens no larger than the area of a few postage stamps, they provided limited detail and perspective. Also, the maps are always oriented north making it more difficult for you to orient yourself to the terrain surrounding you. Regardless, it's difficult to argue with Garmin when it says, "The trouble with ordinary maps is they don't know where you are." On the other hand, after reading this book and obtaining good detailed maps with usable grids, you should be able to tell where you are on any map, whether electronic or paper.

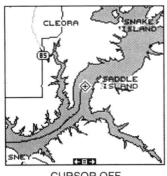

CURSOR OFF

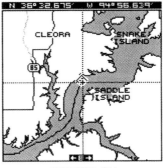

CURSOR ON

FIGURE 5-47
EAGLE ACCUMAP SPORT™ ELECTRONIC MAP DISPLAY

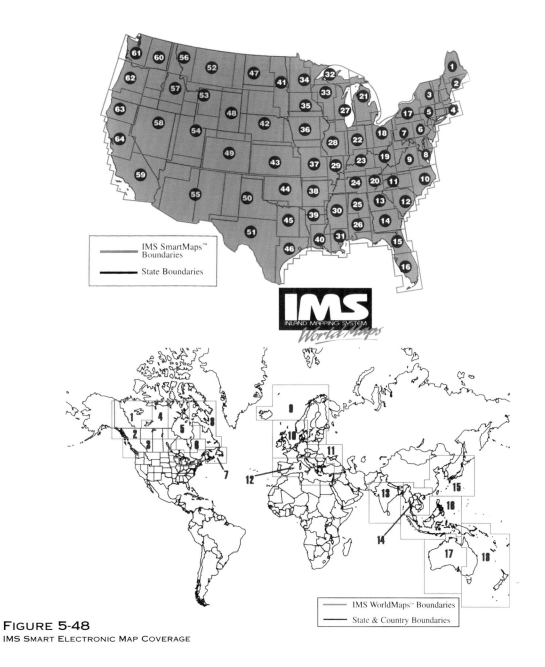

FIGURE 5-48
IMS SMART ELECTRONIC MAP COVERAGE

FEATURES, CHARACTERISTICS & ACCESSORIES

Here is a quick listing of the "bells and whistles," that can be found on various hand-held GPS receivers, some of which have and others which have not already been mentioned. Furthermore, we'll take a look at some of the special characteristics and accessories being made available to enhance their utility, as well.

FEATURES & CHARACTERISTICS

- number and types of available coordinate systems, especially MGRS & UTM
- number and types of available horizontal map datums, especially NAD-27 CONUS
- multiple keystroke unlocking feature to prevent accidental turn on of the set
- battery life and types of batteries accommodated (e.g., alkaline/nickel rechargeable)
- selective erase features (landmark, route, or last location buffer, etc.)
- clear memory (erase all data held in memory and restore factory defaults in setup)
- set alarm parameters w/off & on capabilities (i.e., arrival at destination, CDI/XTE warnings, etc.)
- landmark library sort by alpha/numerical, chronological, proximity
- naming and editing landmarks, as well as icon availability for landmark identification (most useful on plotter screens)
- landmark projections through triangulation and azimuth direction/ distance calculations

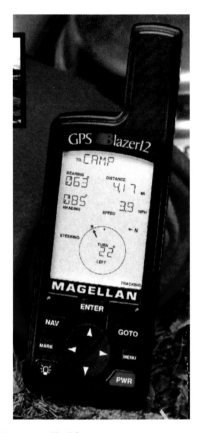

FIGURE 5-49
MAGELLAN BLAZER 12™
(12 PARALLEL CHANNEL RECEIVER)

- adjustable frequency of position sampling and saves in a "lastfix buffer" feature
- averaging features for position (when in a position for an hour or more) and velocity calculations (when on the move) [Note: Position averaging over a period of time can negate most of the error induced by SA]
- compatibility with DGPS beacons broadcasting pseudo range errors from SV signals and NMEA interface with other equipment (e.g., PCs, other GPS units, communications equipment, auto-pilots on boats)
- satellite status reports and position accuracy reports based upon GDOP and its components
- special screens displaying trip odometers, clocks, and stop watches
- numbers and types of graphic and information screens contributing to ease of navigation
- visual and audible alarms
- trip summary reports (where, when, how fast, averages, etc.)
- electronic moving map display
- sun and moon data by location & date
- graphic grid overlay screens for various positions within selected coordinate systems through which you can save waypoints
- calculated projected fuel consumption rates
- automatic light and unit turn-off features to save battery power
- varying memory capacities for storing numbers of landmarks, route segments, and routes
- quick GO TO routing capability
- multiplex vs. parallel channel operation of receiver (numbers of channels up to 12)
- frequency of calculated position updates
- keyboard glow and/or screen lighting for night operations
- adjustable screen orientation
- color screens for easy reading (separating and seeing all the data)
- internal back-up battery to save stored data in memory
- ports used for external power/antenna/data exchange
- map software compatibility (PC)

- waterproof/water & dust resistant/rugged case/non-slip rubberized grips on case
- training simulator
- size, weight, and ergonomic design
- easy to understand and use owner's manual
- type and length of warranty

ACCESSORIES

- lanyards, shoulder straps, and carrying cases
- active external antennas that boost incoming signals
- various external power, data interface, and antenna cables
- external power units
- cigarette lighter adapters
- rubberized dashboard holders
- mounting brackets
- electronic map and chart cartridges

IN SUMMARY

You should now have a thorough mastery of the information and concepts needed to initialize and setup your GPS receiver unit as well as apply the many functions and features available on today's products to your land navigation requirements. Obviously, no single GPS model could possibly include all these capabilities; but the purpose of this chapter will be served if it has prepared you to know which features you prefer on a GPS receiver and you are able to utilize any you may encounter. Although there is no claim that this chapter represents an exhaustive listing and review of the features, functions, characteristics, and accessories available on portable hand-held receiver units, every effort has been made to have it as comprehensive as possible.

In conclusion, the best way to learn and retain navigation skills is to use them. So, gather up your receiver, map, and compass and go outdoors to enjoy what nature and GPS have to offer.

FIGURE 5-50
EAGLE/LOWRANCE GLOBAL MAP 100™

A NEW PRODUCT RECENTLY RELEASED BY EAGLE/LOWRANCE IS THE GOBAL MAP 100 PICTURED ABOVE. THIS POCKET SIZED 12 PARALLEL CHANNEL RECEIVER FEATURES A BUILT-IN DIGITAL BACKGROUND MAP OF THE WORLD WITH ENHANCED DETAIL OF LAKES, RIVERS, STREAMS AND HIGHWAYS IN NORTH AMERICA.   INCLUDED WITH THE RECEIVER IS THE IMS MAPSELECT DC-ROM WITH 39 IMS WORLDMAPS, U.S. NAV AIDS AND MORE. YOU CAN USE YOUR PC TO TRANSFER SELECTED, MORE DETAILED MAP DATA FROM THE CD-ROM INTO YOUR RECEIVER.

HIGHWAY TRAVEL WITH GPS

On Thanksgiving Day, 1895, Frank Duryea demonstrated the practical superiority of gasoline-powered automobiles over a 54-mile course in a $5000 auto race sponsored by the *Chicago Times Herald*. He followed the route from Jackson Park to Waukegan and back on a map that had been printed in the newspaper. This was considered to be the first automobile road map ever published. Soon, thereafter, published guidebooks appeared giving detailed written instructions as to how to proceed from city to city, but it wasn't long before the motoring public was using the easier to follow graphic displays of H. Sargent Michaels' *Photographic Automobile Maps* beginning in 1905. Next, Chapin's *Photo-Auto Maps* entered the market and by 1909 Rand McNally had assumed responsibility for their publication. By 1912, General Drafting had produced a map of Vermont for the American Automobile Association and by 1923, Standard Oil of New Jersey had commissioned a highway map of that state to be offered at no charge to its customers.

Until 1926, Rand McNally and General Drafting were the only publishers of road maps when some former employees of Rand McNally formed Gousha in Chicago. For a number of years, these three publishers provided nearly all the highway maps for the motoring public, distributed mainly through the oil companies. In fact, the Texaco series published in 1929 was the first to cover the entire United States for its customers (**Figure 6-1**).

Today our options in highway navigational guidance are numerous, unfortunately no longer free, and often difficult to select from among so many. Hopefully this chapter will help you navigate through the selection of tools now available and suggest how to effectively apply them to your highway travel in conjunction with America's fabulous world-wide NAVSTAR System.

You might ask why it has taken until the publication of this third edition to include a chapter on highway travel with GPS. After all, we navigate most frequently and for the greatest distances over roads in our motor vehicles. Furthermore, the GPS offers the same navigational advantages and opportunities to the highway traveler as it does to airplane pilots, ship captains, and hikers. The essential reason for the delay is that one necessary ingredient was missing to facilitate the application of GPS to highway travel. There were virtually no road maps available which were compatible with GPS. As you by now have recognized, maps are so vital to

FIGURE 6-1

the effective use of this new technology that nearly half this book is devoted to helping you thoroughly understand and make better use of them.

What has been most exciting for us here at Alexis Publishing is that we have had a great deal to do with creating the circumstances that require this new chapter. We have designed and published what we feel is the first truly useful GPS-compatible road map series, which covers the continental United States (**Figure 6-2**). You can now take along maps from this 26-sheet set and, with a hand-held GPS receiver, easily find your way over the highways anywhere within the 48 contiguous states. We believe that our publication of the maps and the first two editions of this book, along with the many discussions we have held with the major GPS manufacturers, has led to the general acceptance of the concept that a UTM-based coordinate system--rather than LAT/LON--is best for land navigation. Furthermore, we conclude that all these efforts have resulted in the MGRS coordinate format option being made available by the GPS manufacturers today. As we expected, more people are joining the chorus calling for the adoption of the MGRS-UTM as the national standard grid coordinate system for use on all new and revised maps and in conjunction with GPS.

FIGURE 6-2
ALEXIS GPS-COMPATIBLE ROAD MAPS

BACKGROUND

You will recall that the first topic presented in Chapter 3 (Navigating With GPS and a Map) dealt with locating positions on maps using various coordinate systems. Since the heart of the GPS is its capacity to

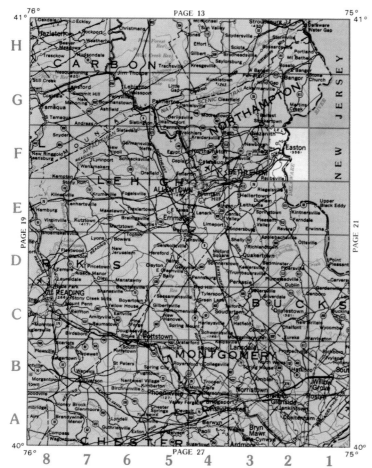

report locations in mathematical terms (grid or geographic coordinates), it is absolutely necessary that usable road maps carry this type of information. It is the map's "grid" that enables us to take the otherwise meaningless numbers used to define a position from the screen of the GPS receiver and place it within the context of the real world places and features surrounding us as they are portrayed on the map.

The old familiar alpha-numeric grid we have commonly seen on our now antiquated road maps is useful only to locate features on the map such as cities, towns, streets, or various other attractions by using that particular map's or atlas' index (e.g., Easton, PA, **F2**, as shown in (**Figure 6-3**)). Nearly all highway maps produced since the early years of the 20th century have carried some variation of this grid pattern with numbers generally being placed horizontally across the top and/or bottom margins and letters being placed vertically along either side. This generic grid used over and over again on various maps is obviously not compatible for use with GPS because it is not part of any standard coordinate system covering an area beyond the margins of each individual map.

Granted, some receivers allow you to program a "user's coordinate system" in which you can theoretically define this generic grid in mathematical terms and use for finding your position; but this approach is rather time-consuming and requires that you develop a separate program for each map sheet you intend to use this way. Besides, you would have to be a bit creative to devise a decimal system necessary to interpolate between the lettered grid lines (e.g., A.3, or would it be A.c?).

Until very recently, few, if any, commercial maps of any type readily lent themselves to use with GPS. The majority of those maps that did were the large-and intermediate-scale topographic quadrangles produced and made available for public sale by the United States Geological Survey (USGS) and the National Imagery and Mapping Agency (NIMA), formerly known as the Defense Mapping Agency (DMA). No question, these maps are ideal for hiking, but just imagine how many dozens of large-scale USGS quadrangles a driver would need and how frequently he would be required to change sheets in order to utilize them in conjunction with highway travel over even moderate distances. A single 1°x 1° area of land surface is covered by sixty-four 1:24,000-scale 7.5-minute x 7.5-minute quadrangles. You will recall that one degree of latitude anywhere on the earth or one degree of longitude at the equator covers only approximately 69 miles (111 kilometers). Although some die-hards who were determined to use their hand-held GPS units for highway travel probably did so, it wasn't a practical solution to the problem. Furthermore, the government's maps aren't updated frequently enough to keep pace with the continuous changes taking place in many areas, particularly with regard to the construction of new streets and highways.

Having recognized this need for GPS-compatible road maps, various organizations began to develop a number of strategies for dealing with it. First, since GPS provided such a successful high-tech solution to the age-old navigational problem of determining position, it was only natural that some would also take a high-tech approach to overcoming this scarcity of maps. One such result was the development of a number of inte-grated onboard electronic map/GPS products such as Hertz' *NEVERLost*, Alpine Electonics' *Acura*, Delco's *Telepath 100*, Sony's *NVX-F 160*, and Oldsmobile's *Guidestar*, to name a few (**Figure 6-4**). In addition, BMW and Toyota presently have factory-installed onboard GPS-based navigation systems available while Amerigon, Clarion, Kenwood, Rockwell, and Sony are among those producing similar products for the auto-motive after-market. Finally, by linking GPS with cellular telephone technology, Cadillac's *OnStar* and Ford's *RESCU* systems can pinpoint your position and sum-mon help or directions when and where you need it through either manual or automatic calls to their special service centers. Certainly, there will soon be many more of these types of products heading to market.

A few of these onboard systems utter voice com-mands as well as offering visual cues to the navigator.

FIGURE 6-4
MAGELLAN'S ON-BOARD GPS UNIT

Some utilize maps stored on CD-ROMs while others call-up images from their hard-disk drives. However, the disadvantages they share are that they are relatively expensive to purchase and support with the necessary digital map data, they cannot be easily transferred from one vehicle to another, and none blankets all areas of the country with a detailed map coverage. Finally, one further limitation is that, while there is no question they will guide you to your favorite park for a brush with nature, they aren't much help when you leave the car and head out into the brush.

Yet another high-tech strategy developed for meeting the scarcity of GPS-compatible road maps is to connect your hand-held GPS receiver to a personal computer. Obviously, the use of either a laptop or one of the new palmtop computers (provided you can read maps that small) makes things somewhat more portable when using this type of integrated system. Some well recognized cartography houses such as Rand McNally, Delorme, and Thomas Brothers, as well as a multitude of nitch market producers like MAPTECH, WILDFLOWER, and ETAK, are providing digitized map software for use in conjunction with a PC and GPS unit. MAPTECH, for example, will sell you collections of USGS topographic map quadrangles at various scales on a CD-ROM (**Figure 6-5**). More than being just a collection of maps, their *Terrain Navigator* software allows you to perform a number of useful functions in conjunc-

FIGURE 6-5
MAPTECH TERRAIN NAVIGATOR CD ROM

tion with their maps. These functions range from labeling capabilities and measuring both straight line and irregular distances to reporting as well as saving landmark (waypoint) coordinates and displaying elevation profiles. This program is usable while navigating in conjunction with a PC and GPS, yet it is also valuable in defining landmarks (waypoints), route planning, and printing paper maps to be carried into the area in which you plan to hike or travel (see **Appendix B**).

Another interesting type of product coming into the market place is represented by *FUGAWI Moving Map Software*, developed by Pinpoint Systems, Inc. of Toronto, Canada. *FUGAWI* allows you to import any raster digital map (either commercially prepared or scanned by you) and, provided you know and input the datum information and the precise coordinates for 3 known points on any chart you have stored in its map library file, the software will correct the map information for rotation, skewing, and differential stretching of the axes caused by photocopying or paper shrinkage. Furthermore, these types of programs are designed to upload to or download from a connected GPS unit any landmarks (waypoints) that may be held within either file. Finally, it will handle conversions among a number of commonly used map datums and will generally operate within the context of either LAT/LON or UTM-based coordinate systems.

You will recall that there are two types of "digital maps:" <u>Raster</u> maps (digital bit-mapped copies of paper charts) and <u>vector</u> maps (charts set in the context of more complex mathematical relationships). Raster maps possess limited flexibility and require relatively unsophisticated operating software programs; whereas, vector maps, which are the essence of the Geographic Information System (GIS) technology, are highly manipulative and require more sophisticated software programs. In any case, for either type of digital map held in memory--so long as the map's main characteristics and parameters are included--the software will, in effect, superimpose a transparent GPS-compatible coordinate system over the cartographic display which allows the GPS unit to control the "moving map" and pinpoint your position at all times with a cursor at or near the center of the screen. Most computer map software applications also allow you to "zoom in" and "zoom out" at will.

Unlike the more expensive integrated onboard systems, you can quite easily move these laptop/hand-held GPS unit combinations from vehicle to vehicle and unplug your hand-held GPS receiver for hikes in the woods. Nevertheless, in addition to the added expense of the computer and special software programs, some disadvantages associated with this strategy are that the equipment occupies the passenger seat of the automobile and laptop computer screens are extremely difficult to read in daylight.

Now, let's turn our attention to another application that is closely related to those we have just discussed. If you "surf" the Internet or read either the popular science oriented magazines or some of the professional journals, you know that GPS technology is also being applied to the task of fleet management, monitoring, and control. In this case, the GPS is quickly becoming the "big brother" watching over the likes of truckers, bus and taxicab drivers, and various public safety and emergency vehicle crews. GPS can help make timely deliveries to customers, improve employee supervision and safety, and track stolen vehicles and cargos. Most of these tracking systems link GPS technology through cellular telephone or radio communications equipment to a PC monitoring system utilizing digital maps back at the companies' or governmental agencies' headquarters.

It should be recalled that some hand-held GPS receiver units (e.g., **Figure 6-6**) also incorporate "moving map" capabilities as an option. Map cartridges are available for various parts of the country (see Chapter 5). While these maps can, without question, be helpful as you travel, the overall perspective and amount of detail included are somewhat limited as compared to either the larger computer-based programs or paper maps. However, there is no question that they are highly portable and rather inexpensive when compared with the other high-tech GPS-map solutions already discussed.

The final strategy to be closely examined in this chapter is one that directly involves Alexis Publishing: It is to provide the driving public with high quality GPS-compatible paper road maps. It is, of course, a low-tech and low-cost as well as a highly portable and usable solution to the problem. These road maps are very

FIGURE 6-6
EAGLE ACCU-MAP SPORT™

similar to the ones you have been using for years; the exception being that they display an easy-to-use standard grid coordinate system that Alexis calls the *Universal GPS (UGPS) Grid*™. Use of this utilitarian grid application renders every map upon which it is placed fully compatible with virtually every hand-held GPS receiver ever manufactured.

In the excitement that comes with the development of highly advanced technological breakthroughs, we are at times slow to recognize that some of the associated products that have served us for years, if slightly modified, could easily take on new applications that bring them into greater utility and demand than ever before. This certainly will be the case for paper maps. You can be certain they won't be relegated to the same status as horseshoes following the invention of the automobile.

There is no question that the high-tech GPS-map interface solutions being developed have important applications in a variety of circumstances; but the substantial value of paper maps at the dawn of this new era of highway navigation with GPS is obvious. First, paper maps generally carry more detail than most "moving map" options. Furthermore, you can view any portion of or the entire paper map sheet which is generally printed at a readable scale. This enables you to gain a broad perspective not possible with the "moving-map" displays found on the "rear view mirror-size" onboard systems, the slightly larger laptop computers, or the tiny screens of hand-held GPS receiver units.

Finally, paper maps can be more easily read (especially in sunlight), which is frequently a problem encountered with the other options.

Another significant advantage offered by paper maps is their economy. As you know, nothing could be less expensive. While there is no question that the high-tech solution to position finding (the use of GPS) is the paramount option available for use in that regard; we must keep in mind that GPS has been kept relatively inexpensive for consumers because the high cost of its research and development--over $13 billion--was borne by the U.S. Government; not the receiver unit manufacturers. What has already been paid for by taxpayers does not have to be passed along to consumers. Conversely, the full costs incurred by manufacturers while developing their high-tech integrated map display/GPS interface technology must be included in the price tags of the new products. Obviously, little of this economic down-side applies to paper maps.

Finally, even for those of you who choose to use either the laptop or onboard highway navigation options, you will find paper maps quite useful when planning a trip. They can easily be carried into your home or office and provide the opportunity for relaxed study, a wider perspective, and a deeper insight into the area to be traveled as you make decisions regarding the most advantageous routes to follow.

HIGHWAY NAVIGATION OVERVIEW

Finding your way over mapped highways, roads, streets, and trails in a motor vehicle while using GPS is fundamentally the same as any other type of land navigation. The major differences are that you will generally be moving at a much greater rate of speed and probably use much smaller scale maps (covering larger areas) that will most likely portray only the most significant features. It is obvious you won't be moving in straight lines suggested by a compass azimuth; nevertheless, keeping track of direction and distance is still very important. On the other hand, you will recall that due to the various types of difficult terrain and other types of features encountered while hiking cross-county, such as cliffs, steep mountains and hillsides, densely vegetated areas, and swamps, you don't very often move over long distances in straight lines while bushwhacking, either.

It is reassuring to know that the same four steps and one cardinal rule for land navigation still apply during highway travel. Chapter 2 taught that when navigating, you must:

Step 1 - Know where you are,

Step 2 - Plan the route,

Step 3 - Stay on the route, and

Step 4 - Recognize the destination.

And, the one cardinal rule reminds us that most people find it easier to keep track of their progress and know which way to turn if they keep the map oriented to the real world around them.

In regard to the four navigational steps, the fact that you are following mapped roadways and employing GPS makes them much easier to accomplish than when crossing a trackless wilderness on foot. Knowing where you are, step 1, is easily accomplished at any time by checking the screen of the GPS receiver and locating yourself on the road or street at the indicated position on the map. The finely-tuned terrain association necessary to overcome the accumulated errors built in by SA and caused by poor GDOP as well as other small errors in the GPS position fix while out in the open countryside is usually not necessary on the highway. You know you're on the road or trail no matter what the position read on GPS unit indicates.

Just as when embarking on a hike, you must not fail to know exactly where on the map you'll begin your travel and where you're headed before sitting down to analyze the portrayal of the terrain and highway system over which you will pass (step 2 - plan the route). Factors to consider when selecting your route might include the time you have available for travel; whether you wish a leisurely scenic drive or a more direct high speed journey; where you may wish to make stops to eat, sleep, or visit along the way; and those adverse or unsafe conditions present that you may wish to avoid (i.e., construction sites, areas where roads frequently wash-out or become impassible with mud during heavy rains or with heavy snows, or, perhaps, dusty roads that might get your freshly washed car dirty).

Step 3 (staying on the route) simply becomes a task of keeping to the selected roads by making the correct turns and heading in the right directions. Occasionally checking your position using the GPS receiver, especially when approaching various decision points, as well as "navigating" a route you have previously set on the GPS unit by using landmarks (waypoints) that coincide with your "decision points" are the tasks most helpful in accomplishing step 3. One helpful hint is that you select your landmarks (waypoints) just short of the actual decision-points (i.e., limited access highway interchanges or turns at key road intersections). This will give you ample warning that the decision point is being approached. It can be especially helpful if your GPS receiver has the capability to sound an audible alarm. Whenever you feel you may have missed a turn, check your GPS position reading against the map and make any necessary adjustments to your travel.

Recognizing your destination (step 4) is generally much easier during highway travel than it is when searching for something like a hunter's tree stand in heavy woods. Nevertheless, if you have never previously seen your destination (a house, office, or store), it may still present a challenge. Again, more frequently checking your position on the map as you approach the destination and/or setting the GPS unit to warn you a few hundred meters short of the objective will help you to accomplish step 4.

In summary, the route-setting and route-following features of your GPS unit will be used differently when negotiating highways than when hiking cross-country. You will select landmarks (waypoints) and delineate routes to define your decision points and then use the route-following (navigation) features only to inform you about how far you are from those decision points at any given time and when you are about to reach one of them to make a turn or arrive at the final destination. Since you must stay on the roadways, you will not follow the more precise navigation information provided by the unit. However, if you happen to be operating without a map, you can use the graphic "pointer" screen to help determine which way to turn based upon the position coordinates of your destination. It is not as efficient a method as using a map, but it will ultimately bring success. Just be prepared to encounter dead-end streets or roadways that, perhaps, unexpectedly turn away from your intended direction of travel.

SELECTING THE PROPER NAVIGATION TOOL (I.E., MAP)

Although no map is perfect, when selecting a road map, you should examine it closely while asking yourself the following questions:

- Does it adequately cover the area in which I plan to travel at a scale that is most usable?
- Does it display an easy-to-read GPS-compatible grid?
- Are the colors and symbols used on the map clearly presented and easily understood?
- Are there clear labels for towns, route numbers, and the names of roads and streets?
- What is the date of the last revision?
- Is direction and scale information presented?
- Who published the map?

The specific information you are looking for in answer to each of these questions is pretty straight forward, but we will explain a bit what you need . Looking at the first question, "does it adequately cover the area in which I plan to travel at a scale that is most usable," the speed of your expected travel is the primary determinant. Generally, the faster you plan to drive (i.e., over interstate highways as opposed to back country roads or city streets), the smaller the map scale (e.g., those showing an entire state) you may wish to choose. On the other hand, large-scale USGS 7.5-

minute topographic quadrangles discussed elsewhere in this book cover limited areas in much detail. These are best for use on jeep trails and old logging roads, just as they are for hiking.

The question of "does it display an easy-to-read GPS-compatible grid," will be discussed in more detail below, but basically you need to have maps with a grid that is reported by your GPS unit. Most paper highway maps currently lack this universal type of grid, but have the age-old "over to E and down to 5" type grid previously discussed.

Understandability of colors and symbols used on the map is key to your interpretation of it. Make sure the symbols are clear—you can determine the difference between a lake and an industrial area (surprisingly, we have used maps that use blue to mark lakes and industrial areas—this was somewhat confusing!). A clear and comprehensive legend or "key" should be present, usually somewhere in the margins. In tandem with this requirement is that labels for towns, highways, and roads be clear. Since not all features are likely portrayed on the map, you can not trust that the "third right" on the map will be the third right in reality, you need a name or route number to go with the road you see on the map. Having natural (lakes, rivers, forests) and cultural markings (parks, schools, government buildings) marked on the map is also very helpful to the attentive driver, as most of us see more than just the center line of the road as we travel (**Figure 6-7**).

FIGURE 6-7
BICYCLE MONUMENT IN TRAFFIC CIRCLE
(ALSO APPEARING ON CITY MAP),
JEDDAH, SAUDI ARABIA

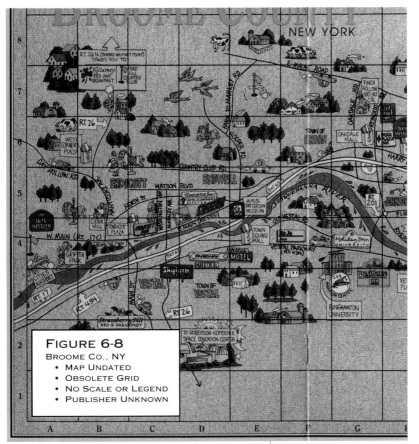

FIGURE 6-8
BROOME CO., NY
- MAP UNDATED
- OBSOLETE GRID
- NO SCALE OR LEGEND
- PUBLISHER UNKNOWN

The date of the most recent revision is very important. If you think about your own neighborhood, you can probably note changes that have occurred recently - "landmark" buildings that have been demolished, roads constructed or moved. An old map can leave you lost and confused in unfamiliar territory that has changed since the map's revision.

Direction and scale of a map is also important. If you do not know which way is north, and you find yourself lost on streets not portrayed on the map, you will have great difficulty getting back on course. Scale is important so that you know when you should be encountering turns or your destination.

Finally, a map's publisher is very important. You want maps printed by a publisher with a reputation for producing accurate and up-to-date charts. If you are unsure, but are familiar with at least some of the areas on the map, spend the time to look at it closely to see if it is accurate.

Be especially wary of maps that do not carry the publisher's name and publication date, as well as maps that appear to be crude representations and are difficult to read.

Figure 6-8 represents a map that does not include a GPS compatible grid, has no legend, reports no scale, shows no publication date, and fails to include the name of the author or publisher. Although it does present a clear, uncluttered appearance, it should not be trusted to be complete nor could it be used in conjunction with GPS.

WHAT SPECIAL REQUIREMENTS DOES GPS DEMAND FROM MAPS?

All maps use colors, symbols, labels, and marginal notes to portray and define the real world around us. But, when employing the GPS, maps must also include a standard coordinate system that facilitates the location and reporting of specific positions in mathematical terms. These position coordinates, in turn, are related through the grid to the maps' graphically displayed inventory of geographic features. In other words, it's not enough to just know that you're here at these coordinates. Instead, you must also know that you're here on this road, approaching that intersection, between these two towns which are both located along this highway. This is precisely why you will need a map as well as a GPS receiver to effectively navigate and derive the most utility from the Global Positioning System.

The grid coordinate system to be applied to highway maps for use in conjunction with GPS must possess the following characteristics:

- relative simplicity and ease of use for the general public
- "understandable" by most GPS receiver units
- maximum utility for use on land

Unquestionably, the UTM grid (more specifically, the MGRS format of the UTM grid) described previously in this book meets all three criteria. Thus, use of this array and labeling strategy works best for those who wish to employ hand-held GPS receiver units in guiding their vehicular travel.

Experienced navigators with either aerial or nautical backgrounds may question why true geographic coordinates (latitude and longitude) were not selected as the basis for guiding movement on these highway maps. The two major reasons are: 1) the graticule does not form a square grid representing consistent distances between its lines of longitude at all latitudes, and 2) it is extremely difficult to conceptualize and estimate fractions or decimals within a system based upon sixtieths (degrees, minutes, and seconds). It is far more practical and accurate to work within a perpendicular grid framework utilizing metric measurements based upon a system of tenths.

There is no argument that LAT/LON readily accommodates long-distance airborne and oceanic routing applications requiring angular directional settings and corrections relative to the graticule; but land-based travelers simply do not plan or execute these kinds of straight line movements. Few trails, streets, or highways follow a given bearing for even moderate distances, and off-road drivers and cross-country hikers generally find it prudent to maneuver around such features as swamps, escarpments, and hills or mountains. Obviously, the navigational challenges for land-based navigators are quite different from those encountered in the air and on the seas.

Prior to reading this book, you may have come to the same conclusions we have stated above, that in order to use GPS most effectively with your vehicle, you need a map that is compatible with GPS. If this is the case, you probably had little success finding one. However, the search can now be over. Alexis Publishing has designed and is presently marketing a series of U.S. highway maps for this specific purpose. The 26 sheets that make up this highly useful package cover the 48 contiguous states and include dozens of large-scale metropolitan area inset maps.

All the maps in the series are presented at a usable scale; have a crisp, uncluttered appearance; and effectively employ color and various other graphic techniques to enhance their readability and make them easy to use. More importantly, each of these maps display and label the locational grid lines in a way that makes position coordinates as uncomplicated to understand and use as a telephone number. Still, the best news is that these maps can be used with virtually every make and model of GPS receiver in service today and for the foreseeable future.

SIDE BAR 1

THE INTERSTATE HIGHWAY SYSTEM

-EVEN NUMBERED ROUTES RUN GENERALLY EAST AND WEST (I-10)

-HIGHWAY NUMBERS INCREASE FROM SOUTH TO NORTH (I-10 TO I-90)

-ODD NUMBERED ROUTES RUN GENERALLY NORTH AND SOUTH (I-5)

-HIGHWAY NUMBERS INCREASE FROM WEST TO EAST (I-5 TO I-95)

-SHORT FEEDER OR CITY BY-PASS ROUTES CONNECT WITH MAIN HIGHWAY (I-690 WITH I-90)

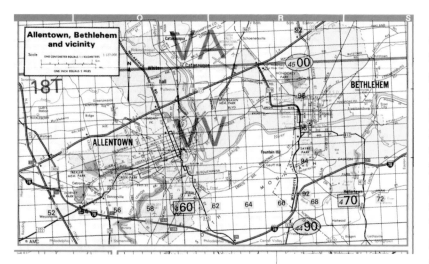

FIGURE 6-9
LARGE SCALE INSET MAP FROM ALEXIS PUBLISHING'S
PENNSYLVANIA MAP SHEET USING THE
GPS COMPATIBLE UNIVERSAL GPS GRID™

These maps use a format of the MGRS/UTM grid system that Alexis has dubbed the *Universal GPS Grid™*. The unique array of grid lines and dual purpose labels found on these maps effectively facilitate their use with GPS receivers reporting positions in either old MGRS (MGRS-1/ ALT MGRS) or UTM coordinate values (**Figure 6-9**). The UTM is, of course, a perfectly square map coordinate system designed for use on land; while the MGRS is merely a simplified method for labeling the UTM. Either or both of these standard grid coordinate systems are routinely programmed into virtually every portable GPS receiver unit manufactured to date.

There was yet another consideration taken into account by Alexis when it designed these maps. The employment and dual labeling of their Universal GPS Grid™ results in these maps being fully compatible with the large- and intermediate-scale topographic map quadrangles produced by the United States Geological Survey (USGS) and frequently used by hikers and other outdoor enthusiasts. Furthermore, Alexis' maps are compatible with the former Defense Mapping Agency's (now NIMA's) military topographic products, as well. In other words, the unique world-wide "grid address" for every location found on any Alexis state or large-scale metropolitan area inset map is identical to and interchangeable with those same position grids found on any USGS or NIMA map. Topographic maps published by the USGS and many of the large-scale military topographic map quadrangles are available for public sale through the USGS' Public Inquiries Offices or by calling 1-800-USA-MAPS. Just ask them to send you catalogs for the desired states and an index of the military quadrangles available to the general public (**Figure 6-10**).

READING ALEXIS ROAD MAP

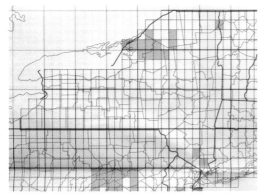

FIGURE 6-10
NY STATE PORTION OF 1:50,000 - SCALE, 15 - MIN MAPPING INDEX OF DMA (NIMA) QUADRANGLES AVAILABLE FOR PUBLIC SALE FROM USGS

In utilizing the *Universal GPS Grid*™, Alexis clearly presents and labels two map coordinate systems commonly programmed into GPS receiver units for use on land. Both the MGRS and UTM coordinate systems utilize the same matrix of perpendicular grid lines; however, each system uses a similar, yet somewhat unique, method for labeling these lines. Certainly, use of its old MGRS (MGRS-1/ALT MGRS) labels are the preferred method for using the maps; however, the UTM labels are also present and can easily be used.

Experienced land navigators agree that the Military Grid Reference System is undoubtedly the easiest to understand world-wide positioning coordinate system ever devised. In the case of these maps, your GPS unit's old MGRS (MGRS-1/ALT MGRS) coordinates locate a position by first identifying a general region (similar to a telephone AREA CODE) (**Figure 6-11a**). They then proceed to identify a more specific locality within that region (analogous to the smaller area covered by a particular telephone exchange) (**Figure 6-11b**). And,

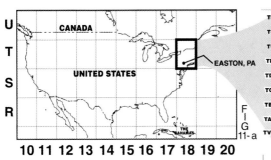

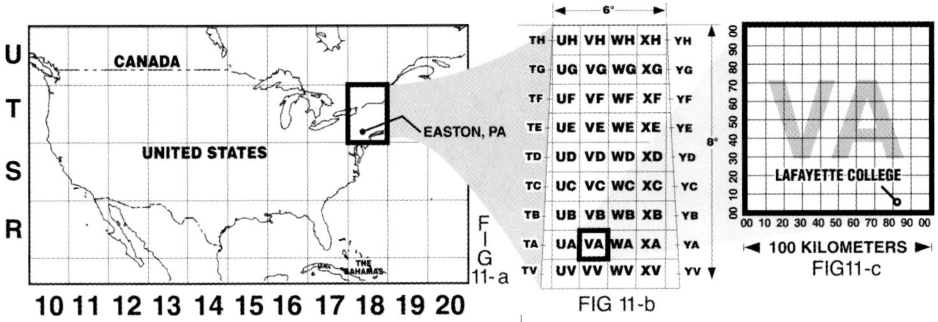

FIGURE 6-11
STRUCTURE OF THE UNIVERSAL GPS GRID™

FIG 11-a

FIG 11-b

FIG11-c

finally, they provide a set of coordinate numbers pinpointing a specific map location (as in the last four digits of an individual telephone number) (**Figure 6-11c**).

A full explanation about reading positions using the *Universal GPS Grid*™ is found under the heading "Map Coordinate Systems: A Practical Application" in Chapter 3.

ORDERING THE ALEXIS ROAD MAPS

FIGURE 6-12
ALEXIS MAP AVAILABILITY BY REGION

After now being thoroughly convinced that not using GPS in your car is seriously under-using the capabilities of your unit, the most useful information we can provide you with is where to obtain GPS compatible maps. The maps come in six sets (**Figure 6-12**), and are available from Alexis Publishing (**1-800-677-7515**).

Region I (4 maps) WA, OR; ID, MT, WY; ND, SD, NE; KS, OK
Region II (4 maps) CA, NV; UT, CO; AZ, NM; TX
Region III (4 maps) AR, LA, MS; MO; IA; MN
Region IV (4 maps) AL, GA; KY, TN; NC, SC; FL
Region V (5 maps) WI; MI; OH; IL; IN
Region VI (5 maps) WV, VA, MD, DE; PA; NJ; NY; ME, NH, VT, CT, RI, MA

As GPS becomes more widely used, it will not be long before city street maps, tourist maps, and strip trip maps, as well as various commercial indexes listing

219

restaurant and motel chains will begin making use of the *Universal GPS Grid*™ to report their locations. In fact, Alexis Publishing would be happy to consult with anyone interested in doing so.

PLANNING YOUR TRIP WITH A MAP

Now that we have discussed how to select a map, we will discuss how to use it to plan your trip. Every successful endeavor takes study and planning and this includes a trip over the highways in a motor vehicle. Of course, overall trip planning requires far more than navigational considerations, but for this discussion we'll stick to those related to route selection and finding your way.

If you wish to move with maximum efficiency making a minimum of mistakes, arrive on time, and generally experience the type of trip you envisioned, then you must study the map closely and select the routes that best match your wants and needs. Here are some of these navigational considerations.

The first is route selection. As was stated earlier, the factors you might wish to consider when selecting a route may include the time you have available for travel; whether you wish a leisurely scenic drive or a more direct, high speed journey; where you may wish to stop along the way to visit or take in sights and attractions; and the desire to avoid adverse or unsafe conditions (i.e., construction sites, areas where roads frequently wash-out or become impassible with mud during heavy rains or snows, or steep and winding roads through particularly rough country that present significant dangers, especially during hours of darkness. For example, your map study may lead you to select a bit longer route to avoid a time-consuming trek through either a highly congested or particularly rugged area. On the other hand, if you're looking for a beautiful mountain vista or babbling brook before which to place your blanket for a romantic picnic lunch, you may wish to head directly into "them there hills."

Here are some other aspects of map study. For certain, you should study the map to learn what features you might expect to encounter along your route and use them to help guide your travel. Don't be a horse wearing blinders and miss all the beauty, culture, history, and navigational hints you are about to pass by. Take note of the rivers, shorelines major highways, railroads, mountain ranges, and so forth that either cross or lie adjacent to your path. Also, study the map to gain a more comprehensive sense of the spatial relationships existing among the roads and highways, towns and cities, and other prominent features found in the area through which you will travel.

In other words, study the published map in order to develop your own comprehensive cognitive map of the area. Don't be content to allow your degree of spatial comprehension about the area to remain so limited that your understanding consists only of memorized routing instructions in tandem as in a simple chain. In short, become someone who really "knows his way around."

A "Family Circus" comic strip once dealt with this issue. It shows the mommy picking up her young daughter and two friends. The first friend lived many blocks from school and was dropped off at her home. Mommy then asked the second child where she lived and she said she could only show her the way if they went back to school first. Many dozens of city blocks later, friend number two was dropped of at her home only two and half blocks from where they had taken friend number one. This is frequently the way we, as adults, find our way in an unfamiliar area.

A thorough map study can help to overcome this disadvantage by providing a "home court advantage." At home, we can find the local grocery store through selection of a virtually unlimited combination or roads and streets without ever having to refer to written instructions or a map. In fact, we could even get there by walking cross-lots because we hold a comprehensive cognitive map of the area in our heads. If you will take the time, you can garner this level of understanding from a map for any area. Just be sure to pay attention to the details. It's obvious that having this type of "mind map" at your disposal will not only pay dividends as you find your way, it will become highly useful whenever you have a sudden change of plans or miss a turn and wish to follow the most expeditious route to correct the error. Generally, this will not turn out to be a simple backtracking.

Two final suggestions for things you might do during a map study are that you (1) highlight in green or yellow your entire route for easy identification while on the go and (2) develop a little "route card" as a memory aid for reference during the move. Make it concise, easy-to-read, and complete. For example, it might read: "Line 1, Exit I-90 onto north I-390 at Interchange 45. Line 2, proceed approximately 5 miles to Interchange 4 and head east on Rt..."

NAVIGATING ALONG THE ROUTE

Once you've selected your route, it won't be long before you're out there following it. In addition to your GPS unit and a map, you'll find that using the trip odometer and a compass will be of great assistance. When the "route card" you developed calls for "a right turn east onto State Route 367 for about 4.5 miles to the intersection with Back Country Road," it is probably easier to press the reset button on the vehicle's trip odometer right there in front of you than it is to set things up to do the same thing on the GPS unit; but, conversely, some GPS units readily report your present position, speed, direction of travel, and distance to the next end-of-leg landmark (waypoint) on a single screen without the need to refer to other screens. Just remember, when you swing into a small parking lot or spot, the automobile may <u>not</u> still be pointed in the direction of travel indicated on the screen. Although the GPS unit will tell you direction while you're moving, it is <u>not</u> a compass.

If you have first studied the map in some detail before starting your journey and then accomplish the following tasks, you should have little difficulty in following your route. Check your GPS receiver periodically to keep track of your progress, direction, and distance traveled; locate and recognize the various "decision points" along the route where you will exit limited-access highways or make turns at road intersections; use your cognitive map to help guide your movement, refer to your simple route card as a memory prompt; and recognize your intermediate and final destinations when you arrive. Certainly, with a GPS unit at your disposal, you will never be, at least in the traditional sense, lost. It is important to keep your sense of direction at all times and to keep the portrait of the area printed on the map aligned, at least in your mind, with the real world surrounding you.

Another helpful hint about following the route is to save all your "decision points" as landmarks (waypoints) in your GPS unit and set up routes with multiple segments from one to the next. While you won't pay much attention to the reports on the screen regarding which way to go and how far--as you will most likely wish to stay on the road--the unit will, nonetheless, report your arrival at each decision point. Better still, if you locate these landmarks (waypoints) just short of the actual exits or intersections, you will have some advance warning that you are about to make a turn. If your unit has an audible alarm built in, you have some additional assurance that you won't miss the turn. Just remember to consider your likely driving speed as you establish your landmarks (waypoints) in advance of the actual decision points. As a guide, it is suggested that you use a two-kilometer lead along main thoroughfares, 1 kilometer in rural or suburban areas, and 200 meters in highly congested urban centers.

While discussing urban centers, they may present a particular challenge to drivers. Maps of large urban areas are often incomplete, difficult to read, or both. Another problem is that few, if any, large-scale urban street maps presently have a grid that is compatible with GPS.

One hint that may help when you become "lost" within an urban area is to consult the inset map for that urban area found in the Alexis highway series and pinpoint your position using GPS. Whether or not the street you are located on appears on the map, you still know where you are located within the entire scheme of things and which direction you are moving; therefore, you can look for streets that do appear on the map to the front, rear, or either side and proceed from there. This beats having to get out of your car in an unfamiliar and possibly dangerous area of a city to ask directions.

OUR "TRIAL RUN"

Before sitting down to begin writing this new chapter, we of course wanted to "road test" the methods we would be advising readers to use. At the time of our trial we only had available to us the prototype Delaware, Maryland, Virginia, West Virginia map sheet of the Alexis series, so we decided a trip from Philadelphia, PA (just slightly north of the map sheet) to Williamsburg,

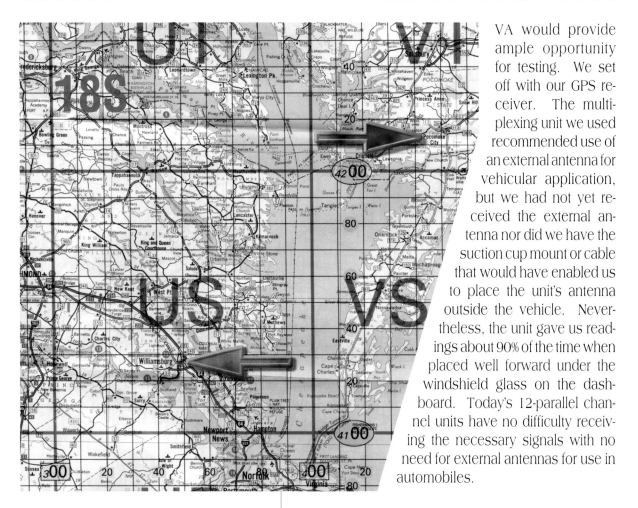

FIGURE 6-13
PORTION OF VA, WV, DE, MD MAP SHEET
ALEXIS PUBLISHING

VA would provide ample opportunity for testing. We set off with our GPS receiver. The multiplexing unit we used recommended use of an external antenna for vehicular application, but we had not yet received the external antenna nor did we have the suction cup mount or cable that would have enabled us to place the unit's antenna outside the vehicle. Nevertheless, the unit gave us readings about 90% of the time when placed well forward under the windshield glass on the dashboard. Today's 12-parallel channel units have no difficulty receiving the necessary signals with no need for external antennas for use in automobiles.

Our route entered the mapped area near Wilmington, DE; proceeded south down the peninsula past Dover and Pocomoke City; crossed the Chesapeake Bay Bridge-Tunnel to Virginia Beach; then proceeded northwest on I-64 to Williamsburg; and, finally, shifted direction again at Richmond to north on I-95 past Washington, Baltimore, and off the map again northeast of Wilmington. As we began our travel in the Chesapeake Bay area (**Figure 6-13**), we quickly realized an advantage of having the maps available that we had not anticipated. Being that we began our journey somewhat late in the evening, we were eager to reach our first stop at Pocomoke City. However, as we traveled south along Route 13 in darkness, we found ourselves passing through many seemingly identical little towns with nothing much in the way of identification to help us pinpoint our position on the map. Having the GPS device available and maps marked with the *Universal GPS Grid*™ helped to alleviate the all too common "are we there yet mommy?" syndrome that we all experience. Since *Universal GPS Grid*™ "locality" squares are 100 km x 100 km (about 62 miles square), estimating travel time is quite simple. When using traditional highway maps, determining when you will arrive at your next destination can be quite cumbersome. First, you struggle to find some sign that will allow you to pinpoint your position on the map—hopefully to within not too many miles. Next, you struggle with a makeshift ruler—perhaps a small piece of paper or your finger joints—to measure how much further you have to go on the map. Finally, you apply your measurement to the scale of miles to find out just how far "7 fingertip lengths" is in actual ground distance.

The *Universal GPS Grid*™ greatly simplifies this process. After obtaining your position using a GPS receiver, you turn to the state map and locate yourself to within one kilometer, as was described in Chapter 3. Since the boundaries of the 'locality' squares are outlined in purple, they are easily recognized and you can expect about one hour of interstate highway driving to cross one either horizontally or vertically; about an hour and a half when proceeding across at a diagonal. Even a child, given a map with your travel route highlighted, can quickly count the squares over which you must still travel and figure out if you will make it to Grandmother's house in time for the roast beef dinner she promised.

While on our journey, we had planned to deliberately get lost, just to see how much the GPS unit/map combination could help us. However, our moment of being lost came sooner than expected, and not in accordance with any plan. As we attempted to find Colonial Williamsburg, we accidentally passed our intended exit from the highway. Quickly finding our location on the map, we were able to get off at the next exit and proceed to Williamsburg without doubling back to the accepted "tourist route" from the highway.

Later that evening we found a situation in which we greatly wished the map could have come to our rescue. Tired from a full day of exploring the historic old capital, we were ready to find our hotel and relax. Unfortunately, the directions given in the guidebook were incomplete and this left us wandering about. Twice we stopped to ask directions, all to no avail. Finally, we located our hotel and found that one of our problems had been that it didn't have the appearance we expected. The large national chain had constructed a building in keeping with the colonial theme and we failed to recognize it when we did finally drive by. Had the hotel been listed in the directory with its "GPS address" we could quickly have located it despite the erroneous directions and unique architectural design.

Not convinced that our experience of being lost near Williamsburg was difficult enough to truly test the capabilities of the map and our GPS equipment, we waited for a more challenging opportunity. As we drove home, we decided to exit off I-95 in Washington, D.C., and attempt to find our way back to another entry ramp of the highway. Once off the interstate, we quickly found ourselves disoriented in a maze of one-way streets. Finally, after spotting a street sign after traveling several blocks, we were disappointed (really a bit happy) to find that the street was not included on the larger-scale D.C. inset map. Turning on the GPS unit, we obtained a position reading and located ourselves on the map. Although this particular street was not in-cluded on the inset, we saw immediately where to proceed and in only a few minutes were again entering I-95 a few miles north of where we had exited. We were relieved to have been successful in finding ourselves and proceeding back to our route without having to stop in a strange city after dark to ask directions.

MOST HELPFUL GPS RECEIVER FEATURES FOR HIGHWAY USE

Not all features available on various hand-held GPS receivers have equal utility for cross-country and highway navigation. Here are the singular features most important to highway travel (most to least):

1 12-parallel channel receiver improves signal reception and eliminates need for an external antenna.

2 coordinate readouts in (easy to use) MGRS as well as UTM coordinates.

3 screen simultaneously displaying present position, track (direction of travel), and distance to next decision point (landmark/waypoint).

4 audible alarm to warn of approaching decision points (availability of this feature could certainly have helped us to avoid missing our exit for Colonial Williamsburg).

5 unit design shape or dashboard holder accessory to facilitate use in automobile.

6 cigarette lighter adaptor for external power to eliminate drain on batteries.

7 if you plan to use digital mapping programs on personal computer, NMEA port to allow upload/download of stored information (e.g., landmarks and routes planned utilizing identified decision points).

Here are two additionl features that do not presently exist on hand-held GPS receivers that could add great utility to their use in guiding highway travel:

1 decision point feature with adjustable size for warning zone alarm feature (beep points)

2 audible route card instruction note feature

The <u>decision point audible alert feature</u>, which would quickly become known as "beep points," are distinguished from landmarks (waypoints) in that they could be used by the highway navigator without setting them up as part of the formal route function on the GPS unit. They would sound an audible alarm (a beep) anytime the driver entered a pre-determined circular distance zone around the specific coordinates assigned to any particular "beep point." Entered either through a key on the unit's keypad or through a menu option on the screen, the navigator could "plug-in" the coordinates of his journey's decision points, which would be designated upon entry as being one of three types: 1) main thoroughfare, 2) rural and suburban, or 3) urban. The main thoroughfare type "beep point" would sound whenever the driver came within two kilometers of its position as a warning that he is approaching an exit to a major highway, the rural and suburban "beep point" would sound when the vehicle came within one kilometer of the decision point, and the urban "beep point" would sound whenever the unit entered within 200 meters of the next turn or the destination. Of course, these decision points would not have to be entered in any particular order, but it might be advantageous to be able to group and save them as belonging to particular "trips." That way they could be used again later or shared with others through downloading.

The <u>audible route card instruction note feature</u> could be added to hand-held GPS receiver units and linked directly to the "beep point" alarm feature. Similar to the key chains that allow you to record your own voice telling where you left your car in the parking garage or lot, you could be given six seconds in which to tell your receiver unit the next set of route card directions to be followed when you press the ENTER key for saving the coordinates of each particular decision point. For example, as you approach the next decision point, your GPS unit would announce, "b-e-e-p, exit at interchange 32 and proceed east for 7 miles on State Route 5," or "b-e-e-p, turn right at Walnut Street and proceed east for two blocks to the brown office building number 265 on the left." This feature would greatly aid in nighttime navigation and provide users of hand-held GPS units with the best of both worlds--the portability and economy of the high-tech/low-tech strategy offered by hand-held GPS units and paper maps) and many of the advantages offered by the on-board and PC-based systems at a fraction of the cost.

OFF-ROAD TRAVEL

Owners of 4WD drive sport and utility vehicles frequently find themselves navigating in three distinct circumstances. First, they must find their way to the location of their recreational driving activity, which requires the same type of highway driving that has already been the focus of this chapter. Once they arrive at the site, they may become involved in driving along primitive roads, such as jeep trails or old vehicular road or railbed traces; or they may travel cross-county.

When negotiating a mapped trail system, navigation takes on many of the aspects of highway navigation already described in this chapter (only much slower) and hiking as described elsewhere in this book (only much faster). One thing is for certain, you will need to use large-scale maps, such as USGS 7.5-minute quadrangles, and as with hiking, you will find it advantageous to pay close attention to the topography of the land as well as the other natural and cultural features in conjunction with the use of your GPS receiver to help guide you along the route. You will recall this is what was referred to as "smart terrain association." Use of your topographic map will more closely resemble its use while hiking; whereas, the employment of your GPS unit will more closely resemble those techniques used for highway navigation. Use of "beep points" (decision points) and routing cards may well prove helpful.

Vehicular cross-country navigation is simply a speeded-up version of hiking with a number of complications and a few advantages. As you know, you can easily walk in places where your vehicle can't go. This makes your study of the map and route selection acumen even more important. On the other hand, both your employment of the topographic map and the GPS receiver will be identical to that of the hiker, but the advantage is that mistakes or longer distances to gain routing advantages are less physically taxing when riding in a vehicle.

In open areas, you may be able to move fairly quickly by terrain association while periodically checking your position readout on the GPS receiver and the map. In areas where visibility is limited due to vegetation, rough terrain, or unfavorable weather and during hours of darkness, you must proceed more slowly in a dead reckoning mode making use of all your GPS unit's routing and navigating features and capabilities, as well as a good compass.

In summary, driving sport and utility vehicles is another recreational pursuit that can be enhanced and made safer through the use of GPS. Hopefully, all who drive these vehicles will be conscientious and take proper care of the ecosystems and not violate the rights of landowners so the sport can continue to be enjoyed for years to come.

ON-BOARD VEHICLE GPS NAVIGATION SYSTEMS

FIGURE 6-14
HERTZ NEVER LOST VEHICLE NAVIGATION SYSTEM™

The easiest way to become familiar with the latest on-board GPS navigation systems is do what we did; simply rent an automobile that is equipped with one. Since not all cities are covered by the necessary digital maps, we rented a car from Hertz which offers this feature in about two dozen locations, including Dulles International Airport near our office in Herndon, Virginia.

Hertz offers what they call the *NEVER LOST* system manufactured by Magellan (**Figure 6-14**). Incidentally, the Hertz model appears to be identical to Oldsmobile's *GUIDESTAR*. On the other hand, the *Acura Navigation System*, developed in conjunction with Alpine Electronics, is, without question, a completely different unit, yet it offers features and functions very similar to that of Hertz and Oldsmobile (**Figure 6-15**).

All three models utilize on-screen-digital maps stored on the hard drive, while the BMW system, for example, stores its maps on a CD in the trunk. Both Magellan and Alpine systems employ a combination of GPS and dead reckoning navigation to improve accuracy. Furthermore, they provide automatic route programming, user selection of routing preferences (i.e., shortest time / most use of FWYS / least use of FWYS), voice directions, and databases holding various types of potential destinations. These points of interests encompass a range of sites from restaurants and gas stations to ATMs and popular attractions.

We were able to operate the Hertz equipment without instruction and received no printed information with the automobile. The menus are clear and simple to follow and the equipment is in no way complex. If you have ever used a computer, you will find the use of the equipment to be quite intuitive.

This unit allows you to navigate to street addresses, various points of interest, or freeway interchanges. It also enables you to toggle between the on-screen map and verbal directions complete with turning arrows. The unit reports how far it is to your destination, as well as the distance to your next exit or turn (decision point). The on-screen map highlights your route and, in the SETUP menu, allows you to select scales of one inch to 1/8, 1/4, 1, 4, and 16 miles. Also, in the SETUP menu, you are given options to have either north or your heading oriented toward the top of the screen. Finally, the SETUP menu is where you select and control the volume for the voice routing instruction option.

Some units, such as the *ACURA/ALPINE* and DELCO's *Telepath*, are built into the dashboard; however, other units, such as the *NEVER LOST/GUIDESTAR* and SONY *NVX-F160* are mounted on flexible stems. Those with flexible stems bring the units closer and allow you to more easily adjust the angle to reduce glare; therefore, they are somewhat easier to read than the dashboard models.

FIGURE 6-15
ALPINE-ACCURA NAVIGATION SYSTEM

MANY PEOPLE LOOK BACK FONDLY ON "SCAVENGER HUNTS" OR "ROAD RALLIES" THEY HAVE PARTICIPATED IN, AND WONDER IF SOMEHOW GPS COULD BE BROUGHT INTO THIS ACTIVITY. WITHOUT A DOUBT IT CAN! IN ADVANCE THE "GPS ADDRESSES" OF SEVERAL "LANDMARKS" (I.E. BUSINESSES, PARKS, SOMEBODY'S HOME IN YOUR GROUP) CAN BE ASSEMBLED. THIS CAN EITHER BE DONE BY ONE PERSON, OR EACH TEAM THAT PLANS TO PARTICIPATE COULD SUBMIT A PREVIOUSLY AGREED UPON NUMBER OF ADDRESSES. EACH TEAM THEN TRIES TO VISIT AS MANY OF THE ADDRESSES AS POSSIBLE AND COLLECT PROOF OF BEING THERE (I.E., PRINTED NAPKIN FROM A FAST FOOD RESTAURANT, BROCHURE FROM A PARK, SIGNATURE OF SOMEONE AT THE HOME IN QUESTION; OR TAKE PICTURES AND USE 1 HOUR PHOTO PROCESSING)—OF COURSE A TEAM COULDN'T GO TO THE ADDRESSES WHICH THEY HAD SUBMITTED. ALLOWING THE USE OF MAPS IS OPTIONAL—OMITTING THEM, IF EVERYONE IS FAMILIAR WITH THE AREA, CERTAINLY WOULD ADD TO THE CHALLENGE!

Navigation features and functions—as well as prices—included on the multitude of systems coming to market vary greatly from model to model. For example; some models include digital maps while others are limited to routing instructions, many include voice directions while others do not, and some will automatically plot your route after offering routing options while others may not even include an on-screen map with your position located.

Since not all streets and roads are included within the mapped areas and a number of areas across the country are not included in the database, it is a good idea to carry backup paper maps. In addition, for lengthy travels outside a particular metropolitan area, you will most likely wish to plan your trip by gaining the perspective and detail offered by a good paper map.

Other organizations such as American Automobile Association (AAA) have been conducting tests on various approaches to utilizing the GPS. According to their web pages on the INTERNET, most of these projects have been focused upon improving efficiency in providing emergency road service (ERS Automatic Vehicle Location, Vehicle Assistance Network, and Computer Assisted Dispatch). In addition, some of these services may parallel those offered with General Motors' *OnStar* and Ford's *RESCU* systems. Triple A presently calls this particular experimental program IVAN (In-Vehicle Assistance Network). Finally, their automobile clubs may soon begin to make on-board systems available to their members.

The technology surrounding on-board GPS navigation systems is new and rapidly changing. No doubt, the models we see today will soon evolve into more sophisticated and less costly products.

EMERGING GPS/ PERSONAL COMPUTER SOFTWARE

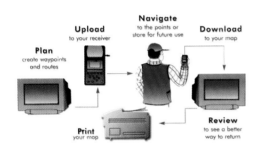

FIGURE 6-16
GPS / PC DIGITAL MAP SOFTWARE SYSTEMS

Digitized map products can be employed with your hand-held GPS receiver in a number of ways. Obviously, you can plug your GPS unit into a PC, laptop, or palm-size computer and establish a "moving-map" capability for navigation. However, as we have already stated, this is often impractical in your automobile and virtually impossible while hiking along trails or cross-country. Nevertheless, these products do have some highly useful and very practical applications for the outdoor enthusiast and general consumer. Figure 6-16 illustrates how this is the case.

The figure shows us that the dismounted outdoors man or, perhaps, off-road vehicle driver can sit at his home computer and call-up a digitized topographic map for any area and upload into his hand-held GPS receiver the landmarks (waypoints) he wishes to select for route(s) or for any other purpose. Or, after he has been out trekking, he might wish to download into his computer any saved landmarks (waypoints) or his entire track for the purpose of replicating his route of travel in the future or to save particular locations, such as beautiful vistas

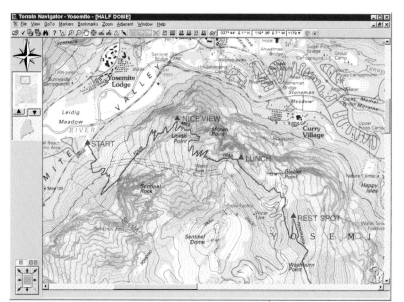

FIGURE 6-17
MAPTECH'S TERRAIN NAVIGATOR TRAIL SCREEN

FIGURE 6-18
DIGITAL MAPPING SOFTWARE OPERATING WITH THE
COMPACT HAND-HELD DELORME PALM PILOT™

or quality fishing/hunting spots. These downloaded landmarks (waypoints), or even the locations of features not found on the map, can then be added to an existing map, thereby, creating a customized topo map showing marked routes, various labeled sites, previously missing features, and so forth using the digital mapping software. Finally, the new custom topo map can then be saved and printed for later use in the field.

For example, MAPTECH's *Terrain Navigator*™ (formerly called *TopoScout*™) software package and digital topo maps allow you to do everything mentioned in the above paragraph in addition to measuring both straight line and irregular distances on its maps, providing both graphic line of sight and elevation profiles across any stretches of terrain covered by the map on your screen, converting track logs into marked routes, and annotating anything on the map that you wish through the use of labels. Furthermore, the coordinates for any map location can be determined by placing the cursor over the spot and reading the display in LAT/LON, UTM, or MGRS values (**Figure 6-17**). The cursor will also generate an elevation readout, but this type of information could also be determined from the contour lines. As the cursor is moved, these readings are continuously updated. And, finally, the margins of the various quadrangles can be

FIGURE 6-19
YEOMAN EXPEDITION MOUSE FOR MAPS™

EMERGING GPS- PAPER MAP ELECTRONIC INTERFACE

viewed in order to gain access to the information contained thereon. Further information about MAPTECH's *Terrain Navigator*™ software and maps, which are included on the CD-ROM packaged along with this book, is found in **Appendix B**. MAPTECH can be contacted at 655 Portsmouth Avenue, Greenland, NH 03840 or by calling **(800) 627-7236**.

DeLorme is another cartography house making available a number of digital map products. It also markets what it calls a "GPS Navigator" for connection with a palm-size computer to provide a GPS/moving map capability (**Figure 6-18**). This GPS enabler will, of course, work with any size computer. DeLorme has been producing maps and atlases for many years.

An English company named YEOMAN, with an office in Annapolis, MD, has recently introduced a product of interest for use in conjunction with hand-held GPS receivers and paper maps. This company obviously recognizes the utility of paper maps and charts. Yeoman calls its light weight and rugged *Expedition* a "MOUSE FOR MAPS™" (**Figure 6-19**). When connected

THIS CHAPTER ON HIGHWAY NAVIGA-
TION WAS WRITTEN BY JENNIFER N.
(DRESCHER) RIEDY, WHO IS SKILLED
IN MAP INTERPRETATION AND THE
USE OF MAP COORDINATE SYSTEMS.
IN PREPARATION FOR THE INSTRUC-
TION OF ROYAL SAUDI MILITARY
PERSONEL, SHE ADAPTED FOR
ALEXIS A FORMER U.S. ARMY MULTI-
MEDIA INSTRUCTIONAL PROGRAM
ENTITLED, "MAP INTERPRETATION
AND TERRAIN ASSOCIATION COURSE
(MITAC)", BY SUBSTITUTING BOTH
REAL WORLD SCENES AND MAP
SEGMENTS ASSOCIATED WITH THE
ARABIAN PENINSULA AND COM-
PLETELY REVISING THE TEXT. MRS.
RIEDY IS PRESENTLY EMPLOYED AS A
CHEMICAL TECHNICIAN FOR AIR
PRODUCTS AND CHEMICALS, INC. IN
ALLENTOWN, PA.

to your hand-held GPS receiver and to its special "elec-tronic grid" map pad, you have a two-fisted capability for obtaining position readouts. The GPS receiver will give you position fixes in the real world while the "Yeoman mouse" will provide them on a map. Furthermore, the GPS receiver will then enable you to guide the mouse through the use of lighted directional arrows to your actual position on the map. Finally, the coordinates of any map position over which you place the sighting "cursor", which is found in the mouse's viewing win-dow, can be saved as a landmark (waypoint) in the GPS unit's library with the click of a button.

This new equipment is the miniaturized version of a product that has seen years of service on ships around the world. It has been made smaller for the land navigator and accommodates use of both LAT/LON and UTM-based coordinate systems. Yeoman can be con-tacted at 222 Severn Avenue, Annapolis, MD 21403 or by calling (410) 263-7335. You can also visit their web site at **http://www.yeomangroup.plc.uk**.

IN SUMMARY

In closing, you will recall that GPS is a rapidly emerging field, and should be of great interest and importance to drivers. It can help anyone from the average vacationing family to rescue workers rushing to an accident. GPS units vary widely in cost and capabilities, and the best selection varies widely from person to person. An outdoor enthusiast will want a portable unit to take on hikes, while a person who will use the unit only in his vehicle may prefer a more complex, "on-board" system.

GPS LAND NAVIGATION PRACTICE EXERCISE

(PLAN AND CONDUCT OR PARTICIPATE)

Whether you are the instructor or the instructed on the subject of navigating with GPS, you may wish to establish or participate in a short practical test to evaluate the effectiveness of your instruction or reinforce the wayfinding skills you are working to develop. This brief chapter will provide some suggestions for setting-up a short LN course and some helpful hints for negotiating one as a participant. As you might suspect, the GPS receiver will prove itself to be a valuable tool in either case.

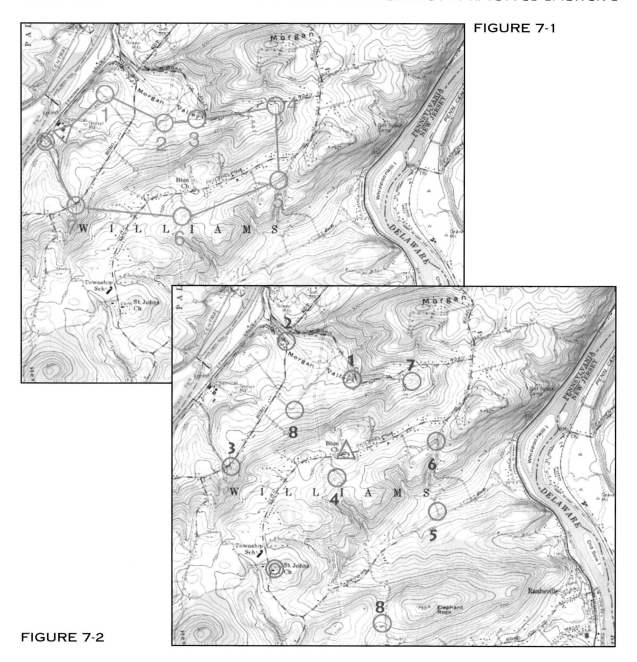

FIGURE 7-1

FIGURE 7-2

BACKGROUND

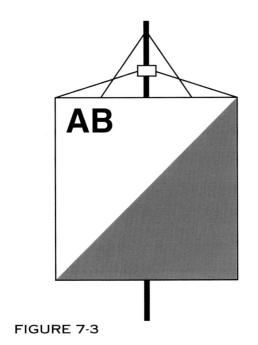

FIGURE 7-3

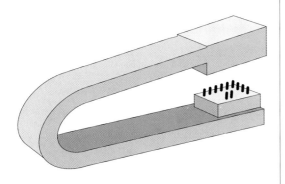

FIGURE 7-4

The design principles and techniques used to establish a simple orienteering course, more specifically a TRIM-orienteering™ course, provide an excellent basis for developing this type of practical, hands-on exercise. It will test not only the employment of GPS, but will encourage its appropriate utilization in conjunction with the terrain, a map, and compass.

Orienteering is both a competitive LN sport and a more leisurely recreational activity using natural outdoor areas and large-scale topographic maps. It may require participants to visit the established control points (waypoints) in numerical order over a specific course (**Figure 7-1**) or at random, as in TRIM-orienteering™. The design of a course with several randomly placed control points is preferred for this activity in order to prevent "following" by the participants (**Figure 7-2**). Each group can be assigned a different set of two or three control points from common start and finish points without all participants having to wait lengthy periods for others to move on ahead and then follow the same route. This method encourages individualized route selection and better guarantees that each team will navigate on its own from place to place over the course.

Each control point is marked by a large orange and white "kite" hung clearly at a distinctive target feature (**Figure 7-3**) and its location is circled on the master control map (**Figures 7-1 and 7-2**). Every control point marker is coded (e.g., AB) and has a punch with a unique pin pattern to mark the score card as proof it was located by the team (**Figure 7-4**).

FIGURE 7-5

Very little equipment is needed to establish and operate a good quality course. Control markers and those unique punches can be purchased at various orienteering supply outlets and the necessary maps obtained from local outdoor stores, bookstores, the USGS or any other appropriate governmental agency or commercial map source. Signs leading the participants off the highway into the test sight and master maps showing all control locations on the course should be fabricated and prominently displayed. Score cards can either be professionally printed or reproduced locally. And, you might consider issuing whistles to be blown in cases of emergency to facilitate finding and evacuating any injured personnel.

You may wish to contact the publishers of **Orienteering North America**, SM & L Berman Publishing Co., 23 Fayette Street, Cambridge, MA, USA, 02139-1111 (617-868-7416); The United States Orienteering Federation, P.O. Box 1444, Forest Park, GA, USA, 30051; or any other nation's Orienteering Federation for the names, addresses, and telephone numbers of reputable orienteering supply outlets.

Finally, distinctly marked parking and start and finish areas are helpful in better managing the various off-course activities associated with the operation of an LN test site. These activities include arriving and departing vehicular traffic, recording the locations of control points found on the master map(s) onto individual maps by the participants (**Figure 7-5**), and waiting for others to start and finish the course.

COURSE PLANNING

Before you start the process of planning an effective GPS LN skill test course, locate and obtain permission to use a natural outdoor site with sufficient area to accommodate the activity and the number of navigational teams you plan to exercise. You will require an area of at least several square kilometers in size. Generally, you should not locate more than two or three control points within a one square kilometer area, and you should plan to establish about twice as many control points as you have navigational teams operating at any one time on the course. Parks, other public lands, and military reservations often present excellent locations for this type of activity.

Next, you must obtain and study a large-scale map of the area to be used (1:50,000 or greater/1:25,000 preferred). This intensive map study should be done while walking over the terrain. Keep in mind the fact that you wish only to provide some practical experience in using the GPS while navigating, not brutally test the physical endurance or special mountain-goat-like or swamp-traversing skills of the participants. In other words, use terrain that is safe and relatively easy to negotiate. Also, be certain the entire course will be covered by a map that is fairly comprehensive and easy to read.

Now, it is time to select the specific locations of your numbered and coded control points. Their locations should be circled and numbered on the map and, later, a day or so before the course is to be used, the control markers accurately placed on the ground and coded with letters to provide proof of their being visited by the participants. The accurate placement of control points on the ground will be covered in the next section.

In terms of the course's length, it is reasonable to expect navigators on foot to cover 3,000 meters per hour during daylight or 1,000 meters per hour in darkness. Thus, nighttime courses can be much shorter, but care should be taken not to make control markers too difficult to find in the darkness. Use of lighted control markers is not suggested because they eliminate most of the challenge.

Control points should be placed on specific, identifiable terrain or other features in order to encourage use of map interpretation and terrain association skills by the participants. Some features that might be used for this purpose include a hill, the upper end of a small draw, lower end of a small spur, point along a small lake or pond shoreline, the point or tip of the arm of a swamp, a cabin, a location adjacent to a stream or road junction, and so forth. Obviously, these features should also be clearly portrayed on the map. Placement of control points on these types of features will not only help the participants navigate to them, but it will also assist you in placing the control markers more accurately on the ground.

Finally, control points should be placed in a way that discourages participants from wandering onto private land, damaging a fragile environment or habitat, and endangering themselves or property in any way.

COURSE SETUP

First, you must clearly mark the parking area, master map viewing area, and your start and finish points and associated waiting areas. In addition, any signs and the master map(s) must be set out.

Next, you must accurately place all control point markers and punches at appropriate locations on the ground. Employ your GPS unit to generally locate your points and then use your map and terrain association skills to fine-tune the markers' specific placements. If a control point is shown on the map at the tip of a small spur, don't locate the marker in an adjacent draw out there on the ground. This will only cause your participants to lose confidence in your course and lead to "heated" discussions after the event.

Before employing the GPS unit to help you locate your control markers on the ground, it is suggested that you manually key in the coordinates and elevations of all control locations as waypoints. Then, you should proceed to each of their locations using your GPS receiver, compass and terrain association skills to correctly place the markers at each of the sites on the ground. It is always a good idea to have another knowledgeable person check your work.

CONDUCTING THE EXERCISE

In addition to a well planned and accurately prepared course, a good LN exercise requires a highly organized operation. Participants should be thoroughly briefed, quickly broken into teams, immediately sent through their paces, given a meaningful after-action review, and an adequate opportunity to have any questions answered.

The briefing should include general and specific safety considerations; the general layout of the course; what to look for and do at the assigned control points; any special cautions or helpful hints; a review of the schedule of events; and when and where to start, finish, wait, and participate in the critique and question and answer session at the end of the event.

Following the briefing, equipment should be checked and participants led to the master maps where they can mark the course control locations and numbers on their individual maps. Next, they should be led to the start waiting area where score cards, with the control numbers circled that the team is instructed to visit, will be distributed to each group. Then, teams must be sent out at regular timed intervals by the event starter.

After everyone has completed the course, all participants will engage in an after-action review to reinforce what has been learned. All questions from the participants should also be answered. It is crucial that the participants understand that their active sharing of experiences during the exercise is key to the effectiveness of this review activity.

HINTS FOR RUNNING A COURSE (AS A PARTICIPANT)

Actually, the first five chapters of this Guide present all the information, concepts, and skills needed to successfully complete a LN practice course or to meet any other LN challenge. It is assumed that by now you know how to employ a GPS receiver, interpret a map, and use a compass. However, a quick review of some helpful hints may serve as a good memory aid just prior to your running a course.

First, you are encouraged to mark on your map the locations of the various control points that make up the course with as much precision as possible. Further, you should take the time to manually enter the locations of your start and end points and any of the controls you are to visit as waypoints into your GPS unit's memory. You should also thoroughly analyze the map to select "functional" and easy-to-follow routes from the starting point to each of the controls you are to visit and on to the finish.

Remember to identify and use handrails, catching features, and navigational attack points where they will aid you in guiding your movements. You might also utilize other controls located on the course that are not required for your particular team's exercise, should they be helpful as guides. Finally, you are encouraged to take maximum advantage of any number of your GPS receiver's many functions and features and to fully integrate its application with your ability to use the terrain, your map, and a compass.

In conclusion, good land navigators exploit any advantage they may have available to them. This includes the fine capabilities of your GPS equipment and any cues offered by either the map or the real world.

IN SUMMARY

This chapter provided some suggestions for setting-up a short LN test course and some helpful hints for negotiating one as a participant. Briefly, you were encouraged to use some of the design principles and techniques to establish a simple orienteering course. Including the capabilities of the GPS receiver and your map and compass while using terrain association skills to establish or to run through a course exercise is an outstanding way to learn and practice the skills addressed in this chapter.

LOOKING AHEAD (IMPACT OF GPS)

There is no question that GPS will have a profound effect upon everyone. In fact, it would not be at all surprising if our letterheads soon include our MGRS/UTM grid coordinates as well as our telephone and fax numbers, street addresses, and zip codes.

BACKGROUND

We increasingly read and hear about GPS in the news as its applications become more extensive; but we are also beginning to encounter it as part of our culture through entertainment and literature. GPS is being mentioned in comic strips, on prime time television and in the soaps, and it is presently finding its way into some first-rate films and best-sellers. For example, award-winning mystery writer Patricia Cornwell in a recent book (*Unnatural Exposure*, G.P. Putnam's Sons, 1997) has her central character, Virginia's chief medical examiner Dr. Kay Scarpetta, learn from a local Richmond area landfill employee that they can now track garbage. "A satellite system that uses a grid. We can at least tell you which trucks would have dumped trash

A GLIMPSE INTO THE

FUTURE

during a certain time period in the area where the body was found."

Evidence of the ever-expanding applications of GPS abound. In addition to the navigation aids, precise surveying capabilities, and vehicular tracking and reporting systems already mentioned, we now regularly encounter the use of GPS across a broad spectrum of activities. They include such undertakings as managing agricultural planting and fertilizing, tracking bird migrations and other wild animal movements, measuring the earth's tectonic plate slippages, creating a spatial inventory of the various components of our vast utilities infrastructures, the covert tracking of people and equipment for espionage and law enforcement purposes, recording the movements of convicted probationers, and determining the whereabouts of lost children.

Furthermore, people are using GPS to assist them in selecting clubs on the golf course, managing and accurately mapping archeological digs, and even recreating historical events. See the article in the October 7, 1997, issue of *GPSWorld*, entitled "Victorio's Escape" describing a century-old cavalry battle between Buffalo Soldiers under the command of Captain Henry Carroll and the Chihenne Apaches being led by Chief Victorio back in the waning days of the wild, wild west. The point being that our imaginations seem to be the only limiting factors when it comes to the applications await-ing this great new technology.

We are entering a world where cellular telephones will report our locations to 911 dispatchers and courts accept the time, date, and/or position stamps of the GPS on photographs and other recorded information as legal evidence. Some "leading edge" catalogs already fea-ture clocks that receive their controlling signals from the highly accurate and very expensive atomic clocks aboard the GPS SVs orbiting the earth. Often, manufacturers making use of the system's time and position applica-tions don't even bother to mention to their customers that it is the GPS which enables their products to function with such accuracy.

Soon, GPS will assist us in sorting through vari-ous computerized "yellow pages" and other kinds of directories by providing those listings that meet proxim-ity requirements to either our present position or some other user-selected location. And, of course, GPS will significantly affect the way the military conducts war. The spatial aspects of command, control, communica-tions, intelligence, fire control, "smart" munitions guid-ance, and logistical functions will ultimately be moni-tored and handled with the aid of GPS through various communications/ computer information networks that make complex and comprehensive real-time decisions possible on the battlefield. Naturally, commercial trans-port, manufacturing, and various private sector logisti-cal operations will soon be handled in a similar fashion.

Through various aspects of modern technology, including the GPS, a company's control over its means for production can now reach far beyond the walls of its own facilities to anywhere in the world. It is now possible to manage the flow of raw materials, components, and subassemblies through a myriad of suppliers, subcontractors, and shippers to finished products, as never before.

Finally, it is already apparent that various GPS applications will make further inroads into what is being called the field of "intelligent transportation." This encompasses the means for the elimination and/or avoidance of heavily congested areas, the development of enroute guidance systems, and the creation of safety backups for the decisions we make and the actions we take while driving a motor vehicle. In other words, we are talking about the rather rapid evolution of "smart" highways and vehicles.

Without a doubt, the most exciting news in recent years regarding GPS was the 1996 announcement by the White House that the United States Government intends "to terminate the current practice of degrading civil GPS signals (selective availability) within the next decade..." The press release detailing this announcement goes on to reaffirm "U.S. commitment to providing basic GPS services, free of direct user fees, for peaceful, civil, commercial, and scientific users throughout the world." The Administration expects this announcement will add 100,000 jobs to the economy and spur growth of the GPS market from $2 billion to $8 billion in the four years between 1996 and 2000.

The highest priorities for further refinement of the technology will most likely focus on 1) further miniaturization, 2) improved signal reception (particularly in areas of heavy vegetation and within the "street canyons" of our cities), and 3) reduced power drain/increased battery life. Obviously, now that manufacturers have broken the "$100 barrier" on their "leanest" models, prices can not be significantly reduced. It is interesting to recall that, according to Motorola vice president Robert Denaro, "...the first commercial GPS receiver was built by Texas Instruments, cost $153,000, and was about the size of the overhead projector. And it drew about as much power. Today, GPS chipsets are significantly under 50 bucks."

Before closing this discussion on the future, there must be at least a passing reference to the geopolitical aspects of the system. While everyone from the Japanese to the French have voiced a concern about the control the Americans and Russians now enjoy over the most advanced and accurate world-wide navigation systems, there appears to be no plan to design a completely new system in the short term. Some European nations have talked about establishing a civil European Global Navigation Satellite System (GNSS1) which consists of the integrated use of both the U.S. GPS and Russian GLONASS (Global Navigation Satellite System) along with four Imarsat-3 satellites to provide correction signals for both GPS and GLONASS data. The second phase being discussed, GNSS2, might at some undefined future date consist of an independent satellite navigation system designed and funded by as of yet undetermined sponsors.

In answer to the obvious question; yes, there are currently some commercial products available that use the signals from the Russian GLONASS system to calculate positions and guide navigation. In fact, there are civilian receivers on the market that utilize signals from both GPS and GLONASS, which, when averaged, provide accuracies superior to those possible when using either system independently. The up side for the use of GLONASS is that the Russians do not now nor do they intend to degrade their signals as does the U.S. Department of Defense (DoD). On the down side, however, GPS is more accurate (discounting SA) and both GLONASS and the dual-system receivers are far more expensive (far fewer having been manufactured) than the comparable GPS equipment. Finally, GLONASS was designed, established, and funded by the former Soviet Union to support its cold war military objectives. The fundamental question now facing Russia is whether its military establishment can continue to maintain this expensive system during difficult economic times when it is unable to pay its soldiers their wages.

The July 1997 issue of GPS World compares the accuracies attained by the GPS and GLONASS systems. According to the article, MIT's Lincoln Laboratory (Massachusetts Institute of Technology) made the following observations on May 24, 1997:

GLONASS	95% horizontal errors of 21.2 and vertical errors of 39.1 meters (no degradation)
G P S	95% horizontal errors of 48.1 and vertical errors of 81.7 meters (w/SA)
GPS+GLONASS	95% horizontal errors of 14.9 and vertical errors of 41.8 meters (w/SA)

IN SUMMARY

This new technology is going to have a profound impact upon our daily lives in ways too numerous to imagine. Some are just now beginning to emerge while others remain completely unforeseen and unexpected. Before this decade began, GPS was virtually unheard of and completely untested outside the scientific community. By January of 1991, it had won us and our allies a major military victory in the Middle East against a powerful tyrant in the short period of just a few days with minimal casualties. Today, GPS has become a household word; and it won't be long before it becomes a regular utility that we won't be able to recall how we ever lived without. It ranks in importance with the development of the internal combustion engine, transistor, and computer chip.

Most fundamentally, GPS is going to generate vastly increased, broad-based interest in geography and maps. The spatial relationships among places and various natural events and human activities will steadily gain our attention. GPS will inevitably contribute to our awareness that we all share the same planet, face the same challenges.

In conclusion, GPS obviously offers great utility to those who wish or need to navigate with precision, but it also holds a similar potential for those who wish to apply and exploit its capabilities in nearly every other endeavor; whether they be academic, scientific, or commercial.

APPENDIX A: HOW GPS WORKS

SOME TECHNICAL TALK FOR THE LAYMAN

Most of us have a certain amount of curiosity about how things came about and how they work, especially when they are spectacular and cost billions of tax dollars. Without delving into the specifics of the complex physics, electronics, and mathematics involved, this is the story behind the development of GPS and how it works.

THE GLOBAL POSITIONING SYSTEM (GPS)

Satellite navigation first arrived during the early 1960s with the establishment of the U.S. Navy's low orbit TRANSIT system. This was certainly an improvement over the limited land-based radio navigation capabilities that had existed prior to that time. Then, in 1973, a team of Air Force officers and civilian scientists working in the Pentagon began developing plans that would completely revolutionize navigation world-wide. In the words of Dr. Bradford Parkinson, one of the Air Force officers who worked on that team; "Instead of angular measurements to natural stars, the new system would use radio-ranging measurements (eventually with millimeter precision) to a constellation of artificial satellites called NAVSTARs." These satellites would be placed in high orbit free of the earth's atmosphere.

According to Parkinson, "The DoD's primary purposes in developing GPS were its use in precision weapon delivery and providing a capability that would help reverse the proliferation of navigation systems in the military." He said the motto adopted by people working on the project was to build a system "that could drop five bombs in the same hole and build a cheap (less than $10,000) set that navigates." The Gulf War demonstrated that the system they developed certainly can drop any number of bombs into almost any size hole and GPS receivers are now available on the consumer market at prices ranging to less than $100. Just twenty-one years and $13 billion after that small planning group first began its work on the project, Secretary of Defense Aspin was able to officially change the status of the GPS in 1994 from "experimental" to "operational."

Today, the GPS is still completely funded and controlled by the U.S. Department of Defense (DoD), although that control is now coming under debate. The system is made up of three segments: 1) space segment, 2) control segment, and 3) user segment, each of which will be discussed.

Presently, the space segment consists of the 24 space vehicles (SVs) of which three are held as active spares, but this number is obviously subject to change. They span 17 feet (with solar panels extended); weigh about 1900 pounds; were built to last about 7.5 years (although they are lasting longer); and orbit the earth in sets of four SVs equally spaced on six orbital planes. These orbital planes are inclined at about 55 degrees with the equatorial plane and at an altitude of approximately 12,500 miles (20,200 kilometers). The SVs' 12-hour orbits repeat the same ground track, as the earth turns beneath them in nearly the same direction, about once each day. More precisely, they arrive over the same ground locatations about four minutes earlier each day (**Figure A-1**).

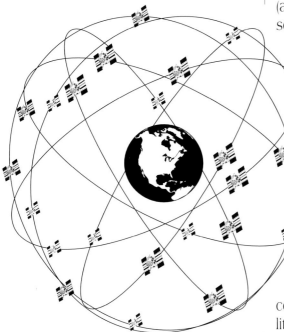

FIGURE A-1
VECTOR ILLUSTRATION OF 24 SATELLITE
GPSCONSTELLATION BY FRANCK E. BOYNTON

Each satellite broadcasts the information needed by any user unit (GPS receiver/computer) to calculate its position. The information contained in these broadcasts includes a reasonably accurate constellation almanac, as well as highly specific satellite ephemeris data, precise time information, and special sequences of coded signals.

Since the user unit must previously have obtained an almanac from any SV, which is good for about six months and contains the general locations of all satellites in the constellation, it knows which satellites' signals to search for at any given time or place in gathering the information needed for the calculation of a position. Of course, this is true only if its last position fix or most recent position initialization by the user was located within about 300 miles of its current location. Whenever the unit has been turned off for more than six months (contains an outdated almanac) or has been moved more than 300 miles since it was last used, a "cold start" is automatically initiated by the receiver unit that can take several minutes while all the necessary preliminary data is collected prior to the calculation of its position. Whenever the unit is in use, almanac data is continually being updated and stored in memory as are the latest time corrections and current position information for the receiver.

The fresh information required from the SVs for each new position update includes ephemeris data (highly precise orbital location information), the time, and those coded signal sequences that are matched by the user unit to the time and identical coded signal pattern being run by its own built-in computer. The minute-time discrepancies measured in nano seconds (billionths of a second) between these pseudo-random codes (so called because they are similar to the random electromagnetic "noise" naturally present at all times) are translated into distance calculations between the various SVs and the GPS unit (time lag x 186,000 miles per second) at the instant the signals were received (**Figure A-2**). In theory, it takes calculations from only two satellites to determine a precise horizontal (two-dimensional) position fix, but, since theory and reality are not the same, information from a third SV is required to improve the accuracy of the fix. We will further discuss GPS signals and position accuracies later.

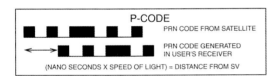

FIGURE A-2

TIME / DISTANCE MEASUREMENT USING THE COMPARISON OF A PSEUDO-RANDOM CODE COMING FROM A GPS SV AND THAT BEING GENERATED BY THE USER UNIT

GPS satellites keep highly accurate time with very expensive atomic clocks ($50,000 to $100,000), but individual user units do not have this kind of time-keeping capability. (Incidentally, atomic clocks aren't powered by atomic energy, they use the oscillations of a particular atom to accurately measure time.) Nevertheless, by knowing the precise orbital locations of all SVs at any given moment, each GPS receiver can compare the information coming in from the satellites and calculate the amount of time error existing on its own clock while continuously (but never perfectly) correcting it. Also, by using information from three or more SVs, the unit can further reduce its horizontal position calculation errors by averaging them out. Finally, use of signals from a fourth SV allows the user unit to report its altitude as well as its horiontal position. This is called a three-dimensional position reading. The end result is a highly accurate postion report each time the navigator requires one.

The control segment consists of a network of tracking stations around the world (Ascension Island, Diego Garcia, Hawaii, Kwajalein), with the master tracking and control station being located at Falcon Air Force Base in Colorado. The tracking stations monitor signals from each of the SVs and compute precise orbital data and clock corrections for each satellite. The control station then uploads the corrected data to the SVs which, in turn, broadcast the information for use by receiver units in calculating positions around the world.

The user segment is made up of all receiver/computer units that utilize the signals broadcast by the

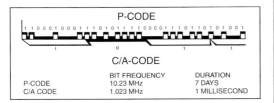

FIGURE A-3
PSEUDO-RANDOM CODES

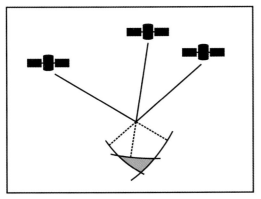

FIGURE A-4
THE PSEUDO RANGES DO NOT ACTUALLY INTERSECT.
THEY DO, HOWEVER, EMBRACE THE DARKENED AREA.
BY CORRECTING FOR THE RECEIVER CLOCK ERROR
MULTIPLIED BY THE SPEED OF LIGHT, THE TRUE
RECEIVER POSITION IS THE AVERAGED POINTS OF
INTERSECTION AMONG THE CIRCLES.

NAVSTARs to calculate positions. These receiver units are basically grouped into two categories: 1) those that use the C/A-code (Course Acquisition), which modulates the L1 carrier signal and is the basis for the civilian Standard Positioning System (SPS), and 2) those that use the P-code (Precise), which modulates both the L1 and L2 carrier signals. When the military operates the P-Code in the encrypted mode (which is most of the time and is referred to as antispoofing), it is referred to by scientists as the Y-code, which, in either case, is the basis for the Precise Positioning System (PPS). Again, both the C/A- and P-codes are called "pseudo-random codes" because they emulate random electrical noise. Nevertheless, they are actually complicated and repeating patterns of ones and zeros (**Figure A-3**). Finally, it is what is called the "pseudo-range" that is measured by the user unit when it matches the satellite's transmitted pseudo-random code with it's own reference code in synchronization between the SV transmitter's atomic clock and the receiver's clock. It is called a "pseudo-range" because no individual calculation is ever quite accurate. Finally, it is from among these "pseudo-ranges" that averaging takes place and position is determined (**Figure A-4**).

The civilian SPS, degraded by selective availability (SA), has a DoD predictable accuracy of 100 meters horizontal, 156 meters vertical, and 340 nanoseconds (billionths of a second) of time. On the other hand, the more accurate military PPS has a predicable accuracy of 22 meters horizontal, 27.7 meters vertical and 100 nanosecond of time.

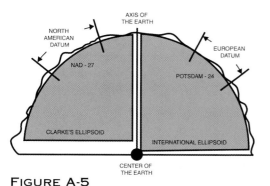

FIGURE A-5

GPS UNITS CALCULATE POSITIONS BASED UPON
LATITIDE AND LONGITUDE AS DETERMINED ON THE
ACTUAL GEOID (WGS-84 DATUM). HOWEVER, THEY CAN
FURTHER TRANSLATE THIS POSITION INFORMATION.

In addition to the C/A and P-codes, the Navigation Message also modulates the L1 carrier. This is how the user units receive the data bits regarding SV orbits, clock corrections, and other system information.

After receiving and calculating the information broadcast from the satellites, the user units, whether they be military or civilian sets, locate themselves in latitude and longitude on the earth's surface relative to Universal Time Coordinated (UTC) on the WGS-84 geoid. From there the unit can translate (calculate) horizontal positions assumed within other spheroid- or geoid-based map datums (e.g., WGS-72, NAD-27, or Ord. Survey G.B.-36), while using any number of horizontal position coordinate systems (e.g., LAT/LON, MGRS/UTM (old), MGRS/UTM (new), or UTM), and at elevations in either feet or meters above or below the WGS-84 geoid (theoretical sea level). See **Figure A-5**.

The position inaccuracies reported by GPS user units are caused by a number of factors. They include slight errors resulting from the SV clock, SV emphemeris data, the troposphere (weather zone up to 15 km aloft) and ionosphere (ionized air zone from about 50 to 500 km in altitude), pseudo-range noise, receiver noise, multipath effects (signals bouncing indirectly off the ground and other objects nearby), and, most significantly, the inaccuracies introduced by the U.S. Government's SA. Selective Availability degrades the general accuracy of the C/A code from about 30 to 100 meters. In fact, the U.S. Government's specifications for SA state that accuracies achieved when using the

Standard Positioning System (using the C/A Code) can only be less than 100 meters 95% of the time.

Although the U.S. Government has stated that the DoD must leave SA in place for security reasons until sometime between the year 2000 and 2006, it never officially explains why it is periodically turned off. In addition to various other occasions, it was switched off during the Gulf War, the landings of our military forces in Samolia and Haiti, and during the dramatic 1995 rescue of downed pilot Captain Scott O'Grady in Bosnia. Certainly, it's no secret that there are far more civilian-type (C/A-Code) GPS receivers than military (P-Code) models, even in the hands the U.S. Armed Forces and its allies, thus it isn't difficult to speculate why they might wish to "beef-up" the accuracy of the C-A code at times when SA's purpose might theoretically have had greater validity.

With the exception of those inaccuracies deliberately caused by SA, both GPS experts and buffs often talk about position errors being measured in such terms as GDOP, HDOP, and so forth. Geometric Dilution of Precision (GDOP) results from the poor geometry that periodically occurs everywhere due to the various satellite positions over the earth's surface. Sometimes, just moving the receiver to give it a clearer "view" of the sky and receipt of signals from additional SVs will resolve this temporary problem. But, at other times, a short wait will change the configuration of signals coming in from those constantly moving SVs (**Figure A-6**).

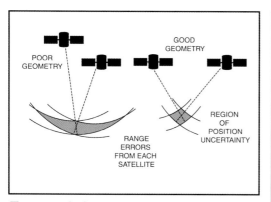

FIGURE A-6
GDOP. WHEN THE USER UNIT IS AT A POINT WHERE
THE LINES OF COMMUNICATION FROM THE SV'S ARE
NEARLY PERPENDICULAR, THE POINT OF INTERSECTION
IS WELL DEFINED. WHEN THE ANGLE BECOMES EITHER
VERY LARGE OR SMALL, THE POINT OF INTERSECTION
IS GENERALIZED AND POSITION CALCULATIONS
DEGRADE IN ACCURACY.

GDOP is made up of the following components, and, while each can be computed separately, they are impacted by covariances that also impact upon one another. The components of **GDOP** include:

PDOP (*Position Dilution of Precision*)
HDOP (*Horizontal Dilution of Precision*)
VDOP (*Vertical Dilution of Precision*)
TDOP (*Time Dilution of Precision*)

GDOP can be calculated by a receiver unit's computer and many hand-held units, including some of the cheaper ones, have a means for reporting the quality of a fix. Some units report the overall numerical value of the GDOP or the PDOP; others report the values for all of the DOPs; while still others use schemes such as "figures of merit" (1-9) and "expected horizontal position error" or "estimates of position error" in feet or meters. These messages generally appear on the unit's satellite status screen along with the strengths of signals being received from each of the SVs in "view." Remember, the strength of a signal has no impact upon the accuracy of the position fix. A weak signal, however, does mean that your set may soon lose the use of that satellite for computing its position.

Finally, position reporting errors can be caused by you, the operator, as well. The most common mistakes made by operators are the setting of the wrong horizontal map datum on the receiver (resulting in up to 1 km of error), misreading the data being reported on the screen, and manually entering incorrect coordinates for landmarks/waypoints and then attempting to navigate to them. You are cautioned that these kinds of operator errors can be significant.

Before ending our review of the user segment of the GPS, we must discuss the two groups of C/A-Code receivers presently available on the consumer market: 1) multiplexing receivers (single channel) and 2) parallel channel receivers. Each uses a different approach to gathering and processing the positioning information broadcast by the satellites.

Multiplexing receivers (single channel receivers) are less expensive and can be slower and somewhat less accurate. This type of receiver feeds data from the various satellites to the unit's computer in series (one after another). In order to reduce the length of time this would normally take between fixes (several seconds), most multiplexing units sample data from a couple of satellites and make a good estimate for "interim" (every second) position updates. Of course, it will usually take longer for both an initial position fix when the set is first turned on (a few minutes) as well as for a cold start (up to 12 minutes or more). These receivers can also experience problems finding and maintaining contact with satellites in places where there isn't a clear horizon-to-horizon view of the sky. Without question, the performance of multiplexing receivers is significantly inferior to that of parallel channel receivers in wooded areas (even with moderate foliage), areas with significant relief (many hills and mountains), and urban places (with several large buildings).

Parallel channel receivers are somewhat more expensive, but the payoffs in speed, a bit more accuracy, and, most importantly, improved signal reception are well worth the investment. Various GPS receiver units operate with from 2 to 12 separate channels, with 12 being the ideal and 8 being sufficient. If the advertising about a particular model doesn't say the unit has the "parallel channel" feature and how many channels it has, you can bet it doesn't.

The more useful parallel channel receiver feeds data from several satellites to the unit's computer in parallel (simultaneously) which calculates everything faster from initial position fixes when turning the unit on to cold starts requiring that all new information be gathered. Furthermore, fully computed every-second position updates are possible, and, as has already been stated, signal reception under adverse terrain conditions is vastly improved. Finally, parallel channel receivers always select from among all the SV signals available those that give every fix the best possible GDOP (least error).

DIFFERENTIAL GPS (DGPS)

This is a strategy developed by scientists to overcome both the inaccuracies naturally incumbent within the system and those artificially introduced through SA. It incorporates the use of a special GPS receiver/transmitter, often referred to as a GPS beacon, surveyed in to a highly precise known position. This unit then monitors its pseudo-range calculations for each of the satellites from which it receives a signal, determines the errors resulting from each of these calculations, and broadcasts corrective data to all "roving units" within the local area being covered. Meter, submeter, and even centimeter accuracy is possible when using DGPS. This precision can be used to guide aircraft onto runways, ships through narrow port entrances, and to conduct property surveys or monitor slight shifts in the earth's surface.

Whenever "real-time" accuracy is not important, such as when inventorying the positions of various components of our nation's infrastructure (e.g., pipeline intersections, valves, or joints), data from "roving units" can be downloaded at a later time into a computer holding the calculations and corrections ascertained earlier by precisely located DGPS equipment. As long as the information carries the time stamp and identifies the satellites used to compute the position fixes, the data can be retroactively corrected for accuracy. This can be done an hour later, next year, or in some future century; it makes no difference.

Many of the moderately priced hand-held GPS receivers presently on the market have the capacity for receiving and using DGPS information being broadcast within a local area. They can't serve as surveying instruments, but they will give you accuracies approaching just a few meters. This DGPS feature may become increasingly useful along navigable waterways, in port areas, and wherever an organization or governmental unit has established DGPS services (e.g., the U.S. Coast Guard network of DGPS radio beacons covering most of the U.S. coastline). Various commercial DGPS services have recently sprung up to cover various size areas, including some rather large regions of the country.

Some pieces of DGPS equipment provide information updates as frequently as every twenty seconds; however, you must be cautioned that they will not remove errors attributable to individual receiver noise or multipath signal bouncing because these errors are unique either to the individual receiver unit or to its particular location.

ANOTHER METHOD FOR INCREASING ACCURACY

Another strategy being explored by GPS manufacturers for improving the accuracy of civilian GPS receivers is through use of the L2 carrier wave (which carries the encrypted Y-code) as a means for further refining the position fix ascertained from the non-encrypted C/A-code modulating on the L1 carrier. The 1996 Federal Radionavigation Plan (FRP) gives them encouragement by stating, "until such time as a second coded civil GPS signal is operational, the DoD will not intentionally reduce the current received minimum radio frequency signal strength of the P(Y)-code signal on the L2 link..." It will be interesting to see what the scientists can do with this new approach in making use of the second carrier wave.

FURTHER INFORMATION

For a more in-depth technical exploration of GPS topics, you are encouraged to contact Navtech Seminars & GPS Supply at 2775 S. Quincy Street, Arlington, VA 22206-2204, call (800) 628-0885 or (703) 931-0503, or visit their web site at www.navtechgps.com. Navtech has an extensive library and bookstore covering every aspect of GPS. Also, more books, Alexis GPS Road Maps, and other GPS links, such as to Navtech Seminars & GPS Supply can be accessed by visiting:

http://www.alexispublishing.com.

APPENDIX B: TERRAIN NAVIGATOR

DIGITAL MAP SOFTWARE CD ROM

Maptech takes U.S. Geologic Survey topographic maps, preferred by hikers, hunters and outdoors enthusiasts, and presents them in a convenient, easy-to-use CD-ROM format. Actual maps are scanned at high resolution and paired with Terrain Navigator software for powerful, digitized mapping. Included with this book is a Maptech CD-ROM, with one topographic map and Terrain Navigator mapping software (formerly called TopoScout).

Terrain Navigator's mapping tools enable quick and easy interpretation and manipulation of map data. Calculate precise distances and land areas instantly with the freehand distance tool. Trace a path and Terrain Navigator will display its elevation profile. Use the line-of-sight option to find what terrain is (or isn't) visible from a mountain's summit. Terrain Navigator lets

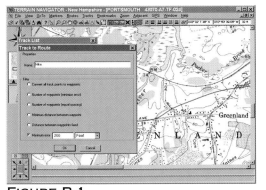

FIGURE B-1
TERRAIN NAVIGATOR™ TRACK ROUTE SCREEN

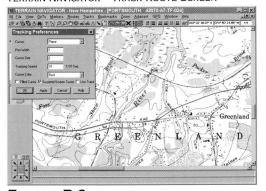

FIGURE B-2
TERRAIN NAVIGATOR™ PREFERENCES SCREEN

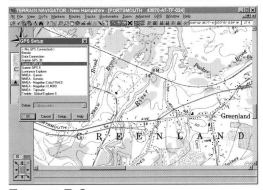

FIGURE B-3
TERRAIN NAVIGATOR™ SETUP SCREEN

you annotate maps with markers and comments, and print out customized versions.

Maptech's digitized map images are georeferenced, which means that every pixel of the image has a corresponding coordinate location. You may select latitude/longitude, UTM, or MGRS coordinate systems. Place your cursor anywhere on the map, and Terrain Navigator will display the coordinates of that exact location. As the cursor is moved, this reading is continuously updated.

Terrain Navigator is especially useful in GPS navigation. This software allows for the direct electronic download and upload of coordinates between a computer and a compatible GPS unit. GPS-generated waypoints, routes and track logs can be imported directly into Terrain Navigator, where they may be displayed on the map. Software tools also let you create and edit waypoints, tracks and routes manually. Terrain Navigator provides several options for converting track logs into routes, with user-defined waypoints. A single track log can provide unlimited generation of waypointed routes, and these routes can always be modified. Users can add their own annotations; for example, to note areas of trail obstruction, scenic views, rest stop locations, etc. Track logs, routes and waypoints may be stored within Terrain Navigator software for future reference. This data can be uploaded to a GPS, for use in the field.

In addition, Terrain Navigator offers a real-time GPS interface capability, which enables live tracking.

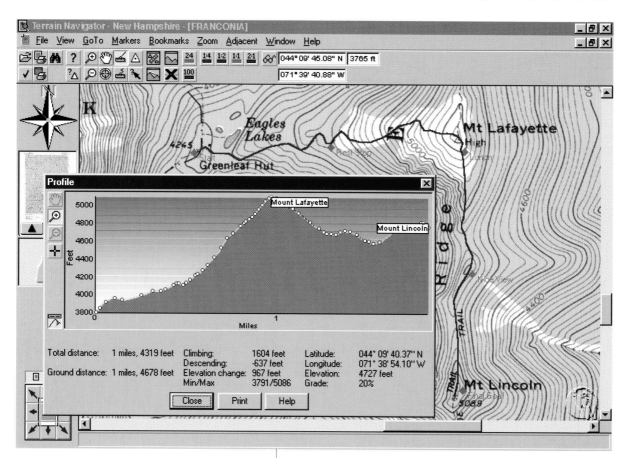

Terrain Navigator - New Hampshire - [FRANCONIA]
File View GoTo Markers Bookmarks Zoom Adjacent Window Help

FIGURE B-4
TERRAIN NAVIGATOR™ BY MAPTECH

With this feature, a person equipped with a GPS and laptop can check the map at any point in a journey to see the current location. This lets travelers track their continuing progress along a trail, and see where they are in relation to points of interest on the map.

Terrain Navigator contains an interactive Help file, laid out in a click-and-learn format. Context-sensitive explanations and hints are readily available at the touch of a button. Maptech is constantly working to refine and improve Terrain Navigator, through the regular release of maintenance updates and upgrades. Maptech's USGS Topographic CD Series, for use with Terrain Navigator, will include full state coverage, on a state-by-state basis, for the entire USA. Generally, each CD contains between 125 and 300 USGS topo maps.

Terrain Navigator may also be used with Maptech's "Take a Hike" CDs, whose coverage focuses on established outdoor recreation areas, such as State Parks and National Forests. Complete coverage for the Appalachian Trail, from Georgia to Maine, is provided in four Take a Hike CDs. Other available titles include the White Mountain National Forest in New Hampshire, the San Juan National Forest in Colorado, the Lake Tahoe/Gold Country region in California and Nevada, and Olympic National Forest in Washington. More titles are being added; Maptech welcomes ideas for areas to include in this growing series.

For further information on available map coverage and navigation software products, please visit www.maptech.com, or call (800) 627-7236.

APPENDIX C

In addition to providing large, medium and small scale topographic maps of the United States, as indicated in Chapter 3, the USGS National Mapping Program has developed an extensive data base of locations within the U.S. referenced by latitude/longitude grid pair coordinates. The data base which includes populated places, schools, harbors, reservoirs, tunnels, etc. is described by the USGS as follows:

"The Geographic Names Information System (GNIS), ... contains information about almost 2 million physical and cultural geographic features in the United States. The Federally recognized name of each feature described in the database is identified, and references are made to a feature's location by State, county, and geographic coordinates." See Figure C-1.

This source of information may be most useful for vehicle travel or when coordinates for the navigator's destination is not readily obtainable from a regional topographic map.

The GNIS is accessible through Internet access at:

http://mapping.usgs.gov/www/gnis

The entire database may be acquired on a compact disk entitled The Digital Gazetteer of the U.S. by contacting any regional USGS Earth Science Information Center or phoning **1-800-USA-MAPS**.

USGS: GEOGRAPHIC NAMES INFORMATION SYSTEM

```
Feature Name: Easton

State: Pennsylvania

County: Northampton

Feature Type: populated place

Elevation: 300

USGS 7.5'x7.5' Map:Easton

Latitude:404118N

Longitude:0751316W
```

FIGURE C-1:

RECORD FROM GNIS QUERY
FOR EASTON, PENNSYLVANIA

APPENDIX D

GPS-COMPATIBLE HIGH-WAY MAPS WITH THE UNIVERSAL GPS GRID™

FINALLY, PAPER MAPS WHICH ALLOW YOU TO USE YOUR GPS

- GIVE EVERY LOCATION A UNIQUE WORLDWIDE GPS ADDRESS

- DETERMINE YOUR LOCATION

- USE WITH VIRTUALLY ANY MAKE AND MODEL OF GPS RECEIVER

- PLOT AND PROGRAM YOUR DESTINATION

- ESTIMATE TIME AND DISTANCE TO NEXT STOP

- LOCATE AND REPORT EMERGENCIES

- PROVIDE OTHERS WITH AN EASY WAY TO LOCATE YOUR HOME OR OFFICE

- OTHER ENDLESS POSSIBILITIES

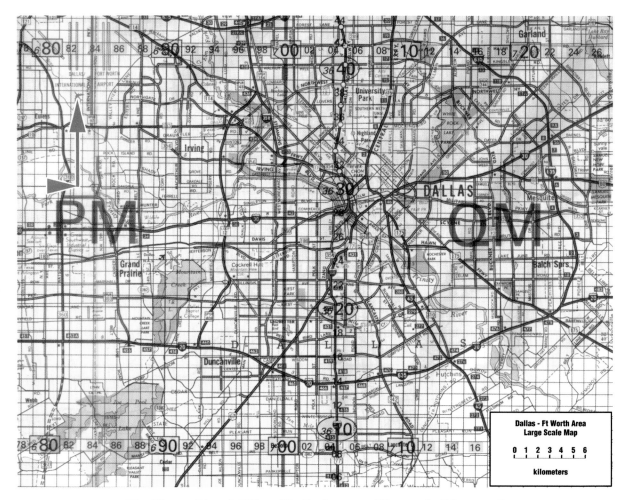

Dallas-Fort Worth International Airport
Large Scale Map

MGRS Coordinate:

14S PM 826 375
(to within 100 meters)

UTM Coordinate:

14 **682**600
3637500 _(to within 1 meter)

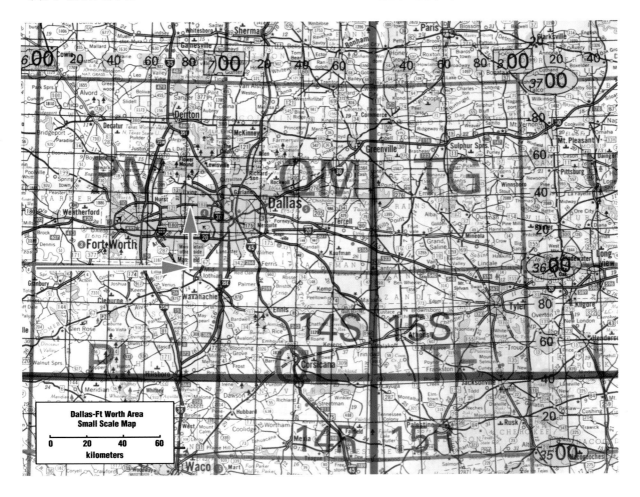

Dallas-Fort Worth International Airport
Small Scale Map

MGRS Coordinate:

14S PM 82 37
(to within 1 Km)

UTM Coordinate:

14 682600
3637500 (to within 1 meter)

GPS VEHICLE NAVIGATION

Nearly every publication or program you see today from Readers Digest to the Simson's is talking about GPS. This exciting new technology is doing everything from assisting farmers in planting crops to determining the distance of a golfer's next shot.

One application most recognized by the general public is the use of GPS for automobile navigation. In fact many car manufactures are now offering GPS Guidance Systems as options in their luxury model cars. Unfortunately these systems can cost anywhere between $1,000.00 and $3,000.00 dollars.

BUT I ALREADY OWN A GPS RECEIVER

As a leading edge consumer, you may have already discovered the many advantages of using GPS in your outdoor/recreational activities. However, if you have tried to use GPS to find your way while driving, you have no doubt discovered that your standard road atlas is of little help. Quite simply, current road maps lack grids which interface with GPS receivers. Even the few maps which have latitude and longitude markings are difficult to interpret.

A COST EFFECTIVE SOLUTION HAS ARRIVED

Now, Alexis Publishing has produced a full set of detailed, inexpensive GPS Compatible Road Maps which accommodate the use of virtually all GPS hand-held receivers. Each map incorporates an easy to interpret Universal GPS (UGPS) Grid™ that enables you to navigate effectively while driving. In addition, a brief narrative found on each map provides a full explanation of the UGPS Grid™ and includes a specific example of how it works.

Roadmaps Available by Region

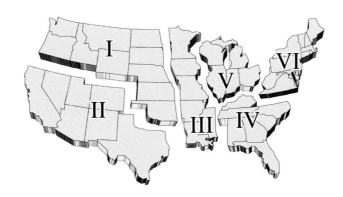

Region	**Maps**	
I. (4 map set)	1. WA,OR	2. ID,MT, WY
	3. ND,SD,NE	4. KS,OK
II. (4 map set)	5. CA,NV	6. UT,CO
	7. AZ,NM	8. TX
III. (4 map set)	9. AR,LA,MS	10. MO
	11. IA	12. MN
IV. (4 map set)	13. AL,GA	14. KY,TN
	15. NC,SC	16. FL
V. (5 map set)	17. WI	18. MI
	19. OH	20. IL
	21. IN	
VI. (5 map set)	22. WV,VA,MD,DE	25. NY
	23. PA 24. NJ	
	26. ME,NH,VT,CT,RI,MA	

APPENDIX E: BUYING A GPS RECEIVER

Readers of previous editions of this book have asked that we include a comparison of hand-held GPS receivers along with specific recommendations to first time buyers for purchasing GPS equipment. We have chosen not to do this only because manufactures of GPS equipment are constantly introducing new makes and models of receivers. Unfortunately, our recommendations about specific equipment would be obsolete shortly after the book was printed.

What we have included here are some of the major issues to be considered when selecting a receiver and a few sources to consult for current information regarding product comparisons and new product releases. We have found that the major manufactures of GPS equipment referenced in Chapter 5 provide a similar range of quality products at competitive prices.

APPLICATIONS

☐ AVIATION
☐ NAUTICAL
☐ VEHICLE
☐ HIKING

The first question to ask yourself when considering the purchase of a GPS receiver is what you will use it for. Each major manufacturer offers specialized equipment designed for maritime and aviation applications. Pilots and sailors should carefully consider the advantages offered by specialized software programs such as built in Jepessen databases or Coastal Loran Navigation Charts before investing in the basic models. Land navigators will discover that different models may be better suited for vehicle applications as opposed to dismounted use.

OPERATING FEATURES

☐ MEMORY
☐ COORDINATE SYSTEMS
☐ DIFFERENTIAL GPS CAPABLE
☐ DIGITAL MAP DIS PLAYS
☐ CARTRIDGE DIGITAL MAPS
☐ AUDIBLE ALARMS

Units should afford you the capability to save several hundreds of landmarks and at least 5 multi-segmented routes. Advances in computer chip technology should offer dramatic increases in these numbers over the near future. Look for a unit that provides you with a capability of using both UTM and the MGRS Coordinate system, as well as LAT/LON. When traveling at high speed in vehicles, an audible alarm feature will allow you to focus your attention on the road rather than your receiver. A receiver with a DGPS capability will provide you with enhanced position accuracy (to within 10 meters) in areas covered by a differential service. Units which either include an internal digital map or allow you to download maps via cartridge or CD are extremely convenient but at a much higher cost. However, at this time, these digital maps (especial those internally stored in the receiver) are not as detailed as USGS topo Quads. or published highway maps.

PERFORMANCE

☐ **SATELLITE TRACKING**
☐ **ACQUISITION TIME**
☐ **SPEED OF POSITION FIX**
☐ **POSITION UPDATES**

Chapter 5 provides an extensive discussion of 12-parallel channel receivers vs. serial or multiplexing units. It is strongly recommended that you select a 12-parallel channel unit due to its vastly superior satellite tracking capabilities. These units acquire a satellite fix more quickly and maintain that contact more reliably, especially from within a vehicle or under a heavy vegetation canopy. Receivers should provide an accurate fix to within 30 meters with Selective Availability (SA) off and to within 125 meters with SA turned on (which is most of the time).

COST

☐ **$100 OR LESS – GENERALLY NOT A 12-PARALLEL CHANNEL UNIT**
☐ **$100-$300 – MOST BASIC FULL-FEATURED MODELS**
☐ **$300 PLUS – INTEGRATE DIGITAL MAP CAPABILITIES**

Expect to pay between $100 - $700 for your first GPS receiver. The least expensive models normally offer two serial channel receptions (multiplexing), that is not recommended. The most expensive models offer integrated moving map software built into the unit. Note that in spite of the general perception among novice GPS users, cost has little relationship to unit accuracy.

UNIT PHYSICAL CHARACTERISTICS

Most units sold today are well constructed and can withstand fairly rugged handling. Check the warranty to be sure of what type of replacement

☐ **DURABILITY**

☐ **SIZE AND WEIGHT**

☐ **BATTERY LIFE**

☐ **SCREEN SIZE, BACK LIGHTING**

☐ **BATTERY BACKUP**

☐ **DETACHABLE ANTENNA**

coverage is provided. A fully sealed waterproof (as opposed to water resistant) unit is a must in any boating situations and preferable for most outdoor recreational purposes. Lightweight units have an advantage if you will spend a good deal of time hiking, but don't overlook the importance of battery life. Units should provide around 24 hours or better. It makes no sense to save a few ounces in unit weight and have to carry a couple extra pounds of batteries. Battery backup capacity is another important consideration. Insist on a unit with internal (lithium) battery backup. If your batteries go dead this internal battery will retain all stored information for up to one year. Some units will only retain this memory for 20-30 minutes while batteries are replaced. . As you might expect, when it comes to screen size, the larger the better; and for nighttime use, back lighting is a must. Detachable antennas allow you to remove the unit's antenna and place it on the roof of you vehicle or boat cabin for clearer signal reception. This can be a plus but has become less significant with the advent of 12-parallel channel receivers.

SOFTWARE INTEGRATION

☐ **NMEA INTERFACE**

☐ **DOWNLOADING LANDMARKS & ROUTES**

☐ **CD-ROM MAP DOWNLOADS**

☐ **PC MOVING MAP SOFTWARE**

☐ **SOFTWARE UPGRADES**

NMEA interface ports are used to connect your GPS Unit to computers or other GPS receivers for the purpose of exchanging data. This connection is used in conjunction with the Terrain Navigator Software (included with the book) to upload or download landmarks and routes. See Appendix B. With a system like Eagle's new Global Map 100, you can add specific regional map detail to an existing generic world map built into the receiver. Other programs allow you to connect your receiver to a PC laptop and utilize moving map software while driving. This option will no doubt become even more significant in the future as the majority of advances will likely be in software development and the NMEA port will allow you to update your device with software upgrades.

ACCESSORIES

☐ **MOUNTS**

☐ **NMEA DATA CABLES**

☐ **CARRYING CASES**

☐ **EXTERNAL ANTENNAS**

Various bracket configurations allow you to mount your GPS unit on the dashboard of your car or boat or to the handlebars of your bicycle. Carrying cases afford additional protection from shock and often allow you to clip your unit on your belt. External power cables or cigarette lighter power adapters assure that your batteries will never fail while in your vehicle. External antennas may be required for use with DGPS

RESOURCES

JOE MEHAFFEY & JACK YEAZEL'S
GPS INFORMATION
www.joe.mehaffey.com

THE CAR CONNECTION
www.thecarconnection.com/cc_gps.htm

GPS WORLD
(218) 723-9477
www.gpsworld.com

TELSON COMMUNICATIONS
(908) 730-9672
www.telson.net

ADVENTURE GPS PRODUCTS
(888) 477-4386
www.gps4fun.com

NAVTECH SEMINARS
(800) 628-0885
www.navtechgps.com

The internet is the best source of information regarding up-to-date evaluations of GPS Equipment. Joe Mehaffey's Web Page is a good place to start. The Car Connection Web Page provides an extensive overview of vehicle navigation systems, although a bit dated.

GPS World Magazine publishes an evaluation of GPS receivers each year. This normally appears in their January Edition. Several companies who sell GPS equipment over the internet also provide up-to-date evaluations of GPS equipment and comparisons between different models and manufactures.

GLOSSARY

(TERMS & ACRONYMS)

Agonic Line	Isogonic line of zero degrees magnetic declination. *see isogonic Line*
Almanac	Data broadcast by each GPS satellite vehicle on the general location and health of all satellites in the GPS constellation. It takes several minutes for a GPS unit to gather almanac information.
Altitude	*see elevation*
Atomic Clock	The highly accurate and expensive quartz clocks placed aboard each NAVSTAR satellite vehicle.
Anti-Spoofing	Encryption of the P-Code which is then referred to as the Y-Code.
Azimuth	An angular measure of direction taken clockwise and usually in degrees from a north reference line (true, grid or magnetic north). *see bearing, course, and track*
Bearing	Within the context of land-based GPS jargon, it is the directional azimuth measured from any present position (PP) to the destination landmark.

C/A-Code	The civilian access-code which is further degraded in accuracy by the U.S. Government's policy of selective availability (SA).
CDI	Course Deviation Indicator. A GPS receiver unit feature that graphically reports the distance one has veered off to the left or right from the course azimuth set between two landmarks (waypoints or checkpoints). *see XTE*
Chart	*see map*
COG	Course Over Ground. The azimuth of your track. *see track*
Cold Start	Whenever a GPS receiver is powered and must locate itself without user initialization or when it must gather fresh almanac information (stale by more than six months).
Contour Interval	The vertical distance between two adjacent contour lines.
Course	Within the context of land-based GPS jargon, it is the directional azimuth measured from any starting point for navigation to the destination landmark (waypoint).
Contour Line	A line on a topographic map connecting points of equal elevation.
CTS	Course to steer. The azimuth of the bearing to your next landmark (waypoint).
Datum	*see map datums*
Declination	*see magnetic declination*
Default	The value or setting automatically selected by the GPS receiver unless another is specified by the user.
Degree	A unit of measure for the arc. Full circle= 360 degrees; 60 minutes = 1 degree; and 60 seconds = 1 minute.

Deviation	*see magnetic deviation*
DGPS	*see differential GPS*
Differential GPS	A technique that uses locally-broadcasted information to GPS receiver units correcting errors in the pseudo-ranges calculated from GPS satellites (including SA errors) in order to improve the accuracy of the position fixes provided by the GPS. A.K.A. DGPS
Digital Maps	Map data stored in either raster or vector formats. Raster maps are simply digitized pictures of maps, while vector maps are those that have aspects which can be manipulated.
Direction	*see azimuth*
DMA	The Defense Mapping Agency, successor to the WWII-era Army Map Service, which has recently been merged with other governmental agency mapping divisions (e.g., CIA & State Dept.) into the National Mapping Imagery Agency (NIMA).
DoD	United States Department of Defense, which owns and operates the GPS.
DOP	Dilution of Precision. A function of the geometry resulting from the positioning of satellites relative to a location at a given time (see GDOP). The components of GDOP (Geometric Dilution of Precision) include PDOP (Position Dilution of Precision), HDOP (Horizontal Dilution of Precision), VDOP (Vertical Dilution of Precision) and TDOP (Time Dilution of Precision).
Easting (False)	The distance value of a point to the east of the western boundary of a UTM grid zone in reference to the zone's central meridian having a value of 500000mE. It is called a false easting due to the slight distortion that comes with portrayal of a spherical earth on a flat surface.

Elevation	The measurement of distance (usually in feet or meters) above or below mean sea level or, most recently, above or below the surface of the WGS-84 geoid. A.K.A. Altitude
Ellipsoid	A flattened sphere described by a mathematical formula representing the theoretical shape of the earth's surface.
EPE	Estimated position error. Reported on-screen in feet or meters and based upon GDOP.
Ephemeris	Precise time and location information regarding the orbital path of each satellite vehicle broadcast from the SV for use by a receiver unit in calculating its pseudo-range from the SV.
ETA	Estimated time of arrival. The time when a destination will be reached based upon the current rate of progress.
ETE	Estimated time en route. The projected time remaining before arrival at destination.
FOM	Figure of merit. A scale ranging from 9 to 1 relative to position accuracy based upon GDOP.
Functional Distance	A concept of distance that considers the time, effort, and level of difficulty involved in moving over the terrain from one point to another. The term was coined by Mike Hagedorn, NYS Forest Ranger.
GDOP	Geometric Dilution of Position. *see DOP*
Geoid	The shape of the earth's theoretical mean sea level surface as determined by gravitational measurements taken by satellite. It is the basis for map datums GRS-80, NAD-83, and WGS-84.
Geometric Quality	GQ is based upon the positions of SVs used in calculating a position fix. Poor GQ affects GDOP, EPE, and FOM.

GIS	Geographic Information System. A rapidly growing collection of spatial data in digital form.
GLONASS	Built by the USSR as the counterpart to the U.S. NAVSTAR GPS; it is presently being maintained by Russia.
GMT	Greenwich Mean Time. Solar time established at the Greenwich Meridian. Very nearly equal to Universal Time Coordinated (UT) established for use with GPS.
GO TO	A feature on some GPS receiver units that allows the user to push a button, select any saved landmark (waypoint), and navigate directly from the PP to that destination.
GPS	NAVSTAR Global Positioning System. It is made up of three segments: 1) space segment, 2) control segment, 3) user segment.
Graticule	The lines of latitude and longitude on a map which establish a system of true geographic coordinates.
Greenwich Mean Time	Local Time at Greenwich, England. Also known as Zulu Time
Grid North	The direction along or parallel to a UTM/MGRS grid line toward its north end.
Grid Reference Box	Marginal information included on some maps reporting the UTM Grid Zone Designation(s) and 100,000 Meter-Square Identification(s) covered by the sheet.
Grid System	A series of evenly spaced perpendicular grid lines, such as in the Universal Transverse Mercator (UTM) grid system, that makes it possible to locate a position on a map using x- and y-coordinates.
Grid Zone	UTM Grid Zone. One of 60 six-degree wide segments that encircle the globe between the latitudes of 80 degrees south to 84 degrees north. The perpendicular UTM grid is then constructed within each grid zone using the intersection of its central meridian and the equator as the point of origin.

Grid Zone Designation	The label given to the six-degree wide (longitude) by eight-degree high (latitude) areas within the MGRS version of the UTM Grid system. Vertical Grid Zones are numbered from west to east beginning at the International Dateline (180° longitude) and horizontal rows are lettered from south to north beginning at 80° south latitude and running to 84° north longitude. (The top row encompasses a latitude of 12°.) They are referred to as REGIONS on Alexis Road Maps.
GRS-80	Utilizes nearly the identical dimensions of the earth as WGS-84 and was derived in much the same way. *see WGS-84*
HDOP	Horizontal Dilution of Precision. *see DOP*
Heading	*see track*
Initialization	Providing a GPS receiver unit with its current position whenever it has been moved more than 300 miles since last calculating a position fix and setting the correct local time when it has been moved to a different zone. Whenever the user fails to provide this initial position or when the unit must collect a more current almanac, it will initiate a "cold start" which takes several minutes.
International Date Line	The meridian of 180 degrees longitude at which time it is midnight (start of a new day) when the sun is directly over the prime meridian.
Isogonic Line	A line denoting points of equal magnetic declination (variation). Magnetic variation does gradually shift and the USGS publishes updates about every ten years. See Agonic Line
L1/L2	Two channels used by NAVSTAR SVs to broadcast timing, ranging, almanac, and ehemeris information to GPS receiver units.
Landform	An individual terrain feature that can be identified and classified (e.g., hill, saddle, valley, draw, ridge, spur, cliff, depression, cut, or fill).

Landmark	A location (usually an easily recognized natural or man-made feature) that serves as a guide to land navigation. The position coordinates of these locations are also referred to as "waypoints" or "checkpoints" and may be saved in the memory of a GPS receiver for later use in "go to" destinations or to define various legs when establishing a multi-segment route.
Latitude	The angular measurement in degrees, minutes, and seconds north or south of the equator as measured by parallels running east and west and perpendicular to the vertical meridians. A location can be from 0° to 90° north or south latitude.
Legend	Section of information found on a map defining its colors and symbols.
Locality	see One Hundred Thousand Meter-Square Identification
Longitude	The angular measurement in degrees, minutes, and seconds east or west of the prime meridian (generally the Greenwich meridian) as measured by meridian lines running north and south and perpendicular to the horizontal parallels and converging at the poles. A location can be from 0° to 180° east or west longitude.
Magnetic Declination	The angular differences between true and magnetic norths caused by the fact that the magnetic poles are not coincident with the geographic poles (e.g., magnetic north pole is over 1000 miles from the geographic north pole at a location near Bathurst Island in northern Canada). A.K.A Declination
Magnetic Deviation	Errors to the compass needle caused by the proximity of ferris metal and/or the flow of electrical current. Very commonly encountered in boats and vehicles. A.K.A. Deviation
Magnetic North	The direction of the attraction of the north-seeking arrow on a magnetic compass.
Magnetic variation	see magnetic declination

GLOSSARY

Map	A graphic representation—usually on a plane surface and at an established scale—of the natural and cultural features found on the surface or a portion of the surface of the earth. Topographical maps show both the horizontal and vertical relationships of the features portrayed, usually through the use of contour lines. A.K.A. Chart
Map Datums	Vertical and horizontal reference systems based upon the ellipsoid or geoid serving as the mathematical model denoting the size and shape of the earth's surface for mapping purposes. Setting incorrect horizontal datum selections on a GPS receiver can significantly degrade position accuracy on a given map.
Map Features	Four classifications of features are generally portrayed on maps: terrain, vegetation, hydrography (water) and culture (man-made).
Meridian	*see longitude*
MGRS	Military Grid Reference System. A simple alphanumeric format for reporting UTM grid coordinates. Developed by the U.S. military, it is generally recognized as the easiest to understand and use map coordinate system developed to date. There are presently two versions of MGRS—the newest for use in conjunction with maps whose datums are based on the WGS-84 geoid. However, most U.S. maps are constructed using the NAD-27 horizontal map datum, which is based upon the Clarke 1866 spheroid, and thus make use of the older version of the MGRS.
MGRS Coordinates	Position coordinates derived from the simplified Military Grid Reference System labeling feature of the Universal Transverse Mercator (UTM) Grid System.
Microrelief	The subtle shape of the ground that can be interpreted between contour lines by closely observing their shapes (sweeping curves to small wiggles).
Mil	A unit of measure for the arc. 6400 mils = full circle.

MITAC	Map Interpretation and Terrain Association Course. First developed for the U.S. Marine Corps by the Naval Personnel Research Development Center, further refined by the U.S. Army Research Institute, and adapted for use in Arabia by Alexis. *See SOSES*
MOB	Man Overboard A feature on some GPS receiver units that, with the push a button, automatically marks the PP, and navigates back to the spot where the "man went overboard".
NAD-27 CONUS	The horizontal map datum, named North American Datum-1927, which in the United States was indexed in 1927 to a point on Meade Ranch, KS, and is based upon the Clark-1866 elipsoid. Most U.S. maps are based on the NAD-27 CONUS.
NAD-83	The horizontal map datum, named North American Datum-1983, which is based upon the GRS-1980 geoid. GRS-80 and NAD-83 are virtually the same as WGS-84 and can be used with hand-held GPS equipment interchangeably.
Navigation Functions	GPS unit features and capabilities dealing with the guidance of a navigator along either a simple GO TO or a more complex multi-segment route.
NAVSTAR	Navigation System with Time and Ranging The name of the U.S. Government's satellite global positioning system. At times, the SVs (artificial stars) are referred to as NAVSTARS.
Neatline	The edge of a map's portrayal on the paper. The margin lies outside the neatline.
NIMA	National Mapping and Imagery Agency is the current successor to the Defense Mapping Agency (DMA).
NMEA Interface	National Maritime Electronics Association standards for electronic devices used in navigation applications.

Northing (False)	The distance value of a point relative to the equator within a UTM grid zone. It is called a false northing due to the slight distortion that comes with the portrayal of the spherical earth on a flat surface.
One Hundred Thousand	The 100,000 meter squares formed by the basic grid lines established within UTM grid zones at 100 kilometer intervals are identified by dual letters and called 100,000 Meter-Square Identifications within the MGRS and referred to as LOCALITIES on Alexis Road Maps.
Parallel	*see latitude*
Meter-Square Identifications	
P-Code	The highly accurate location data broadcast for military use. It is generally encrypted and is then known as the Y-code.
PDOP	Position Dilution of Precision. *see DOP*
Position Fix	The determination of the coordinates of a position using triangulation calculations from known positions, terrain referencing, or a GPS receiver unit's calculations of its pseudo-ranges from three or more SVs.
Position Functions	GPS unit features and capabilities dealing with the calculation and reporting of position.
PP	Present position.
PPS	Precise Positioning Service. The usually encrypted, highly accurate positioning service (GPS) offered by the DoD to its military subscribers.
Prime Meridian	The Meridian of 0° longitude which runs through Greenwich, England and divides the earth into the eastern and western hemispheres
Raster Maps	*see digital maps*

Region	*see Grid Zone Designation*
Representative Fraction	The scale of a map with map distance being represented by the numerator and ground distance by the denominator (e.g., 1/50,000 means that one meter on the map represents 50,000 meters (50 kilometers on the ground). It is also written as a proportion 1:50,000.
Route Functions	GPS unit features and capabilities dealing with the planning and creation of routes.
Route Segment	A portion of a multi-segment route, often referred to as a leg, as defined between two landmarks (waypoints).
Satellite Vehicle	SVs make up the artificial star constellation of NAVSTAR GPS, each broadcasting information used by receiver units to calculate positions.
Selective Availability	SA is the U.S. Government's policy to degrade the accuracy of the data required to compute a position fix using the civilian access channel.
Setup Functions	GPS unit features and capabilities dealing with unit initialization and various reporting options and parameters built into the set (e.g., speed and distance units, datum selections, coordinate systems, elevation units, screen contrast).
Signal Quality	SQ has little effect on position accuracy, however, a poor SQ immediately preceedes the loss of signal reception from that satellite.
Smart Terrain Association	Utilizing terrain association navigation techniques in conjunction with the advantages of GPS.
SOA	Speed of advance. *see VMG*

SOG	Speed over ground. The speed at which the GPS unit is moving with respect to the earth's surface.
SOSES	The five physical characteristics used by navigators to reference specific terrain features in the real world to their maps utilizing shape, orientation, size, elevation, and slope. *see MITAC*
SPS	Standard Positioning Service. The less accurate positioning service (GPS) offered to nonmilitary subscribers which is further degraded by Selective Availability (SA).
TDOP	Time Dilution of Precision. *see DOP*
Terrain Association	A land navigation technique based upon observing the terrain in the real world and associating it with what is interpreted from the map. *see SOSES*
Terrain Feature	*see landform*
Terrain Referencing	*see terrain association and SOSES*
Three-D GPS Mode	Use of signals from four or more SVs by a receiver to calculate a position fix. This is more accurate than a fix calculated in the 2-dimensional mode and includes elevation information.
Track	Within the context of land-based GPS jargon, it is the azimuth of the direction of movement.
True Geographic Coordinates	Map coordinates reported in terms of latitude and longitude. They are considered as being true because they have not been distorted by a flat rendering of the portrayal of the earth's surface.
True North	The direction from a position toward the geographic north pole.
TTG	Time to go. The estimate of time required for the GPS unit to reach the destination landmark (waypoint) based upon the current rate of advance.

Two-D GPS Mode	Use of signals from three SVs by a receiver to calculate a position fix. This is less accurate than a fix calculated in the 3-dimensional mode and includes no elevation information.
Universal GPS Grid™	The UGPS grid is used on Alexis Road Maps. It utilizes the UTM grid based upon the NAD-27 CONUS horizontal map datum and includes both UTM and old version MGRS labels. It can be used in conjunction with virtually every hand-held GPS receiver unit ever manufactured.
Universal Time	A very precise version of Greenwich Mean Time. It is also called Universal Time Coordinated.
Universal Transverse Mercator Grid	The UTM grid coordinate system that is universally used throughout much of the world and utilizes regularly spaced perpendicular grid lines. It is considered to be the best position reporting system for use on land. When used in conduction with MGRS, it is a superior grid coordinate system for use with GPS in that it is accurate, easily understood, and highly convenient.
USGS	United States Geological Survey, part of the Department of Interior, is the primary mapping agency of the United States Government.
UT	*see Universal Time*
UTM Coordinates	Position coordinates derived from the Universal Transverse Mercator Grid System.
Variation	*see magnetic variation*
VDOP	Vertical Dilution of Precision. *see DOP*
Vector Maps	*see digital maps*
VMG	Velocity made good. The portion of the GPS unit's velocity which results in closing the distance with respect to the destination landmark (waypoint).

Waypoint	*see landmark*
WGS-84	The horizontal map datum, named World Geodetic System-1984, is based upon world-wide satellite gravitational measurements that have rendered a highly accurate size and shape for the earth's theoretical mean sea level which has an irregular form called a geoid. Most U.S. maps are currently based on the NAD-27 CONUS datum, but future maps around the world will be constructed using the very accurate WGS-84 datum for both horizontal and vertical measurements.
XTE/XT	Cross-track error. The distance a GPS receiver unit is off course. A graphic display of XTE is found on some unit's screens and is referred to as CDI.
Y-code	The highly accurate location data transmitted for military use after being encrypted. *see P-code*
Yeoman Mouse	An electronic tool facilitating the digitizing of data from paper maps.

ABOUT THE AUTHOR

NOEL J. HOTCHKISS

Noel Hotchkiss has been actively involved for the past dozen years in the field of map reading and land navigation with GPS as a consultant, training program designer, instructor, and author. In addition to the three editions of this book, he has written a number of instructional materials and various articles related to the topic. He also played an important role in the design of Alexis Publishing's revolutionary new series of GPS road maps.

From 1985 to 1990, Mr. Hotchkiss worked as a land navigation (LN) subject matter expert and instructional design consultant with the U.S. Army Research Institute (ARI) LN Training Team at the Infantry School, Fort Benning, Ga. From 1991 to 1994, he served as a consulting instructional program designer and contract LN instructor for Alexis International, Inc. on a project involving the military forces of the Kingdom of Saudi Arabia.

While serving as a consultant to the U.S. Army ARI, Mr. Hotchkiss authored several LN research and training reports and programs as well as various articles appearing in professional military journals. In addition, he traveled to several service schools and various civilian organizations reviewing their LN training procedures in search of ways to improve the Army's overall performance in this crucial skill area. While testing some of the new experimental programs developed by the ARI, he instructed soldiers enrolled at the 10th Mountain Division's "Light Fighter School" at Fort Drum, NY. In Saudi Arabia, he had the opportunity to instruct soldiers attending the Royal Air Defense Forces Institute in Jeddah using the training programs he developed for Alexis. This included the introduction of the newly developed hand-held GPS equipment as a primary tool for land navigation.

Since the publication of the first edition of his book, Mr. Hotchkiss has been invited to speak on the subjects of GPS navigation and maps at national conferences, and he has been asked to discuss a number of questions relative to maps, grid coordinate systems, and the application of GPS with many of the manufacturers. In addition, several producers of digital map systems have discussed a number of questions and related issues with him. Finally, Alexis Publishing has been told that this book is frequently used as a common reference by those who field questions from customers who have purchased hand-held GPS receivers, and it is also referred to by title in many product manuals.

Mr. Hotchkiss earned an AB degree in social science, MA in social studies education, and MS in education administration at Syracuse University. He has also completed some graduate level study in the field of instructional design, development, and evaluation. His formal military education includes completion of the Armor Officer Basic Course (AOBC), Armor Officer Advance Course (AOAC-RC), several tactical intelligence courses, a commanders' course, and Command and General Staff Officer College Course (C&GSC-RC).

Commissioned through the R.O.T.C. program at Syracuse University, Lieutenant Colonel (USAR, Ret.) Hotchkiss' assignments included two years in the 2-63d Armor, 1st Infantry Division; eighteen years in the 27th Brigade, NYARNG; and four years with the 1159th U.S. Army Reserve Forces School, 98th Division (Training). He has served as a tank platoon leader, battalion and brigade intelligence and operations officer, mechanized infantry battalion executive officer, and Area Commandant for officer and NCO education system programs.

From 1976 until his retirement in 1998, he served as principal at the Jordan Elbridge High School near Syracuse and is presently working with colleagues to launch a new business providing pre-employment background checks on school personnel.

ACKNOWLEDGMENTS

First, I wish to thank Wayne J. Gleason at Alexis USA, Inc. for suggesting that I write the book and having his fine training organization serve as its publisher. Also, Art Lipscomb continues to work magic with his combined graphics and computer skills to accomplish the cover design, develop many of the illustrations, and layout the entire manuscript for publication. With their continued releases of updated versions of this book and the publication of their unique and highly useful series of GPS compatible road maps, Alexis Publishing is making valuable contributions to the advancements being made in the use of this new technology.

I would also like to thank Mike Carney at Eagle/ Lowrance, Spencer Lee at Magellan, and Mike Kahn at Garmin for their assistance and quick responses to questions and requests for materials on their products. These efforts are greatly appreciated.

Next, I must recognize the fine contributions made by Jennifer N. (Drescher) Riedy who wrote the new Chapter 6 Highway Travel with GPS and for her adaptation of the "Map Interpretation and Terrain Association Course (MITAC)" for Alexis. Some of that material has been added to Chapter 3 (NAVIGATING WITH GPS AND A MAP).

The next acknowledgment goes to both Neri (Tom) Terry, recently retired major in the Marine Corps and an active advocate for the adoption of the UTM grid/ MGRS labels as the standard coordinate system for the U.S.A. (*GPS WORLD*, 4/96), and Chief Warrant Officer-2 Scott Maxner, cartographic officer for the G2 section, 10th Mountain Division, Fort Drum. These people reviewed the Second Edition and made excellent suggestions for improvements in the book. Many of their suggestions are reflected in this new publication and their efforts are greatly appreciated.

Recognition must also be given to the fine research work done during the late 1980s by the Fort Benning Land Navigation Team of the U.S. Army Research Institute for the Behavioral and Social Sciences (ARI). I thank Lt. Col. Art Osborne (USA, Ret.) at Litton Computer Services, Inc. and Dr. Seward Smith, Chief of the ARI Fort Benning Field Unit, for involving me in their highly successful project to improve Army LN training.

Finally, both Alexis Publishing and I wish to thank Warren Hart for his valuable contribution in copy editing the manuscript of this third edition. Nevertheless, all errors, whether in content, layout, or use of the English language, are to be attributed to me.

INDEX

INDEX